Canada, Scandinavia and Southern Africa

Canada
Scandinavia
and
Southern Africa

Edited by

Douglas Anglin
Timothy Shaw and
Carl Widstrand

**AFRICANA
PUBLISHING
COMPANY**
A division of Holmes & Meier Publishers, Inc.
30 Irving Place, New York, N.Y. 10003

The Scandinavian Institute of African Studies has served at Uppsala since 1962 as a Scandinavian documentation and research centre on African affairs.

The views expressed in its publications are entirely those of the authors and do not necessarily reflect those of the Institute or the institutions where they are engaged at present.

© 1978 Nordiska afrikainstitutet
ISBN 91-7106-143-6
Printed in Sweden by Uppsala Offsetcenter AB, Uppsala 1978

Contents

Preface

Since 1963, the Scandinavian Institute of African Studies has organized a variety of international seminars. As a part of its function as a Scandinavian documentation and research centre on African problems, the Institute has sought to choose topics for these international seminars that would be of interest to academics as well as to planners, administrators and politicians. These topics have included refugee problems, boundary problems, problems of adult education, the role of mass media, co-operative development in East Africa and problems of land-locked countries in Africa. Scholars from abroad – primarily, of course, from Africa – have been invited to discuss their particular topics with Scandinavian specialists and other interested persons.

Another of our principle tasks over the years has been to promote and sustain the interest in African affairs among Scandinavians. Seminars comprise one way of doing so at an academic level. During these seminars, however, we have also attempted to offer "another point of view" on a variety of topics. The profile, strength and vigour of our institute depends, therefore, to a great extent on our being able to call upon in our discussions with experts from Africa and abroad a large number of Scandinavian scholars with backgrounds and views widely differing from those held in other African studies establishments.

We have also been interested in the studies on Africa and the policies on development of countries like the Netherlands and Canada. We felt that considerably more progress could be achieved towards sustaining the general interest in African affairs and in South Africa in particular, if we could pool our resources with a Canadian research institution to explore jointly the policies on Southern Africa of a group of countries not directly involved in great power politics in Africa.

So, after years of planning and discussion, the first joint Scandinavian-Canadian Conference on an African topic was held in Ottawa from 19 to 22 February 1978. The Conference was intended to examine and discuss Canadian and Scandinavian perspectives on and policies towards the states of Southern Africa, and to analyse and compare the different development strategies and political economies that have emerged in the region in recent years. A rather diverse group of Scandinavian, Canadian and African scholars, officials and activists was deliberately invited to attend as indicated in the list of participants at the end of this volume. However, they all shared a concern for the promotion of justice in Southern Africa and a firm conviction that fundamental change in Southern Africa is urgently necessary and ultimately inevitable, though they differed both on the nature of the changes

7

needed and over strategies for achieving them. The Conference was sponsored by the Scandinavian Institute of African Studies (Uppsala), The Norman Paterson School of International Affairs, Carleton University (Ottawa), and the Centre for African Studies at Dalhousie University (Halifax).

Neither the Conference itself nor this collection of papers were intended to offer a definitive or comprehensive analysis of Southern African affairs. Rather, they were designed to reflect the range of current analyses of regional problems and prospects and to describe and debate Scandinavian and Canadian responses. I hope that this focus constitutes the distinctive contribution of both the Conference and its proceedings. Inevitably, however, given the range of issues and interests, neither the discussions nor the publications could be exhaustive. Some comments in this collection may be overtaken by events occurring either after the Conference or after its publication. Nevertheless, I remain convinced that these papers offer new and important insights into some of the prospects for conflict and change in Southern Africa.

The present volume concentrates on the relations between Canada-Scandinavia and Southern Africa. A companion volume Conflict and Change in Southern Africa: papers from a Scandinavian-Canadian Conference edited by Douglas Anglin, Timothy Shaw and Carl Widstrand (University Press of America, 1978) incorporates a variety of analyses, perceptions and ideologies and discusses the position of the front-line states, the liberation movements and prospects of change within South Africa.

The Conference and hence this publication could not have happened without the ready agreement of participants and my co-editors, the invaluable work of assistants and secretaries and the timely generosity of several funding egencies. In the latter regard it is a pleasure to record the financial assistance of the Canada Council and the Department of External Affairs in Ottawa, Carleton University and the Faculty of Graduate Studies at Dalhousie and the invaluable assistance of the staff of the Norman Paterson School of International Affairs, Carleton University.

Finally, gratitude is due to our contributors for agreeing to the inclusion of their revised papers in this volume. I should take this opportunity to point out that all of the conferees and contributors came to and participated in the Conference in their personal capacities. The papers presented here are their own and should not be taken to represent the official policy of any of the institutions with which they are presently connected.

Carl G. Widstrand
Uppsala, June 1978

Carl Widstrand

Introduction

1978 is the international anti-*apartheid* year. It is therefore very appropriate that this seminar was organized in 1978. This was, however, pure coincidence as the seminar has a rather long history. This history is important, *not* because it is especially outstanding in the history of seminars of the world, but rather because the *changes* the seminar has undergone reflect the rapidly changing situation in Southern Africa.

Professor Douglas Anglin and Dr Tim Shaw, my Canadian coorganisers of this meeting have been discussing the content, focus and direction of the seminar for more than five years. The original ideas were these:

– Here were two areas of the world, Scandinavia and Canada, somewhat – if one may use the simile – on the outer track: *not directly* involved in making great power policy on Southern African questions. We also like to think they were not dependent on any other grouping for shaping their own policies. This is a debatable point and *realpolitik* is of course something else, as we shall no doubt hear during the days to come.

– There were also some common problems between these areas when it came to deal directly with South Africa and the countries of Southern Africa. One such trivial problem is that whatever policies these countries chose to pursue, Canadians and Scandinavians had to have some official policy vis-à-vis them. We have to have some policy towards private enterprise in our own countries. We thought we could not control their relations with South Africa or the countries in Southern Africa.

– We are or were also *unimportant,* in a positive sense, it probably would not matter economically if we withdrew from South Africa. But the importance of such a step by unimportant countries could be very great indeed. I only have to mention the reaction to the recent Canadian move to withdraw the commercial consuls and export support for transactions with South Africa. Even though it may be characterised as a cosmetic move it has caused dramatic and irritated reactions in South Africa.

Discussions on these topics over the years lead to two conclusions, one concerning the structure, the other concerning the form of the seminar.

Structure of seminars and seminar architecture may seem more important to organisers than to participants. Our original idea on the structure of the seminar was to use South Africa as a back drop, not to deal directly with the republic but to look at its influence on the future development in the other countries. The discussion should be focussed on what we consider important, i.e. our relations or the Scandinavian and Canadian relations with the states whose fate is in one way or another connected with the general situation that South Africa's policies have created in the area.

I would like once again to stress the words "*our* relations", *us*. It is our policy options. The future of Southern Africa is in the hands of the Africans and we make no pretension at all telling them what to do. This seminar should be about us, because we have a job to do in the Western community: we have to try to exercise influence on those who influence the politics of South Africa. They are in the Western world. The West is the decisive force shaping South African policy. At present and still for a long time to come South Africa will move in the direction into which it will be pushed by the Western powers. It is our job to push them.

These were some of the ideas, from four, five years ago. Some are still valid but it may be instructive to see how our attitudes have changed over time. It is certainly instructive to list briefly the major events over the last five years that have made our views change:

1. The collapse of the Portuguese empire in Southern Africa. The *victory of FRELIMO* in Mozambique upset the whole idea of a white buffer zone for the *apartheid* regimes, towards the north.

The economy of the illegal regime in Rhodesia was weakened by the problems of not being able to transport goods through Mozambique.

The new opportunities for the Zimbabwe freedom movements to have bases in a liberated Mozambique also played a major role. FRELIMO's victory was also an inspiration for the black population of South Africa itself, symbolized by the demonstrations that organisations within the Black Consciousness movement held in the summer 1975 to congratulate FRELIMO on their victory.

The outcome of the war in Angola was a setback for the South African-US-Zairian combination and for the Angolan organisations supported by them. The myth of the invincibility of the South African war machine was shattered and this again was a stimulus for the black population of South Africa.

2. For the *liberation of Namibia* the MPLA victory was very important, but a more important factor is that without SWAPO participation no lasting solution is possible in Namibia.

3. The *situation in Zimbabwe* has changed drastically. The guerilla war has become more intensive and better organized, especially through the alliance between ZANU and ZAPU in the Patriotic Front. The African states decided in 1977 to channel their support via the OAU to the Patriotic Front. The deliberations concerning an *internal settlement* will therefore only further sharpen the conflict.

4. The cooperation between the *frontline states* is a new and important phenomenon: there is a unity in supporting the Patriotic Front. They constitute an embryo of a more solid group of independent states to counterbalance the military and economic power of South Africa.

5. The *development in the Republic itself* has caused earlier ideas to change among

both researchers and policy makers. Five years ago many people talked about detente, dialogue, of giving time a chance, about the change in the conditions of the black worker, about gradual change and pressure from foreign economic interests and about cooperation with Prime Minister Vorster to "solve" the problems in Namibia and Rhodesia. Those are positions that are not presented or discussed with the same interest today: the Polaroid experiment, the Oppenheimer thesis have gone the same way as other fads and fashions, be they hemlines, pop music or the green revolution, or Leon Sullivan's "six principles". It is necessary to remember that recently other events in the republic are also important.

   – The drastically increasing armament of South Africa;

   – the massacre of school children and others in opposition after Soweto, the increasing brutality and escalation of torture and police murder;

   – the continued forced movement of peoples;

   – the peculiar "independence" of Transkei and Bophutu-Tswana;

   – the eradication of the last remains of open opposition: both Black Consciousness Movement and the white liberal or radical opinion;

   – the continued occupation of Namibia.

All these events have given a mortal blow to the idea of a peaceful solution that many of us believed in some years ago. More and more people now also understand the truth in the analysis put forward by the liberation movements for quite some time: one has to understand South Africa not only in terms of ideology of race and *apartheid,* but also that we are dealing with a colonising and oppressive and exploitative economic system. In the words of the former Swedish Prime Minister Olof Palme: "Neutrality towards the existing and coming struggle in Southern Africa is impossible. Between the exploiters and the exploited there is no middle ground. We cannot escape the question: Whose allies do we want to be? Which side are we on?"

   6. A lot of interesting information surfaced on the *relations* between the *apartheid* regime and the powers in the West, and with Israel and Iran. The documentation is overwhelming both from the research community and the activist organisations on continued investments in the republic, increasing nuclear collaboration, support from the International Monetary Fund and on the close cooperation with the NATO apparatus.

   7. A final fact I would like to mention in this catalogue of changes since we began thinking about this seminar – and which you incidentally can see from the papers presented and from the compositio of the delegations, is the much wider debate on conditions in Southern Africa that has developed over recent in our countries.

While there have been changes in official policy towards the recognition of liberation movements and towards putting international pressure on the apartheid regime, it is equally clear that informed public opinion to a much greater extent wants a more decisive policy. To this group one can today also count many of the researchers who for many years have worked on Southern African problems. The demands concern a clear cut break with the present policies of the UK and the USA, a break in military and economic cooperation and an increase in the direct support of the liberation movements. The interesting thing in Scandinavia is that this opinion has spread far outside the more militant activist groups. I would suggest that you have a look at the composition of the group that signed the final declaration of the South Africa hearing in Oslo in October 1977 which is in the conference documentation.

It is unnecessary to underline the importance of the participation of representatives of the liberation movements and the Frontline states at this seminar. We are very grateful and honoured that they found time to join us. Their presence stresses again the seriousness of the situation in Southern Africa and it will remind us of the important work that the struggling liberation movements and the Frontline states carry out now, in Southern Africa.

Against the background of these changes in Southern Africa itself, the changes in our priorities for research and changes in the climate of opinion in our own countries, we hope that this seminar will be a useful Scandinavian-Canadian arrangement. Because of the difference in background among the participants in research and administration, in their nationality and political opinions we are assured of a wide range of views, an elucidating debate and an exchange of information and ideas for research and for political action.

I. Economic and Military Linkages and Leverage

Steven Langdon

The Canadian Economy and Southern Africa

After years of agitation by Canadians concerned about oppression in Southern Africa, the Canadian government in late 1977 revised its policy on economic relations between Canada and South Africa. Policy moved from a position in which trade and investment were being promoted between the two countries (via Canadian trade commissioners, export credits and investment guarantees), to a position closer to passivity toward such economic interchange – although South Africa does continue to benefit from Canadian Commonwealth trade preferences. This Canadian policy change has been of some symbolic significance in the growing international pressure on the South African regime, but it still falls a good deal short of the positions advocated by a number of church, labour and university groups and by the social democratic opposition party in Canada – who have supported active government *discouragement* of Canadian trade and investment in South Africa, sometimes extending their arguments to proposals for a full economic embargo of that country. From the perspective of such groups, the interesting political economy questions are why it has taken the Canadian government so long to shift its policy, and why that symbolic shift has not been extended to measures that would have actively discouraged Canadian economic ties with South Africa.

An analysis of the economic ties that exist between the two areas is essential background to answering those questions. That is what this paper examines, presenting a profile, first, of trade connections, and then of investment links. After that we return to consider these political economy questions, by advancing some notions on the dynamics of change in Canadian-South African economic relations. As an introduction to the whole analysis, though, we first present a brief review of the contemporary context of Canadian economic development.

The Contemporary Canadian Economy

Considered as an advanced capitalist economy, the Canadian economy suffers from a number of serious and deep-rooted structural problems, exacerbated in the present context by a prolonged and damaging downturn in the capitalist business cycle. That downturn has taken the official Canadian unemployment rate from a

1974 low of 4.9% to a (seasonally-adjusted) rate in December 1977 of 8.5%. And it has resulted in the most recent year (1977), in combination with continuing inflation and a government wage and profit-margin control system, in a situation where real disposable income per employee in Canada has stagnated.

This prolonged cyclic downturn, though, and the failures in Canadian macroeconomic policy that underlie it, are only a part of the problem. More deep-rooted are the structural difficulties of the economy that intertwine around: very large trade deficits on end-product manufactures; very heavy trade dependence on the United States; extremely high levels of foreign control in Canadian industry; and severe regional inequalities.

Over the 1971–1976 period, Canada has typically run a small surplus on its merchandise trade, a large deficit on its non-merchandise current account and a large surplus on long-term capital account. The structure of this trade, however, has become more and more skewed to resource sector exports and end-product imports over this period. By 1976 the annual Canadian trade deficit on end products had reached $3.6 billion in 1971. The Canadian economy has clearly become relatively less able to compete in manufacturing export markets, with consequent unemployment pressures in that sector. The expansion in the resource sector, given the capital intensity of most resource extraction and processing, has not countered this pressure; and this expansion has also made the Canadian economy more subject to the volatile ups and downs of resource product prices. Thus, the drastic post-1974 declines in most mineral export prices were leading factors in prolonging the present cyclic downturn.

This structural reality, in part, reflects the traditional protectionism of Canadian trade policy. Canadian manufacturing remains highly protected by world standards (for example, Canadian manufacturing tariffs average 9.6% compared to 8.7% for the EEC countries – with especially high rates in rubber and wood products, textiles, household equipment, furniture, clothing and footwear). These barriers have cushioned the incentives that would have enforced more world-competitive manufacturing and consequent end product exports from Canada. Moreover, they have left many Canadians – especially in Quebec – working in lower-wage, labour-intensive industries. With the recent dramatic rise of Third World exports of such simpler manufactured goods, the insulation around these inefficient Canadian industries has become less effective, imposing heavy unemployment pressures that focus in a politically discontented region. The result, given the poor industrial adjustment mechanisms that Canada has in place to shift workers and capital from problem industries to new opportunities, has been a desperate erection of new import barriers – that are bound to make much of Canadian manufacturing even less internationally competitive in the future.

The long-run impact of protectionism is only part of the manufacturing problem, however. Another major factor is heavy foreign ownership of such industry. As of 1974, foreign firms controlled 99% of capital employed in the rubber industry, 96% in automibiles and parts, 85% in chemicals, 71% in electrical goods, 63% in agricultural machinery and 57% in transportation equipment – for an overall control of 57% of total Canadian manufacturing capital employed.[1] It can be expected, in such circumstances, that manufacturing in Canada will not be characterized by heavy innovation, product development and aggressive export marketing efforts – since most Canadian-based firms will be adjuncts to foreign multinational enterprises organizing such efforts from their head offices abroad.

This foreign ownership pattern has also added a further pressure in the recent Canadian economic context through stepped-up outflows of funds. Interest and dividend payments abroad have raised the deficit on that item in the Canadian balance-of-payments from $1.1 billion in 1971 to $2.6 billion in 1976, while service payment outflows have also escalated, raising the deficit on that item from $765 million to $1.435 million; the great bulk of these payments flow from affiliates to their parent firms abroad.[2]

Any Canadian attempts to respond to these manufacturing industry inefficiencies, foreign ownership patterns, related end-product trade deficits, and associated employment problems are complicated by two factors. First, over 1974–1976, some 66.1% of all Canadian domestic exports went to the United States, including 82% of Canadian end-product exports; the immense range of markets Canada served there, some under special tariff-free access, plus the aggressive trade strategies of the U.S. government, tended to reduce the leverage a Canadian government could have in organizing or assisting better penetration of such a market. Second, the traditional suspicion between government and business in Canada means that it is difficult for the state to organize and plan industrial restructuring in Canada to establish more efficient manufacturing industry – as through French indicative planning. This absence of state-business co-operation in Canada has also made it difficult to organize effective investment shifts to respond to the serious regional inequalities in the country.

Nevertheless, within these constraints, there have been some limited government attempts to respond to these manufacturing/employment problems. Most important, the government has consciously tried to penetrate new markets for Canadian end products, including the EEC countries and the Third World (strict Canadian procurement conditions in the context of a relatively large aid program assist in this). Moreover, the Canadian government has worked anxiously to support those few Canadian-controlled multinationals that have emerged on a world scale – on the assumption that such international operations would generate improved Canadian exports and high-wage jobs. More recently, the government has also tried energetically to pull business into closer consultation with it – and to control wages so as to assist manufacturers to improve their cost competitiveness more quickly.

In short, the Canadian government has made a limited attempt to respond to the serious difficulties in the contemporary capitalist economy of the country, though this attempt could hardly have been successful in solving either the structural or the cyclical dilemmas of that economy. It can be argued, indeed, that only radical strategies to deal with foreign ownership, and socialist investment planning to

17

restructure manufacturing, could be expected to cope with these serious dilemmas. But the fact remains that the approach that has been taken by the Canadian government in this context represents a significant backdrop to that government's policy on South African-Canadian economic relations. It is to an examination of those relations that we now turn.

Canadian Trade Relations with South Africa

Canada and South Africa do not conduct extensive trading relations. As Table 1 shows, Canadian exports to South Africa have represented well under one-half of one percent of total Canadian exports since 1971, with the percentage value shrinking significantly from 1968–70. Even in absolute terms, the data show a decline in the value of such exports in the last two years. Nor are Canadian imports from South Africa very significant in Canadian import totals – though there has been something of an increase in their relative importance in the last half of the 1968–77 period. This increase has meant that in the last five full years in the table, Canada has run a deficit in trade relations with South Africa (reaching a total of $176.4 million over 1972–76) – compared with a surplus of $128 million over the first four years in the table. While this change in Canada's net trade balance with South Africa has reflected some shift in the relative advantages gained by each side in this exchange relationship, however, the main point to emphasize remains how marginal the whole relationship is for the Canadian economy.

Are there perhaps some particularly strategic commodities, though, that enter into this trade? Tables 2 and 3 provide detailed data on recent flows to test this question. Imports, as Table 2 shows, concentrate around raw sugar and a number of other raw or semi-processed products, none of which appears to be difficult for the Canadian economy to obtain elsewhere. In that sense, these commodities could hardly be called strategic. Significant exports, though, as Table 3 shows, cover a much wider range. While none of these commodities could really be considered a crucial input into the South African economy, the details of this range do convey a rather unusual pattern. Although there are some raw and semi-processed items noted in Table 3, what is most striking is the importance of capital goods and finished manufactured products in this list (from mining machinery to combines to motor vehicle parts). This is the export profile of a mature, successful manufacturing economy – a profile which, in general, we have noted above, is not reflected in Canadian trade relationships.

This points to a rather important reality in Canadian export trade to South Africa, brought out more dramatically in Table 4. To a much greater extent than in the rest of the world, Canada exports mainly manufactured end products to South Africa. Comparing lines 2 and 3 in Table 4 makes this clear. This means that when Canadian trade in manufacturing is analysed, South Africa emerges as a more important export market than the declining percentages in Table 1 above would suggest. This is brought out in a slightly different way in line 4 in Table 4. In considering a strategy to build markets for manufactured goods *outside* the United States (as discussed in section 1), the South African market would loom quite large to Canadian officials – with over 4% of such Canadian sales being made in South Africa in 1975, for example.

Overall, then, Canadian trade *is* marginal with South Africa, when considered from the perspective of the Canadian economy as a whole. However, Canadian exports to South Africa are much more sophisticated, being heavily skewed toward end products, compared to Canadian export patterns to the world as a whole. This has undoubtedly made South African trade seem more significant to the Canadian economy for those emphasizing the penetration of non-U.S. manufacturing markets as the solution to Canadian economic dilemmas. The South African market is one that Canadian manufactured goods have clearly had some success in penetrating.

Canadian Direct Investment Relations with South Africa

Until quite recently, Canada has been notable in the context of direct investment flows primarily as a major net recipient of such transfers of capital and technology. As Table 5 shows, however, there has been quite a marked shift in this pattern since 1973; in balance-of-payments terms, Canada has become a net exporter of direct capital investment. Detailed data show that this Canadian direct investment abroad is dominated by a very small number of firms (17 enterprises in 1973 accounted for 64% of Canadian direct foreign investment), is undertaken mainly by Canadian-controlled corporations (79% of such foreign capital stock was Canadian-controlled in 1973), and is increasingly focused in Third World countries.[3] Recent increased flows abroad, indeed, can be explained in terms of a very small number of Canadian resource corporations investing heavily in a few large Third World mineral extraction projects. Overall, these data reflect the growing significance of a number of Canadian multinational enterprises in the international capitalist economy (including Noranda, Massey-Ferguson, Comincok Consolidated Bathurst, Inco, Alcan, Brascan, Moore Corporation, MacMillan-Bloedel, Canada Packers, Distillers Corporation-Seagrams, Domtar and Stelco).

Tables 6 and 7 provide details on the South African role within this pattern. They indicate an increase in Canadian direct investment in South Africa in the 1971–1972 period, but a generally decreased level in more recent years – though significant Canadian direct investments are clearly still taking place as of 1975–1977 (with over $34 million in new flows there in that period). What is most striking about the data, though, as shown in Table 6, is the very small proportion of such investment from Canadian-controlled corporations (only 23% in 1975). Unlike most Canadian direct investment abroad, that in South Africa is clearly controlled by non-Canadian multinational corporations (such as Ford, in particular, and Falconbridge). For *Canadian* multinationals, as the last column in Table 6 indicates, the South African connection is very marginal to their activities.

19

Table 8 provides a somewhat fuller profile of Canadian direct investment in South Africa. Most important, it indicates that only a small number of Canadian-based firms are active in South African investment (a total of 28, and 10 of these clearly have quite limited investments – see the "other industries" row). Those few investments valued at over $8 million each account for 77% of total investments in 1975, a level of concentrated ownership that reflects the pattern in Canadian direct foreign investment as a whole. Where the South African pattern diverges most from the usual is in the heavy emphasis on manufacturing investment (it accounts for 79% in 1975; in overall Canadian direct foreign investment in 1973 only 50% was accounted for by manufacturing).⁴ Mining and smelting activity also looms larger for Canadian investment in South Africa – while financial and utilities investment is much less important there than in the overall Canadian investment pattern. Canadian banks are involved in international financial consortia with which South Africa deals, but they have not made direct investments in South Africa, unlike their activities in many other parts of the world.⁵

It should be stressed that the small number of firms involved in this investment process, plus the large size of some individual projects, mean that a number of large corporations based in Canada have important subsidiaries, quite significant to corporate wellbeing, operating in South Africa. This is an important political economy reality, considered further below, even though the data do show how marginal Canadian investment in South Africa is for the overall Canadian economy. Such Canadian-controlled companies as Massey-Ferguson and Alcan have quite large South African operations, and so do non-Canadian multinationals based in Canada (the latter firms also have an important political influence within Canada, based on important operations in Canada); of these latter, Ford is undoubtedly the most significant. The fact that these operations in South Africa are concentrated in manufacturing has a good deal to do, too, with the heavy Canadian manufacturing exports to South Africa discussed above. This is suggested by the heavy flows, shown in Table 3 above, of trucks, motor vehicle parts, tractors and combine reapers from Canada to South Africa (coinciding with the major Canadian direct manufacturing investment in South Africa). One could probably account for the high Canadian exports of capital equipment to South Africa in the same direct investment context.

There is a further facet to the Canadian-South African direct investment relationship that should be noted, too – particularly in any assessment of economic leverage that might be exerted from Canada on South Africa. In fact, direct investment controlled by South African corporations in Canada looms larger than Canadian direct investments in South Africa. Table 9 indicates this, though somewhat imprecisely; "African" investment in Canada is, in practice, virtually the same as "South African" investment – but small differences may, nevertheless, exist.

The Political Economy of Change in Canadian-South African Relations

The patterns of relationship discussed in the two previous sections, taken in the context of the Canadian economy, help to answer the questions posed at the beginning of this paper: why has it taken so long for the Canadian government to amend its economic policies toward South Africa, and why have these amendments not taken the direction of active discouragement of Canadian-South African economic ties? These questions arise with even more force in the light of how marginal this review has shown these ties to be to the Canadian economy as a whole.

The explanation of Canadian government policy would appear to lie in the serious structural problems of the domestic economy, and in the responses which government has made to those problems. As the section on the Canadian economy suggested, the weakness of Canadian manufacturing as reflected in high end-product trade deficits, massive foreign ownership and heavy trade dependence on the United States, has led the federal government to promote both Canadian manufacturing penetration of non-U.S. markets and the growth of Canadian multinational enterprises. In terms of such an effort, the South African connection must have looked quite important to government officials. South Africa *was* a market which Canadian manufacturers had penetrated successfully, selling considerable end products (including capital goods) there. And there were a number of significant Canadian multinationals with important operations in South Africa (even if most "Canadian" direct investments in the country were non-Canadian controlled).

This would explain why officials in the Department of Industry, Trade and Commerce fought so hard to prevent any economic break with South Africa, and why "realists" in the Department of External Affairs accepted this view. In the Canadian political economy, the very particular interests of those manufacturing firms organizing South African trade and investment – particularly given the government's very narrow conception of an industrial strategy for Canada – weighed much more heavily than the pressures for change from liberal and social democratic groups.

The recent amendments in government policy, indeed, almost certainly resulted from the greatly increased focus on the South African issue at the international level, rather than from changed balances in power among domestic political forces in Canada. Canada has made a symbolic political gesture in the context of growing pressure from the OECD industrial capitalist countries on the South African regime. But it is likely that the impact of this on Canadian economic links with South Africa will be almost negligible; trade within the framework of multinational enterprises does not need trade commissioners to promote it, and the Canadian direct investment in South Africa is so concentrated, and largely organized by such a small number of big firms, that the elimination of investment guarantee insurance will be meaningless. Expanded trade and investment by smaller Canadian firms will be somewhat discouraged; but these are not leading factors in the Canadian-South African relationship anyway.

The suggestion is, then, that more substantive change in these economic links is ruled out in the present context of Canadian political economy by the prolonged economic recession in Canada, by the more fundamental structural difficulties in the economy, and by the narrow policy strategy which the federal government has adopted to deal with these problems of Canadian capitalism.

The implication of that is that rather basic shifts in the Canadian political economy are essential to any serious Canadian policy change on South Africa. There *are* various elements of economic leverage in the Canadian context that determined political leaders could use – including the freezing of South African assets in Canada, an embargo on Canadian imports from South Africa, and exchange controls to prevent any capital transfers to South Africa. However, these levers will not be used unless: a) South Africa becomes a much more dramatic domestic political issue in Canada (and, given Canada's constitutional problems and internal economic troubles, that is most unlikely); or b) a change occurs in the domestic political context inside Canada, leading to quite different strategies toward Canada's manufacturing weaknesses, and to much reduced influence for the small number of large corporations that now dominate Canadian-South African economic relationships.

Conclusion

The major conclusion of this paper is that South African economic ties are, in fact, of very marginal significance to the well-being of Canadians as a whole. A much tougher Canadian policy stance toward South Africa would impose virtually negligible economic costs on Canada.

Despite this, the overwhelming moral arguments for strong moves against the institutionalized racism of South Africa have had a minimal impact on Canadian policy. This paper has suggested that the reasons for this can be found in the particular character of Canada's links with South Africa – Canadian manufactured goods penetrate South African markets better than they do much of the world, and Canadian multinationals have some important investments there. Facing serious economic difficulties domestically, Canadian policy-makers have responded through a narrow industrial strategy which tries to penetrate non-U.S. manufacturing markets and to promote Canadian multinationals. This strategy has meant the Canadian government has not been prepared to move significantly against South Africa on the economic level.

The implication is that major shifts in the relative strength of Canadian political forces – and consequent overall economic strategy changes within Canada – will be essential requirements in the taking of serious Canadian policy initiatives against the white South African regime.

Notes:

1. "Ownership and Control of Capital Employed in Non-Financial Industries, 1974, *"Statistics Canada Daily,* Dec. 16, 1977, pp. 3–4.
2. See "Business Service Receipts and Payments, 1973-Special," *Statistics Canada Daily,* July 14, 1975.
3. See S.W. Langdon, "Canadian Private Direct Investment and Technology Marketing in Developing Countries," Background Study for the Economic Council of Canada, 1977, chap. 1.
4. Statistics Canada, *Canada's International Investment Position, 1971–1973,* (Catalogue 67–202 Annual), Table 5.
5. See E.W. Clendenning, *The Euro-currency Markets and the International Activities of Canadian Banks,* Ottawa: Economic Council of Canada, 1976, chap. 8.

Table I. *Canadian trade with South Africa, 1968–1977*

Year	Value of Canadian Domestic Exports to South Africa *($ million)*	As Percentage of Total Canadian Domestic Exports	Value of Canadian Imports from South Africa *($ million)*	As Percentage of Total Canadian Imports
1968	$68.3	0.52%	$39.3	0.32%
1969	78.5	0.54	45.9	0.32
1070	104.0	0.63	45.7	0.33
1971	62.8	0.36	54.6	0.35
1972	43.9	0.23	58.9	0.32
1973	64.7	0.26	81.1	0.35
1974	93.3	0.29	117.2	0.36
1975	132.2	0.41	193.8	0.56
1976	96.3	0.26	155.8	0.42
1977 (9 months)	59.9	0.19	51.4	0.24

Source: Statistics Canada, *Imports by Country,* issues from 1969, 1971, 1974, 1976, 1977; *Exports by Country,* same years.

Table 2. *Major Canadian imports from South Africa, 1974–1977*

Commodity	Value of Flow ($000) 1974	1975	1976	1977 (9 months)
canned fruit	3026	4337	2822	466
raw sugar	69063	134117	95091	23835
wool	2017	2478	4825	1530
other crude non-metallic minerals	1959	3746	4578	1267
wood pulp	–	6729	3709	–
steel plate and sheet	691	582	2057	1327
iron and steel and alloys	10985	14093	10931	4904
other non-ferrous metals and alloys	1785	3689	5264	2542
natural and synthetic gem stones	3184	3808	559	737

Source: Statistics Canada, *Imports by Country,* 1976, 1977.

Steven Langdon

Table 3. *Major Canadian exports to South Africa, 1974–1977*

Commodity	Value of Flow ($000)			
	1974	1975	1976	1977 (9 months)
Zinc ores and concentrate	4999	2416	2731	–
Sulphur	5489	8752	11008	8009
Wood pulp	3878	3210	6813	3921
Paper	6620	4524	1296	927
Synthetic rubber and plastic material	920	1009	1152	134
Plastics – basic shapes	1627	1517	869	788
Steel plate and sheet	2081	5073	–	7
Basic metal fabricated products	1002	955	996	786
Basic products – other non-metallic minerals	4372	4122	5383	1651
Materials handling machinery	1062	884	1153	537
Other general purpose industrial machinery	530	1999	737	239
Drilling/excavating/mining machinery	1098	1271	1274	1297
Metalworking machinery	820	1504	2666	1138
Construction machinery	558	1466	1410	42
Other special industries machinery	433	1481	1273	568
Combine reaper-threshers	531	1429	2796	2171
Tractors	1142	2489	128	23
Trucks, truck tractors and chassis	14739	44458	15399	13462
Other motor vehicles	320	472	3893	1750
Motor vehicle parts	7012	13938	8669	2279
Other telecommunications equipment	1269	1092	672	347
Electric lighting and distributing equipment	1034	801	1340	1014
Other measuring, laboratory, medical and optical equipment	1320	1429	1341	840
Office machines and equipment	1318	1690	426	808

Source: Statistics Canada, *Exports by Country,* 1976, 1977.

24

Table 4. *Canadian exports of end products to South Africa, 1974–1977*

	1974	1975	1976	1977 (9 months)
1. Value of Canadian Exports of End Products to South Africa ($000)	40,062	84,709	51,397	31,255
2. Canadian End Product Exports to South Africa as Percentage of Total Canadian Exports to South Africa	42.9%	64.1%	53.4%	52.2%
3. Total Canadian End Product Exports as Percentage of Total Canadian Exports	29.2%	32.0%	33.5%	34.0%
4. Canadian End Product Exports to South Africa as Percentage of all Canadian End Product Exports Outside the United States	2.7%	4.1%	2.3%	1.8%

Source: Calculated from Statistics Canada, *Exports by Country,* 1976, 1977.

Table 5. *Canadian capital inflows and outflows for direct investment, 1967–1976*

	Direct Investment Flows Into Canada	Out of Canada	Surplus (+) or Deficit (–)
1967	$691 million	$125 million	+ $566 million
1968	590	225	+ 365
1969	720	370	+ 350
1970	905	315	+ 350
1971	925	230	+ 695
1972	620	400	+ 220
1973	750	785	− 35
1974	725	775	− 50
1975	630	650	− 20
1976	− 90	550	− 640

Note: It should be stressed that this table covers only inflows and outflows of capital; it ignores reinvested earnings, either by foreign corporations in Canada, or by Canadian corporations abroad.

Source: Statistics Canada, *Quarterly Estimates of the Canadian Balance of International Payments,* 24:3, Jan., 1977, pp. 26–27, 56; *Canadian Statistical Review Weekly Supplement,* Mar. 25, 1977, p. 2.

Steven Langdon

Table 6. *Stock of Canadian direct investment in South Africa, 1968–1975*

Year	Book Value of Canadian Direct Investment in South Africa ($ million) (a)	Book Value of Canadian Controlled Direct Investment in South Africa ($ million) (b)	(a) As Percentages of All Canadian Direct Foreign Investment	(b) As Percentages of All Canadian Controlled Direct Foreign Investment
1968	58	14	1.26%	0.46%
1969	65	12	1.25	0.36
1970	73	12	1.18	0.30
1971	111	27	1.70	0.58
1972	106	30	1.58	0.55
1973	105	26	1.34	0.42
1974	109	34	1.17	0.45
1975	119	36	1.11	0.43

Source: Statistics Canada, *Canada's International Investment Position* (67–202 Annual), 1968–1970, 1971–1973 issues, table 4; *Statistics Canada Daily,* Dec. 12, 1977, p. 3; unpublished data from the Balance of Payments Division, Statistics Canada.

Table 7. *Canadian capital outflows for direct foreign investment in South Africa, 1970–1977[a]*

Direct Investment Outflows Year	Net Outflows[b]	Net Outflows to South Africa at Percentage of Total Canadian (% million)
1970	− 2	0.6%
1971	− 30	13.0
1972	− 13	3.3
1973	+ 11	−1.4
1974	− 4	0.5
1975	− 18	2.8
1976	− 11	2.0
1977 (9 months)[c]	− 5	n.a.

Notes:
a. As with Table 5, it should be stressed that this table ignores reinvested earnings.
b. A negative entry in this column indicates a net outflow from Canada; a positive entry indicates that capital repatriation to Canada has led to a net inflow to Canada.
c. Data for this year, for technical reasons, underestimate overall outflows to South Africa.

Source: Unpublished data, Balance of Payments Division, Statistics Canada.

Table 8. *Industrial sector and size composition of Canadian direct investment in South Africa,*
1972–1975

Book value of Canadian direct investment in South Africa	1972	1973	1974	1975
Divided by industry sector: (Number of firms in brackets)				
a) Manufacturing	$74 million (12)	$73 million (9)	$82 million (9)	$94 million (9)
b) Mining & Smelting ⎱	(9)	$31 million (11)	$25 million (11)	$24 million (9)
	$32 million			
c) Other Industries ⎰	(9)	$1 million (6)	$2 million (8)	$1 million (10)
d) TOTAL	$106 million (30)	$105 million (26)	$109 million (28)	$119 million (28)
Divided by size of investment in the foreign concern:				
a) Over $8 million	$78 million	$79 million	$82 million	$92 million
b) $1–8 million	$23 million	$21 million	$22 million	$22 million
c) Under $1 million	$ 5 million	$ 5 million	$ 5 million	$ 5 million

Source: Unpublished data, Balance of Payments Division, Statistics Canada.

Table 9. *African-controlled direct foreign investment in Canada, 1966–1975*

Year	Total Book Value Controlled ($ million)	As a Percentage of Book Value of All Foreign Controlled Direct Investment in Canada
1966	$74	0.3%
1967	113	0.4
1968	141	0.5
1969	369	1.1
1970	553	1.5
1971	603	1.5
1972	571	1.3
1973	544	1.2
1974	579	1.1
1975	501	0.9

Source: As in Table 6; *Statistics Canada Daily,* Jan. 10, 1978, p. 4.

John S. Saul

Canadian Bank Loans to South Africa

One assumes that the pairing of Canadian and Scandinavian "perspectives and policy options" vis-à-vis Southern Africa which structures this conference represents a mere matter of institutional convenience and not some return to the bad old days of the fifties and sixties when Canada, with Sweden, slipped by, on the international stage, as a sensitive and humane "middle power", in, but in some vague way not of, the imperial camp, perhaps even a neutral, certainly a supporter of oppressed peoples everywhere. Whatever the truth of such an image with respect to Sweden (or other Scandinavian countries), in Canada's case it was spun almost exclusively out of rhetorical posturings and bore no real relationship to the reality of our economic, military and political alignments.

To be sure, some were taken in by this image, both at home and abroad. Thus President Nyerere, for all his other virtues no clear-eyed analyst of imperialism, could startle Canadian progressives (in 1969) with the notion that he did not find Canada's "comparative power intimidating, but rather a reassurance in world affairs" and praise Lester Pearson, the old Cold Warrior himself, for showing "Canada's acceptance of the principle of human equality and dignity". Closer to the mark, surely, was Marcellino dos Santos, Vice President of FRELIMO, who, in an interview on CBC-Radio (1973) concerning Canada's role vis-à-vis his own people's struggle for human equality and dignity, was asked whether his cause was receiving any help from Canada. His reply:

Really, Canada has made many statements but . . . I must say frankly that, knowing and having heard that Canada (has) said several times . . . but knowing that Canada is doing nothing real to help the liberation movements, one should at least ask: is . . . the Government of Canada sincere. We don't believe it, and we hope that Canada will try to show us that it is really sincere.

To what would dos Santos attribute "this ambiguity (sic) in the attitude of Canada" the interviewer continued. "I'm forced to accept that Canada continues to think it preferable to have relations with colonialist and fascist regimes than with people who are fighting for their freedom and their dignity". It was no accident that, on the occasion of Mozambique's celebration of its independence in June, 1975, the new FRELIMO government chose to ignore pressures from Canada to be an official guest and instead invited two delegates from the Canadian liberation support movement to represent Canada – to represent, as it was put to us in Maputo, the Canadian people – many of whom had supported the Mozambican liberation struggle over the years – and not the Canadian state – which had not.

Indeed, quite the contrary. As dos Santos suggests, Canada's stance regarding Portugal's colonial presence is quite a revealling one. On this subject the conclusion reached several years ago by the Toronto Committee for the Liberation of Portugal's African Colonies (now the Toronto Committee for the Liberation of Southern Africa – TCLSAC) in its book *Words and Deeds: Canada, Portugal and Africa* seems a fair one. The Committee found a pattern of "rhetorical commitment to the cause of popular freedom on the one hand and 'business as usual' with the oppressive white minority regimes on the other". As demonstrated in detail in that volume, Canada's support for Portuguese rule took three inter-related forms:

Economically, our bodies corporate and governmental partook readily, and greedily, of the spoils available from the superexploitation which Portuguese hegemony guaranteed in its African holdings. In doing so, we chose to ignore that such economic activity also helped bankroll an otherwise shaky Portuguese economy in its feckless military endeavours. Militarily, through uncritical acceptance of the NATO connection which married the arsenal of the West to Portuguese colonial purposes, Canada made itself, willy-nilly, a partner of the Portuguese. Perhaps most galling of all, on the diplomatic front our spokespersons also served the cause of Portuguese oppression and Western imperialism well by undermining, systematically, the claims of the liberation movements – and of the African people – to their rightful primacy in arbitrating the fate of their own countries. . . (In short) Canada's official record with respect to Portugal's African colonies was a bleak one indeed.

Note the title of this book: *Words and Deeds*. The phrase captures the essence of Canada's role, an essence which even Prime Minister Trudeau, in one of his rare moments of candour, also underlined several years ago when noting our similar posture with reference to South Africa: "It's not consistent. Either we should stop trading or we should stop condemning". In practice, of course, Canada under Pearson's and Trudeau's leadership has continued to do both.

There are a number of themes that could be pursued here: our long-term record of silent complicity within NATO regarding the military linkages established between western capitalist countries and, not just Portugal, but also South Africa, or our above-mentioned penchant for down-grading the claims of liberation movements to represent the legitimate aspirations of their peoples and the legitimate (necessarily non-peaceful) means for the latter's liberation (our gesture of humanitarian aid as outlined in Ladouceur's paper introducing only a minor qualification to this pattern). One could also explore the reasons for our having played the role we have: the imperatives of our dependent economy and the instrumentalization of our state to service the activities of multi-nationals working from a Canadian base, the logic of our own indigneous and unrepentantly capitalist system (cf. the brilliant exposition in Langdon's paper which is, however, almost too brilliant in its pursuit of some special explanation for the rather matter-of-fact nature of our on-going corporate links with South Africa), our political (and uncritical) encapsulation within the "western alliance" under the thumb of the United States (thanks in no small part to the activities of that exemplary Lester Pearson), our cultural imprisonment within the ideological framework of modern liberalism, domestic and global, and so on.

But since our subject is the banks, it is the substance of our economic stance towards South Africa which is the primary issue. And, as Trudeau has emphasized above, it is precisely here that the gap between words and deeds is most evident. More recently, Trudeau's words have again spoken volumes. Despite his articulation of the usual pieties at last June's Commonwealth Conference, Trudeau was pressed to go further. The Canadian press then characterized him as "firmly resisting the urgings of black Commonwealth leaders to clamp down on the operations of Canadian companies in southern Africa" and quoted him as saying "as far as the private sector is concerned we will not interfere in trade nor investment". Geoffrey Stevens of the *Globe and Mail* took him up on one aspect of this in a refreshing manner:

Mr Trudeau is on shakier ground when it comes to some of Canada's own double standards. Mr Kaunda had urged the Commonwealth to unite to end the "exploitation and plunder of Namibian wealth". At his press conference yesterday, Mr Trudeau was asked whether he supported that appeal and whether, if he did, the Canadian Government would take action against Falconbridge Nickel operations in Namibia (which is illegally controlled by South Africa). The Prime Minister replied that his federal Government had caused Crown corporations to withdraw from South Africa, but said no action is contemplated on Falconbridge. "As far as the private sector is concerned, we are not interfering in existing trade (and) investment. This distinction between publicly owned and privately owned Canadian companies is not one which impresses any African.

Nor should it impress any of us at this Conference.

To be sure, the times they are a-changing in Southern Africa. Vis-à-vis Portugal in Africa Canada was prepared to follow, in hand-me-down fashion, the preachments of Kissinger's infamous NSSM 39. But Kissinger's own game plan was soon in flux. Too late in Mozambique, too late in Angola, to guarantee neo-colonial regimes, Kissinger sought to move more quickly in Rhodesia and Namibia to ensure the transition to pliable black governments before an escalation of the struggles there opened up genuine revolutionary possibilities. As he put the point to the Senate Foreign Relations Committee in May 1976, "we have a stake . . . in not having the whole continent become radical and move in a direction which is incompatible with Western interests. That is the issue." Or as his then side-kick Anthony Crosland emphasized with reference to the Geneva conference spawned by Kissinger: "if the British government gave up hope, there would be no doubt who would eventually win on the battlefield. But if the issue were settled on the battlefield it would seriously lessen the chance of bringing about *a moderate African regime* in Rhodesia and would open the way for *more radical solutions* and external intervention of the part of others". (emphases added)

Nor has much changed with the ascension of Carter to the Presidency. The premises for African action were spelt out clearly by U.N. Ambassador Andrew Young when he was asked the following question last year: "Some foreign policy observers have said that the U.S. has two foreign policy options in southern Africa, one being neo-colonialism and the other being out-right support of the minority government of South Africa. Could you just comment on this idea and what kind of options we have in southern Africa?" His answer:

I don't even see that many. I don't think that the United States has but one option and that's neo-colonialism.

This is clear, if difficult, enough for Rhodesia/Zimbabwe and Namibia, much more complex for South Africa. But surely some reform, some kind of liberalization, is possible there too: South Africa as Selma, Alabama. Unfortunately for Young this is not an historical comparison which stands up very well to serious scrutiny, yet it is necessary to note it here despite that fact. For it is within the framework of such a shifting American policy that one must locate Canada's initiatives of December last, initiatives which have earned Canada's Southern Africa policy a considerable amount of international attention. First and foremost, they stand as a signal to South Africa that the West is nervous about the direction of developments there, and about the escalation of confrontation which is in train. In this respect, Canada is not far off Andrew Young's wave-length. Secondarily, of course, such initiatives are also a signal to those in Black Africa who will still listen that Canada remains on the warpath for freedom.

On the warpath, but once again largely rhetorically. Seriously scrutinized the policies announced in December reveal themselves to be far more symbol than substance. Thus the work of the re-called Trade Commissioners in facilitating Canada-South Africa economic links will merely be carried on by locally hired personnel, while the withdrawal of Export Development Corporation facilities affected only one long dormant account and *not* the more crucial government to business account. No word yet on the trade preferences which bring South African sugar to Canada on a protected basis, no word on the tax-relief afforded Falconbridge on its illegal Namibia operations. Every indication that Industry, Trade and Commerce will continue to facilitate trade tours of businessmen to South Africa and the like, even if we can expect rather fewer of the fulsome articles which have been periodically published in *Commerce Canada* extolling the virtues of the South African investment climate. No indication, certainly, of any *positive* action to stem Canadian corporate activity in South Africa, no indication of any concern as to the propriety of Canadian bank loans to the South African government. As Trudeau indicated in London, the private sector remains sacrosanct. Moreover, as External Affairs Department spokesmen have made perfectly clear (e.g. Mr Harry Carter speaking recently in Toronto) this – this token gesture – is all that can be expected by way of government action for the forseeable future.

What, then, of the links of Canada's private sector to the South African economy, links about which the Canadian government waxes so indifferent and claims such impotence. Though any number of corporations might be focussed upon, the above-mentioned involvment of Canadian banks in direct loans to the South African government is a particularly apt target for a number of reasons.

The large bank loans – now running to a total of 2–3 billion dollars – made available to South Africa by various consortia in recent years has been of great significance in strengthening the latter economy (and the entire oppressive apparatus which it underwrites) at a very crucial time. Certainly it would be difficult to overestimate the importance of the extensive credit made available by the international financial community in the "dark days" after Sharpeville. If the economy (and the state) is in somewhat parallel straits at the present time – in fact, if anything, the "crisis" is probably more structural now than in the early 60s and therefore more serious – then success in forestalling the activities of the banks involved in these loans must represent an especially weighty blow against apartheid. All the more so when one considers that such loans are directed to such important ends as meeting shortfalls on balance of payments and financing the state's Iron and Steel Corporation – of obvious significance to South Africa's armaments industry – and the Electricity Supply Commission – overseer of South Africa's growing nuclear capacity, among other things.

The negative impact of such loans for the bulk of the population in South Africa is unequivocal. Though there are strong and, I think, even overwhelming arguments against any form of western economic involvement in South Africa – after all, we have Vorster's assurance that "each trade agreement, each bank loan, each new investment is another brick in the wall of our continued existence" – the direct transfer of monies to strengthen the oppressive South African state yields fewer ambiguities than all other economic links. As the Canadian Task Force on the Churches and Corporate Responsibility has put the point, "To say that some South African Government departments or agencies can operate to the benefit of black South Africans is to fly in the face of history. Apartheid is the official policy of the South African Government and of all its departments and agencies".

The banks are particularly central institutions in our own domestic economy. Indeed, if there is an indigenous core to our capitalist class the work of Naylor, Clement and others would suggest that it lies in the financial sector. Thus in pin-pointing the role of the banks and in combatting them Canadians who seek to aid in the liberation of Southern Africa may well find themselves contributing to their own liberation.

The banks, while powerful, are also vulnerable. Unlike corporations such as Falconbridge which have little reason to solicit public support, Canadian banks are very much concerned with matters of "corporate image" and with institutional advertising. Like Gulf Oil (Canada) Ltd., a target of support groups several years ago because of its Angola entanglements, the banks may feel the cool wind of protest more quickly than some other corporations. Certainly the experience in Holland, where two of the largest Dutch banks agreed to suspend all loans to South Africa after an intensive protest campaign there, suggests that potential for the success of popular resistance to such activity does exist.

There are already many groups and individuals across Canada who are active on the bank campaign and there is the promise that more popular energies – directed *against* the banks and *against* the government – can be released by such a campaign. Here we run ahead of our story, but it is a significant point to which we will return.

To undertake the kind of detailed analysis of the current vulnerability of the South African economy necessary fully to situate the importance of foreign loans would require a paper in itself. Suffice to note here that a fundamental factor is deep contradictions which run right through the heart of the South African economy. Though profits are promised upon cheap labour, the very cheapness of the labour and the attendant structure of maldistribution domestically makes for a market constraint; moreover, adventures abroad, like that in Angola, and the breakdown of détente have made the expansion of markets in Black Africa a slower process than had been hoped by South African leaders. Yet, simultaneously, so sophisticated has South African secondary industrialization become that the import bill for machinery and advanced technology has steadily increased. To these factors must be added the unsettling fluctuations of the gold price, plus the due bills for those vast infrastructural projects which the South African government undertook at a time when that price was at its zenith. In addition, the inflow of capital on private account, while by no means stopped, is a more uncertain element in the wake of Soweto. And then there is the vast and tremendously expensive expansion of the military machine. As the *Christian Science Monitor* observed of one of the most recent loans by an international consortia: it comes ". . . at a time when South Africa is suffering from a decline in its financial fortunes. . . Racial unrest has created uncertainty about South Africa's future stability and has contributed to a slowdown in foreign investment."

What are the facts of Canadian bank involvement in the vast network of international banking consortia which has been established in the 1970s to channel money to South Africa? Evidence of both the loans themselves and of the role of Canadian banks first surfaced when documents (the so-called "Frankfurt Documents") were first leaked (in 1973) from within the U.S.-based multinational firm, the European-American Banking Corporation. The materials revealed, in the words of a brief from the Corporate Information Centre in the United States, that "a group of forty banks from the Unites States, Europe and Canada have been jointly involved in direct loans totaling over $210 million to the South African government and its agencies since late 1970". Three of Canada's five major chartered banks – the Canadian Imperial Bank of Commerce, the Toronto-Dominion Bank, and the Bank of Montreal – were found to be involved, in at least one case (a loan to ISCOR) putting up over 50% of the amount involved between them. (A fourth Canadian bank – the Royal Bank of Canada – was found to be implicated in later loans.)

This much we know as hard fact – but it was still early days in the loans to South Africa game. The volume of money involved has increased enormously and so, one assumes, has the stake of the Canadian banks. Not that it is easy to find out the further facts of the matter. The four banks have been most cagey indeed about making information available, pleading "client confidentiality" and "established business practices" when fending off inquiries from church delegations and other interested parties. Some information does filter through. When, in March 1976, a consortium loan to ESCOM was announced by Citibank officials the latter mentioned Canadian bank involvement. And South African sources tied Canadian banks into other 1976 loans of up to $338 million, with possible additional

33

John S. Saul

involvement in a major balance of payments loan that same year. Yet only the Bank of Montreal has been even (minimally) candid, answering a 1977 Annual General Meeting question about such transfers with the comment: "Yes, we still have outstanding loans with that client".

Others have been more evasive in their responses to probings by the Task Force on the Churches and Corporate Responsibility (see this group's excellent pamphlet *Bank on Apartheid* from which the following quotes are drawn):

Toronto Dominion Bank: "The Bank's policy has remained the same . . . the limited request of the churches not to grant loans to the South African government is an oversimplification of the issue . . . there would not be much business in South Africa in that case."

Canadian Imperial Bank of Commerce: "We examine all applications, and from time to time we may make loans but we will not disclose them."

Royal Bank: "We are convinced our fundamental policy is sound, ethical and responsible, and it has not changed since last year . . . we anticipate and accept accountability for the direct and indirect economic and social consequences of our economic decisions."

Certainly none will deny the significance of such loans. And all will go to elaborate lengths to defend these "hypothetical" loans as liberalizing or as non-political or as carefully chosen to be only of benefit to all the people of South Africa!

The case against the banks is clear then, although inevitably neither they nor the Canadian government are prepared to take that case very seriously. Fortunately, however, the matter does not end there. Other Canadians are not so sanguine about these matters and are much more responsive to the virtually unanimous call for an end to such loans (and other western economic involvements) by all South Africans who have sought seriously the overthrow of the apartheid system there – liberation movements like the African National Congress (ANC), political organizations like the South African Student Association (SASO) and the Black People's Convention (BPC) which have been active in recent years, liberal critics like the Christian Institute of South Africa. As Paul Ladouceur's paper underscores, there is a constituency in Canada who will rally against Canada's destructive links to South Africa, and against the Canadian government if need be, one which found expression in the *Black Paper* of 1971 and in the People's Forum on Southern Africa held at the time of the Ottawa Commonwealth Conference of 1973. Such a constituency is now beginning to find renewed expression in the campaign against the bank loans.

The initial impetus for this campaign has come from the churches. Fortified by the undertakings of American and European churches on the issue and building on the exemplary research work of Renate Pratt and others, the aforementioned Task Force on the Churches and Corporate Responsibility – an ecumenical body including representatives from the Anglican, Catholic, Lutheran, Presbyterian and United Churches – launched its effort several years ago, working to educate and rally its own constituency while also carrying on a dialogue, through private meetings and interventions at AGMs, with bank officials. Their premise: "Bank loans to the government of South Africa and its subsidiary agencies are a vote in cash for apartheid." This theme has been picked up by activists in other spheres, for example at several universities, notably at the University of Toronto; moreover, the Ontario Federation of Students, representing 140,000 college and university students, has condemned the banks' policies and has removed its funds from the banks concerned. Other provincial student federations are following suit, as is the National Union of Students, the organization which represents all postsecondary students in Canada.

Non-governmental organizations throughout Canada, such as OXFAM and CUSO are demanding that Canadian banks cease their loans and are conducting campaigns to focus public pressure, while a number of support groups are beginning to launch direct action campaigns around the issue – keying to demonstrations and the like around such dates as March 21 (Sharpeville) and June 16 (Soweto). Some twenty support groups from across the country held a meeting, jointly sponsored by CUSO and TCLSAC, in December, 1977, to co-ordinate their activities and to plan future strategies. And there are growing indications that trade unions will also be more aggressively involved in such a campaign, building on the precedent of the speech by Joe Morris (President of the Canadian Labour Congress) to the United Nations' Special Committee on Apartheid when he affirmed that ". . . if we condemn apartheid, we must also condemn those investing in it: those directly or indirectly helping to maintain this rabid system."

Obviously these actions are not at the core of our governmental life, nor are those who press them forward likely soon to become part of a movement which can realistically hope to seriously challenge the parameters of imperial dictate, capitalist rationality and bourgeois dominance which shape, in the last analysis, our South Africa policy. But it would be a mistake to ignore them altogether. Indeed, it would be unfortunate if this Conference's concern with "policy options" were to direct itself only to the possible actions of governments. Unfortunate not only because, with reference to Canada, this is a particularly grey and unpromising terrain, but also because concerned elements of the citizenry have "policy options" beyond what our state is constrained to do. By resisting the government and the corporations, such elements can certainly give resonance to the actions of the peoples of Southern Africa who are fighting for their freedom – a sense of solidarity which is important to the latter as the invitation from FRELIMO cited above gives eloquent testimony.

Furthermore, by keeping alive the question of Southern Africa, by exposing government duplicity and corporate opportunism, by forcing as many dealings as possible into the light of day, these concerned elements, if unlikely to fulfil their hopes, can at least make a contribution to restraining the powerful from doing the worst they might otherwise do. They can also contribute, through such actions, to the enlightenment of more and more fellow citizens regarding the realities of the Southern African situation. This is of considerable importance, especially when one realizes that, whatever the short term accomplishments of such activists, they must probably think of themselves as preparing, first and foremost for the (inevitable) day when the South African situation escalates even further. Then it will probably be necessary to resist even more strenuously the logic of a Canadian political economy

35

which would otherwise draw Canada further and more firmly onto the wrong side of that struggle. It seems to me important that all Canadian delegates to this Conference take seriously their own individual responsibilities – their own "policy options" – within such a possible scenario.

Abdul S. Minty

Scandinavia, Canada and the Arms Embargo

The international arms embargo against South Africa has been considered to be one of the most important decisions of the United Nations to counter-act the apartheid system. During 1963–64 the Security Council adopted resolutions calling upon member States to cease the supply of arms and military equipment to South Africa. This decision was a major victory for the independent African States and for the newly formed Organization of African Unity.

Britain, the U.S.A. and Germany

Britain was South Africa's traditional arms supplier and it had a formal military alliance with the Republic in the form of the 1955 Simonstown Naval Agreement. In 1963 Britain and the United States of America undertook not to supply South Africa in future with any weapons which could be used to enforce apartheid. However, they qualified this decision by assuring South Africa that all outstanding contracts would be fulfilled and that spares for equipment already supplied would be exempt from the embargo. The Anglo-American arms embargo was interpreted and implemented over the years in different ways by succeeding governments – and sometimes the same government was successfully pressed to enforce it more strictly. The Federal Republic of Germany, though not a traditional arms supplier to South Africa, undertook to abide by the United Nations embargo even though it was not a UN Member at that time. The policies of these three countries with regard to the embargo have been similar. In general they denied South Africa combat equipment – though helicopters, transport aircraft and other major items were sometimes supplied. Nevertheless these were substantial loopholes in their embargo which enabled South Africa to obtain components and so-called dual-purpose or civilian equipment, neither of which were considered to be the"grey area". In addition, the Republic was provided with instruments, military patents and licences as well as experts to help build up an internal armaments industry. Most of the major Western arms producing companies either set up subsidiaries in South Africa or entered into special associate relationship with local enterprises. Thus the arms embargo, as operated by Britain, the United States and the Federal Republic of Germany only covered a small range of equipment and was virtually made meaningless by the extensive military co-operation established under the guise of "normal trade".

Canada

Canada had supplied some military equipment to South Africa prior to the UN embargo. Like the other major Western powers, Ottawa also declared its intention to continue supplying spare parts for equipment already supplied to the Republic. However, as diplomatic and political pressure mounted against the supply of spare parts Canada was the first, in 1970, to seal this loophole. However, it placed no restriction on the flow of investments or the transfer of technology to assist the South African domestic arms production programme. The nature and extent of this form of Canadian co-operation has not been well publicised but when Ottawa was asked to impose governmental control over patent and licence transfer one official explained to the AAM (Anti-Apartheid Movement) in May 1977 that it was not an important aspect since other countries had more extensive arrangements of this nature with Pretoria.

France and Italy

France openly isolated the arms embargo from the very outset and soon replaced Britain as South Africa's major arms supplier. Most of South Africa's modern aircraft, tanks, ships, missiles and ammunition is of French origin. When African and international pressure was exerted sharply France undertook not to supply particular types of equipment but soon reassured Pretoria that it could obtain those items with ease: it provided South Africa with virtually all the military equipment needed by the Pretoria regime.

Italy formally pledged itself to the arms embargo but in fact provided South Africa with substantial quantities of aircraft particularly well suited for counter-insurgency operations. It also made arrangements for Aermacchi aircraft of two types to be made in the Republic in large numbers under licence. These aircraft are powered by Rolls Royce engines made under British licence in Italy and subsequently exported to South Africa.

Scandinavian Policy

The Scandinavian governments have a traditional anti-apartheid policy which is markedly different from the major Western powers. However, it is only Sweden which can be considered an arms producer though both Denmark and Norway have local enterprises which make important components for military equipment.

Sweden

South Africa has a small quantity of Bofors guns which are of Swedish origin, mainly acquired prior to the arms embargo – some of them could have been acquired from

Sweden at that time although this weapon is also produced by other countries under licences. Swedish policy and regulations are probably the most strict in relation to the arms embargo, though once again through subsidiaries such as Asea in South Africa it is possible to supply certain equipment to the South African defence forces both directly and indirectly. For this loophole to be closed the government would have to operate direct control over the production and sales policy of its companies which operate in the Republic. Until Volvo recently ceased its major operations in South Africa it would have been true to say that the armed and police forces could have obtained motor vehicles of Swedish origin without much difficulty.

Norway

As is the case with all South Africa's trading partners there are various Norwegian products which could be acquired by the South African armed forces. Just over two years ago Swapo captured considerable equipment and material from the South African forces following a successful assault in Namibia and found Norwegian tinned fish among the rations of the occupying army. It is not known whether trade of this nature is conducted directly with the South African military authorities or state institutions or via civilian enterprises in the Republic – what is known is that the "normal trade" policy of the Western countries does not place any specific ban on supplying so-called civilian products to the Pretoria regime even if it is intended for the armed forces.

In 1975 the AAM protested to the Norwegian government at the fact that the Norwegian armed forces were in fact using some sighting equipment made in South Africa. The military authorities explained that it was purchased during the early 60's from a British firm and no one had noticed that the equipment itself was clearly marked "made in South Africa". This example illustrates the difficulty which sometimes arises out of Western alliance relationships where one or more members such as Britain enjoy military co-operation with South Africa which in turn directly involves other allies such as Norway.

Denmark

The South African Navy acquired a Danish tanker in 1965 which is still in service. It is not clear whether this purchase was made directly from Denmark or via some third country. Indeed it is not even known whether the Danish authorities consider this transaction to violate the international arms embargo against South Africa.

Secondly, a certain quantity of Danish equipment appears to have been used in the manufacture of the Advokaat naval communications system based at Silvermine near the Simonstown Naval Base in South Africa. In June 1975 the Anti Apartheid Movement published certain confidential documents which were presented to the United Nations Security Council. These documents revealed that although several West German companies had joined together to manufacture the

Advokaat system they used components from various Nato countries including Britain, France, the United States of America, Denmark and the Netherlands. The official Nato forms which revealed these items and their national origin described both the actual items and the source of supply in code. Hence, it became impossible to establish which companies had been involved though of course, the code is known by all Nato Members.

There were official denials by Denmark about the sale of military components to South Africa. If the sales were in fact not made directly to South Africa then it is likely that the equipment in question was supplied via the Federal Republic of Germany or some other third country.

This case shows even more directly the way in which alliance relationships are exploited by certain western countries with the connivance if not support of their governments. No doubt it could be argued that if one Nato member placed restrictions on the sale of certain military equipment to a fellow member of the alliance, even such equipment destined for South Africa, it would strain if not seriously jeopardise the relationship between the countries concerned. Thus in matters of this kind alliance considerations virtually become paramount even where it conflicts with declared official policy and firm international obligations to the United Nations.

The NATO dimension

Like Canada, two of the three Scandinavian countries, Denmark and Norway are Nato Members. The documents published by the AAM in June 1975 also disclosed that the Nato Codification System for spares and equipment had been provided to South Africa. This System is in fact a data collection and recording system whereby Nato Members are able to simplify the process of quality control as well as the ordering of a wide variety of military and other equipment for their armed forces. By virtue of providing it to South Africa the Pretoria regime is able to exploit the full benefits of this Codification System and also saves millions of Rands. Also, its Advokaat naval communications system was constructed by using the Nato Codification System for spares and equipment and this inevitably makes it much easier to operate Project Advokaat and both replace and update its components.

In the controversy which followed the AAM revelations Nato Headquarters was quick to claim that the Codification System being made available to South Africa did not involve any military relationship with the Republic and in any case the System itself did not have any military significance. Since 1975 the AAM has made extensive representations to all Nato Members urging the Alliance to formally withdraw the System from South Africa and to prohibit the supply of all Nato data to the Republic irrespective of whether it is classified or not.

Canada, Denmark and Norway have given the AAM express assurances that they do not provide the Codification System to South Africa. It appears as if any Member of Nato may freely supply the System to a non-Member unilaterally although it does appear difficult to accept that this is done without any joint consultation or within a certain defined policy context. Nevertheless the AAM has persisted with its demands that the Nato Ministerial Council should make a binding decision to eliminate South Africa from benefitting from the System.

Canada and the two Scandinavian countries have so far resisted the call of the AAM to raise the matter formally at Ministerial level and propose a ban. Indeed, no Nato Member has undertaken to do so. Norway, however, did according to press reports express regret at the Ministerial Meeting in Oslo in May 1976, that South Africa had been granted the Codification System.

Neither Canada nor Denmark have taken any formal steps to secure a common Nato policy on this question. It is particularly surprising that even the smaller Nato Members which do not directly provide the Codification System to South Africa refuse to take a joint position against the actions of the major Members. This is particularly disconcerting since presumably all the data fed into the Nato Codification System for Spares and Equipment by countries such as Canada, Denmark and Norway is in fact supplied to South Africa by some of the other Members.

Although the extension of the Codification System to South Africa may not be as important as other forms of external military collaboration with the Republic it does reveal how sensitive most western governments are when it touches on defence matters. And it is precisely because of the secrecy and special sensitivity which surrounds military matters that South Africa is able to enlist considerable direct and indirect western support for its military establishment.

In May 1976 Britain informed the AAM that it would no longer supply Nato data to South Africa. This leaves the United States, the Federal Republic of Germany, France and Italy which have so far not taken such a decision despite persistent representations.

The Cape Route

As a result of domestic and international pressure Britain terminated the Simonstown Agreement with South Africa in 1975. However, this development has not reduced the emphasis being placed on the importance of the Cape Sea Route by certain western countries and particularly their defence bases. It is argued that since Europe's oil supply comes around the Cape South Africa inevitably becomes an area of major strategic importance to the West. It is also claimed that in view of the continued expansion of the Soviet navy it is important to come to some arrangement with South Africa to monitor developments in the South Atlantic and Indian Oceans. These considerations have been pointed to by Britain over the years to maintain the Simonstown Agreement and even to supply arms to South Africa.

However, the so-called strategic importance of the Cape Route has led to other developments within the Nato Alliance. There have always been right wing lobbies in the major Nato countries which have sought close military ties with South Africa and even advocated a formal alliance relationship with the Pretoria regime. The influence of these groups has often been underestimated despite the fact that they represent fairly powerful forces in the western countries.

In 1974 Nato authorised a SACLANT study about the importance of the oil route for the western Alliance. With remarkable speed the demands of the right wing lobby appeared to bear fruit. But there are devious difficulties for the Alliance to appear to cooperate too closely with South Africa and therefore, some of the smaller Nato Members insisted that the study should in no way involve South Africa. This was agreed.

The Saclant study is secret and not available to the general public. Representations made by the AAM to Nato Members about this have produced the response from some of the smaller countries that there is no question of any Nato involvement with South Africa. Despite these assurances it is difficult to conceive of major Nato operations around the Cape Route which would not involve South Africa.

It is South Africa which has the most modern sea and airports in the region; which already has regular exchange of naval and military intelligence with the major western powers; whose Advokaat system not only monitors naval and maritime traffic in the Southern Oceans but conveys this data to the major western powers. Besides, Nato serving and retired officers have publicly declared their desire for a formal alliance relationship with South Africa. It is also remarkable that although the Nato Treaty expressly limits its operations to the North Atlantic area there should be a joint decision to study the feasability of operations around Southern Africa. All these factors provide sufficient grounds for serious concern and anxiety in Africa and the rest of the world about the real intentions of the major western powers.

Indeed, despite formal and public assurances, denying any Nato or western military collaboration with South Africa these statements conflict with much of the known and admitted evidence. Last year the African National Congress of South Africa published certain secret documents about military relations between the Federal Republic of Germany and South Africa. Among them was a letter from a senior German naval officer to the South African defence attache in Bonn which mentioned a discussion within Nato about extending the Treaty area to cover the South Atlantic and that the report had been passed on to South Africa. If there are no military relations with South Africa and none are intended why is South Africa provided with secret Nato reports by certain Nato Members?

South Africa's Strategic Importance

All these developments raise serious anxieties that a western reliance on a stable and secure South Africa as an integral part of the western defence system, could lead to a severe crisis in western policy as the apartheid system becomes more vulnerable and insecure. Economic, military and political considerations in the major Western capitals could easily lead to increased interventionist tendencies on the part of these powers to help preserve the security and stability of South Africa. Thus, the so called strategic importance of South Africa to the west can easily lead the major western powers to come into direct confrontation with the African liberation movement.

The Mandatory Arms Embargo

In November 1977 the UN Security Council adopted a mandatory arms embargo against South Africa under Chapter VII of Charter. This decision, though important, has limited value because it only forbids the export of armaments and spare parts to South Africa and leaves a host of loopholes open. The statement made on behalf of AAM to the UN Special Committee Against Apartheid in December 1977 gives details about the areas which still need to be covered. (Document No. A/AC/115/L.485 16 December 1977).

In effect it is impossible to enforce an effective arms embargo against South Africa unless its trading partners are prepared to exercise greater control over their economic transactions with the Republic. As long as considerations of preserving 'normal trade' with South Africa remain paramount the arms embargo is only likely to be partially effective.

If it is genuinely believed that it is improper to provide the South African armed forces with external assistance then it should not be too difficult to devise and implement appropriate measures. So far western policy regarding the arms embargo has been shifted steadily by increasing African and international pressure and not by a basic acceptance in western capitals that South Africa should be denied all forms of military assistance. This absence of political will to act decisively against South Africa is illustrated even more clearly and dramatically when it comes to the issue of ending economic relations with the Republic.

Canadian and Scandinavian Policy

It is inevitable that the policies of certain western governments towards Southern Africa are influenced to a considerable extent by their own relations with the major western powers. This also means that they refuse to join in the universal condemnation of named western powers which collaborate closely with the South African military establishment.

No one now doubts that South Africa has nuclear capability – a situation brought about by close collaboration with the major western powers. South Africa's massive military capability and its nuclear potential constitutes a grave threat to the peace and security of Africa and the world.

It is therefore vital that the international arms embargo is made effective and all the loopholes sealed. The Scandinavian countries and Canada can adopt an even more active foreign policy than they have done so far. Scandinavia has a traditional policy of supporting the African liberation struggle and Canada has played a

43

valuable role both within and outside the Commonwealth context on Southern African issues.

Canada and the Scandinavian countries can initiate joint measures against South Africa and secure the support of other western countries such as the Netherlands for future united action. This collection of countries can, as a first step, agree to apply a strict arms embargo against South Africa and impose a total freeze on all new investment to that country. They should take initiatives to bring about a programme of economic sanctions against South Africa and work for the immediate imposition of a total oil embargo.

More should be done to support the African liberation movements and these movements should be recognised as the authentic representatives of their countries.

There are of course some difficulties for Canada and the Scandinavian countries to adapt more meaningful measures: the relationships of some of them to South Africa's major trading partners either through defence relationships or because of EEC interests present serious obstacles to a more enlightened policy. But these obstacles have to be overcome in the wider interest of their own peoples as well as of that of Africa and the world.

II. Development Assistance

Roger Leys

Scandinavian Development Assistance to Botswana, Lesotho and Swaziland

The main purpose of this paper is to provoke a debate about the strategy and content of Scandinavian aid[1] to the "rand" states of Botswana, Lesotho and Swaziland in southern Africa. Historically, these states have been part of the trade and labour markets of the Republic of South Africa and the achievement of political independence has not altered significantly the historical structure and form of their "dependence". Aid policies designed to achieve economic growth and social redistribution must understand the character and type of this dependence. Most of the evidence presented in this paper indicates that analysis of this kind has not been undertaken and that the Scandinavian states have pursued eclectic and ad hoc policies. Furthermore, there has been little if any attempt to coordinate these aid policies both within Scandinavia and in relation to the humanitarian assistance given by the Scandinavian states to the victims of apartheid.

The first section of this paper seeks to provide a framework for the analysis of the political economy of the BLS states and includes a brief summary of some principle characteristics of these states stressing specific and unique characteristics. The second section summarizes (a) the aims of Scandinavian aid policy and (b) a number of selective criticisms of the content of bilateral and multilateral aid programmes. The third section details and discusses Scandinavian "humanitarian" assistance to victims of apartheid in the Republic of South Africa and highlights certain ambiguities and inconsistencies between development aid to the BLS countries and a "progressive" image of hostility to apartheid and limited support to those who seek to oppose it.

The Political Economy of the BLS States

Introduction

The primary problem facing development programmes and aid strategy in the BLS states is their economic integration with, and subordination to, the Republic of South Africa. Exactly how this economic and, to a degree, political subordination is to be analysed is, however, a difficult and contentious problem.

47

A relatively uncontentious starting point is the nature and operation of the economic links between the BLS states and the Republic of South Africa (RSA). The BLS states and RSA are, according to the agreed articles of the South African Customs Union, a free trade area as regards the movement of goods, services and capital. The Customs Union has, clearly, exacerbated uneven development within the region. The RSA's powerful and dynamic growth centres have tended to pull production factors from the weak peripheries and have hence contributed to a polarization of centre-periphery relations within the region.[2]

The operation of the Customs Union has certain obvious consequences for development strategy and aid policy to the rand states. Goods and services for aid projects – such as, for example, the 40% of soft state loans for local purchases – tend to stick to the fingers of South African capitalists. Aid projects to the rand states could not function without purchases in the Republic. A further point is that, even projects purchases abroad, unless subject to specific exemption, are subject to South African tariffs. Such tariffs, as part of the customs pool, are redistributed through the common authority – administered by the Republic's Customs and Excise – to BLS and, today, these comprise in toto over 50% of total government revenue of the rand states. These government revenues are, in fact, indirect subsidies from consumers and aid agencies to the BLS governments. The question this raises is whether, given the general character and policies of these regimes, such revenues do in fact serve redistributive purposes.

But the problem of how the relationship between RSA and the BLS states is to be analysed cannot be limited to the operations of the customs area. The key problem is one of analysing key historical and current trends in the political economy of the BLS states that are directly related and subordinate to development trends in the RSA itself.

However, the growth pole approach is heavily criticised by radical and marxist social scientists who argue that this form of analysis cannot comprehend the historical dynamic of the process which has led to the "blocking" of the development of productive forces and relations in South Africa's peripheries. The rand states are not peripheral in the sense that southern Sjælland is peripheral to the growth pole of Copenhagen nor of Northern Jutland to the growth areas of central and southern Jutland. Rather, the BLS states have, historically, been assigned specific functions in terms of the process of primitive and reproductive capital accumulation in the RSA. The generic function of the BLS states, including the reason for their colonization, has been to provide cheap labour to white capital. This process has, far from being "natural", been accompanied by political and social violence and political independence has done little to alter this picture.

Statement of the generic function, however, requires modification and historical specification for each of the BLS states. In terms of the scope of this paper such an analysis cannot be made. Rather, what we can do is to sketch certain key characteristics of the political economy of each of the rand states in order to assess the impact of development efforts and aid programmes.

Botswana

Historically, Botswana (formerly the British Protectorate of Bechuanaland) has been only a marginal "labour reserve" of the Republic of South Africa. Since the beginning of this century some ten percent of the economically active population has worked as migrant labour in the RSA – in mining and in agriculture. The bulk of the rural population "subsist" on cattle grazing. Since the early seventies, the rapid exploitation of Botswana's large mineral reserves has also been a distinct feature. Botswana has, in southern African terms, a remarkably democratic political system which, however, is strongly weighted in favour of traditional chiefs, of large cattle owners and a growing petit bourgeoisie. Despite the evidence of an absence of wide disparities in wealth, there is considerable evidence of substantial and growing rural poverty and also of increasing social differentiation. These trends will only be sketched here but are clearly vital to understanding development strategy and for evaluating development assistance.

The Republic of Botswana has a total land area of 581,000 square kilometres and an estimated population of 650,000 (1971 census 630,379) with an estimated population growth rate of over 3%. Population density is hence 1.12 per square kilometre but this figure disguises the fact that some 80% of the population are concentrated in the eastern belt of the country along the railway line with more fertile arable land (including the block concessions of some 30,000 square kilometres of freehold land to European farmers). Some 86% of the native Tswana population live in the rural areas and 80% of these are concentrated on rural townships of between five and thirty thousand villagers. With a Gross Domestic Product of 87.6 million rand in 1971/72 average per capita annual income was R 140.[3]

Cattle grazing is the backbone of Botswana's rural economy. The national herd is estimated at some three million and sales of cattle to the Botswana Meat Corporation's abattoir at Lobatsi is the principal source of money income. The traditional system of cattle grazing, based on the principle of communal grazing rights allocated by the local chief, distinguished between herd ownership and grazing. Traditionally, rural chiefs controlled usufruct rights to cattle and granted grazing lands, raised taxes and imposed tributes.

However, the development of commodity production in cattle, particularly since the expansion of the Lobatsi abattoir in 1954 and the subsequent development of a substantial market in beef to Western Europe has tended to undermine many of the redistributive mechanisms in traditional society. The key to successful cattle farming has been not so much access to grazing as such but, in this parched land, access to water – to water: to wells, dams and boreholes. Power to allocate land, traditionally the province of the chief is today vested in the Tribal Land Boards. By 1971 it was reported that 90% of potential cattle-post land had been preempted by land allocations and borehole rights.[4] The consequence of this development has been a growing tendency towards inequality in cattle ownership. The Agricultural Census of 1867/68 revealed that 29% of all households owned to cattle at all and

49

a further 21+ owned less than ten – the number thought sufficient to meet such "basic needs" as subsistence, tax payments etc. The Rural Income and Distribution Survey (1974/75) estimated some 45% of rural families below a very basic poverty datum line.

It was stated earlier that Botswana has been only a "marginal" labour reserve of the RSA. A crude estimate of some 60,000 Tswana work in the Republic. Of these some 20,000 are employed by the Chamber of Mines and the bulk of the remainder as farm labour on European farms. Evidence from the 1974/75 Rural Income Distribution Survey indicates that only a small proportion, perhaps 15% of wages are remitted by migrants to rural households and hence wage labour does not make a substantial contribution to gross national income. A second form of labour migration has been internal to Botswana, partly as cattle and farm labour on white-owned freehold farms (some 3,000) and partly as semi-wage labour in the traditional cattle economy. Finally, rural-urban migration is of increasing importance in Botswana. The urban population has grown from some 3.9% (21.400) in 1964 to 14% (100,000) in 1976.

The evidence points to the conclusion that the relatively low but, in relative terms, fairly constant stream of migrant labour to the RSA is a function of rural poverty. Although labour migration is spread fairly evenly throughout the country and the majority of the rural male population have worked in the Republic labour migration is also, traditionally, a function of poverty. Schapera's famous studies of the thirties and forties indicated that young men went to work to pay the bride price but, by the forties, there was considerable increase in the migration rate among married men, especially among men without access to land.

In the early seventies it was expected that the exploitation of Botswana's vast mineral resources – particularly copper, zinc and diamonds – would produce an "economic miracle". The National Development Plan 1973–78 estimated that the copper-nickel mine at Selebi-Pikwe and the brine deposits at Sua Pan would alone bring an eight-fold increase in the contribution of the mining sector to GNP between 1970/71 and 1977/78. In 1971, meat and cattle produce constituted ca 91% of total exports but it was projected that by 1978 mineral exports alone would constitute some 72% of total exports.

This optimistic view of the possibilities of a Botswana economic miracle has had to be readjusted in two important respects. Firstly, due partly to the catastrophic fall in copper prices in recent years and partly to management problems at the Anglo-American mine at Selebi-Pikwe mineral production has not fulfilled expectations and consequently the projected growth in GNP has not been achieved. Secondly, the actual nature of the mineral exploitation, exclusively under foreign control, management and capital has only brought marginal returns. Government revenue returns have fallen well below projections and the contribution to employment has been very limited. Mineral exploitation in Botswana is par excellence of the enclave variety, with almost no backward or forward linkages.

A fourth aspect of Botswana's political economy that we will touch on here is the nature of the political system. Superficially, Botswana is a democratic and multi-party state with a considerable freedom of expression. There are legal opposition parties to the ruling Botswana Democratic Party and a relatively efficient government bureaucracy. Furthermore, Botswana has traditionally harboured refugees from the Republic and from the white regime in Rhodesia. As a Front Line state, Botswana has offered diplomatic support to the Zimbabwe Patriotic Front and has been subject to military attack by the Smith forces. Government development policy stresses the development of the rural sector and the active participation of the rural population in the development effort.

This picture does, however, tend to blur the fundamentally conservative character of the government – dominated by an alliance of traditional leaders and a nascent petit-bourgeoisie that has pursued a technocratic development strategy that has done little to affect the living conditions of the bulk of the rural population. The class basis of the ruling elite is indicated by Holm's study of members of Parliament and District Councils in three southern districts of Botswana.[5] The survey showed that 47% of members of Parliament sampled and 59% of district councillors had paternal kinship ties with local chiefs and headmen. Further that 76% of members of parliament owned more than 50 head of cattle (compared with 12% of the total population owning more than 50 head of cattle) and that one third of MPs and district councillors were traders – owning small shops and businesses, shebeens (beer halls) etc.

This partial study of the rural elite buttresses the argument of Osborne[6] that the ruling Democratic Party has pursued a *technocratic* development strategy that has done little to benefit the mass of the rural population. Mobilization schemes such as the Pupil Farmer Schemes have tended to elevate a small group of rural entrepreneurs: Community Development schemes have been based on Famine Relief Food-For-Work principles and the proportion of the national budget devoted to extension work in the traditional rural sector has been less than 5%. The technocratic nature of development policies that have largely bypassed the mass of rural poverty is a key point that we will return to in the examination of Scandinavian development strategy in the next section.

Lesotho

Lesotho is , and has been since the last century, the labour reserve par excellence of the RSA. Wage labour on the mines, farms and industrial sector of South Africa is critical to the subsistence of the mass of the rural population. Efforts since independence in 1966 to promote industrialisation have had only marginal impact on GDP and employment and, indeed, income from migrant labour has, since independence been in increasing proportion of national income and state revenue. Hence Lesotho's future is seriously threatened by the efforts of the Chamber of Mines and the South African state to substitute South African black labour on the mines at the expense of foreign labour. The development of a Basotho migrant working class is not reflected in Lesotho's political institutions. The traditional chiefs and headmen have a strong grip on the state apparatus through the ruling Basotho National Party which seized power in 1970. The absence of mineral wealth and the ecological decline that pressure of population on land resources has caused make it imperative that development and aid strategy are geared to an understanding of Lesotho's integration into the South African working class. But such an analysis is not evident from a perusal of development strategy and aid policy.

The kingdom of Lesotho, an enclave within the RSA, has a total land area of 30,350 square kilometres and an estimated population of 1,180,000 (1975). Population density is thus 38 per square kilometre, largely concentrated in the lowlands and foothills on the 13% of cultivable land. Gross domestic product for 1974/75 was estimated at R70 million, i.e. a per capita GDP of R59. By contrast, earnings of migrant workers in the RSA were estimated for 1974/75 at ca. R95 millions for Basotho working in the South African mining sector and earnings of migrant workers in other sectors of the RSA at ca. R75 million. Hence the total earnings of Basotho migrant workers in the RSA more than doubled GDP.[7] The actual contribution of these earnings to national income is hard to estimate but in both absolute and proportionate terms is considerably higher than Botswana. 60% of total earnings of migrant workers have, since 1975, been deposited as deferred pay in Lesotho's National Development Bank. It is estimated that some 35% of the total earnings of migrant workers accrue to rural households.

The numbers and proportion of the economically active population working in South Africa are also hard to derive. Accurate figures are only available for recruitment to the mining sector of which the bulk are recruited through recruiting stations that are wholly-owned subsidiaries of the Chamber of Mines. Ca. 50% of the economically active male population are, at any one time, employed in South Africa and this has been a fairly stable trend since the Second World War.

Since independence in 1966, Lesotho has made considerable efforts to promote domestic employment and industrialisation through an "open door" policy to foreign capital, including South African capital, promoted through the agency of the Lesotho National Development Corporation. But the absence of mineral wealth, apart from two small diamond mines, and increasing competition from South Africa's own "homelands" for the handicraft market has limited Lesotho's industrialisation to two small handicraft and light industrial enclaves in the towns of Maseru and Leribe. The manufacturing sector as a whole produces less than 10% of GDP. The most dynamic sector of the domestic economy has been the tourist industry, catering to the white South African tourist market, which today amounts to some 18% of GDP. Today the "modern" sector of the domestic economy employs some 27,500 (1975) of which the government sector represent one third. In the plan period 1970/71 – 1974/75 paid employment in the modern sector increased by some 6,000 falling short of the plan target of 10–15,000 new jobs.[8]

Despite these efforts there are strong indications that Lesotho's dependence on migrant labour to South Africa has increased since independence. The numbers employed in the mining sector have risen fairly steadily: –

Table 1. *Recruitment and employment of Basotho labour in South African mines 1969–1974*

1969	83,000
1970	87,000
1971	93,000
1972	99,000
1973	110,000
1974	104,000
1975	111,300 (estimate)

Source: Second Five Year Development Plan 1975/76 – 1979/89 page 14.

This compares with a total employment in the modern sector of the domestic economy of 27,500 (1975).

Despite the considerable increase in both the numbers and the real wages of Basotho in South Africa in this period, particularly in the mining sector, the long term prospects of expansion in this sector are bleak. The Chamber of Mines and the South African state here have a common interest in the "internalisation" of the labour supply. Growing black unemployment in South Africa and the political "instability" of the mining sector's foreign labour reserves – Malawi, Mozambique and Lesotho which have historically supplied some 75% of the black mine labour force have led the mining industry to embark on a massive campaign to increase the rate of recruitment of South African blacks. Today, over 55% of black mine workers are recruited from within the Republic. So far the effects of this policy on the recruitment of Basotho labour have not been felt (despite a temporary suspension of new recruits in March, 1977). But it is clear that, in the long run, Lesotho cannot plan for an absorption of even a stable proportion of her economically active population in the RSA.[9]

The class character of the political regime in Lesotho is only partially disguised by a radical, anti-apartheid stance in foreign policy. Of all the Southern African rand states, Lesotho developed in the colonial period the most radical political movement, the Basotho Congress Party (BCP) which was originally affiliated to the African National Congress of South Africa. While participating in the contest for political power at independence in 1966, the BCP maintained and developed its links with the South African Liberation Movement. In the contest for political power the BCP was defeated by the more conservative Basotho National Party which, under Chief Leabua Jonaathon, won a majority of seats in Parliament on a minority vote in 1965. The BNP was largely a party of the traditional chiefs and was supported by the Catholic Church. In 1970, the BNP, now confident in its grip over the country, held a general election. The results of the election indicated a clear victory for the BCP, particularly in the more isolated mountain districts that had been centres of BNP traditional support.[10] While election results were coming in, Jonathon declared a state of emergency and seized power. BCP leaders were gaoled and fled into exile. In the following "clean-up" the BNP consolidated its hold on the state apparatus and

53

a considerable number of BCP supporters in government service were dismissed. The BNP rules largely by the distribution of government patronage and it has openly used such patronage to consolidate control. While foreign aid donors have largely resisted attempts to ensure that aid projects and monies are spent on BNP sympathisers their freedom of action has been considerably limited.

Swaziland

The kingdom of Swaziland may be characterized as a type of "internal colonialism" to the profit of foreign capital – in plantation agriculture, forestry, mineral exploitation and tourism – at the expense of a rural peasantry living in conditions of extreme poverty. Far from pursuing a policy of economic independence from the RSA, the government of King Sobhuza has actively promoted and encouraged its links with South Africa. The ruling traditional elite has a firm grip on political power since the dissolution of Parliament and suspension of the constitution in 1973 and has, further, profitted personally from the boom in the modern sector. With a positive trade balance and large foreign reserves promoted by a development strategy that has encouraged large income disparties, it is difficult to make a case for development assistance to Swaziland.

The current population of Swaziland is estimated at some 550,000 (1966 population census 375,000 and a growth rate of 2.7%) on a total land area of 6,704 square miles giving a population density of ca. 75 per square mile. According to the World Bank Report of January, 1977 BNP per capita is estimated at ca. R400 – making Swaziland a relatively rich country in African terms.[11]

The backbone of the Swazi economy is the modern sector of plantation agriculture (sugar and citrus fruits), forestry (wood and paper), mineral exploitation (asbestos and iron ore) and an expanding tourist sector: –

Foreign-owned enterprises are responsible for most modern activities and even in commercial agriculture these account for over 90 per cent of production. The country is dependent on ten foreign-owned and run establishments for almost all its entire production and all commercial production. The export trade is largely in the hands of foreigners and even the distribution system and most of the wholesale and retail trade, at least in urban areas, is controlled by foreign-owned enterprises. The expanding tourist sector is almost entirely in the hands of expatriates. (International Labour Organization Employment Mission *Reducing Dependence,* June 1976).

This modern, capitalist sector of the Swazi economy has developed rapidly in the sixties and seventies (at an annual average rate of 7% since independence in 1968) and has been based on an export market boom – particularly in the sugar industry and woodpulp. In 1968 imports represented 57% and exports 71% of gross domestic product.

The rapid expansion of the export-based modern sector has taken place within a largely stagnant rural traditional sector in which the mass of the Swazi population live. Little if any effort has been made by government to utilize the surplus thus generated for the mobilization and development of the rural sector. Indeed

Swaziland had, until 1976, a positive trade balance and large capital and service inflows that were allowed to accumulate as savings in South African banks. There is an estimated surplus bank liquidity of ca. Rand 25 million with large government deposits in the South African Central Bank.[12]

The result of this liberal development strategy has been to give rise to vast economic inequalities. The problems of this type of "dual" economy are stated frankly in the National Development Plan: –

The economy is unbalanced. It is dominated by foreign interests and the contribution to GDP of the Swazi sector is low. The latter has been estimated to be no more than a third. For this reason, the distribution of income is highly skewed, with a disproportionate amount accruing to foreign capital in the form of profits and to the expatriate labour in the form of high wages and salaries." (source: Swaziland Second National Development Plan 1973–1977 page 9)

According to the ILO Employment Mission referred to earlier, the per capita income of Swazis on Swazi Nation Land (ca. 55% of total land area) was in 1974 Rand 53 as compared with Rand 506 for Swazis in urban areas. By contrast, the average p.c. income of non-Swazis in 1974 was Rand 1, 782.

Swaziland's political economy can be characterised as a form of internal colonialism in which foreign capital on alienated land (ca. 45% of total land area) employs migrant labour – both Swazi labour and, traditionally, on the sugar plantations Mozambican labour at below subsistence wages. Parallel to this form of internal colonialism has been a relatively stable trend of migrant labour to the Republic. This trend is, today, on the increase. E.g. mine labour recruitment was in 1974 9,000, in 1975 16,000 and in 1976 25,000.

The class character of the Swazi state is a complex interweaving of the traditional ruling class and a Swazi bourgeoisie. The traditional Swazi National Council rules openly since the royal "Coup" of 1973. But the National Council is not so "traditional" as to keep its fingers from the profits of the modern sector. A special fund of the Council invests in industry, agriculture and tourism. The police force and the South-African-equipped army enforces this type of political system under which opposition parties have been suppressed, their leaders gaoled and meetings of trade unions banned.

Unlike Lesotho and Botswana, the foreign policy of Swaziland is openly conservative and the government has done the minimum in its power to support and harbour political refugees. On occasions, the police has openly collaborated with the South African police against political refugees from South Afrca.

The Swazi government is also taking active steps, in direct cooperation with the RSA to limit trade with the Republic of Mozambique. A key feature of these endeavours is the construction of a railway line bypassing the line of rail to Maputo in Mozambique and linking up with the South African railway network in Natal Province. Construction has in fact started on a 25 million rand 100 kilometre long railway line from the outskirts of Mbabane to the southern border linking up with the South African railway system and providing direct access to South African harbours. According to authoritative sources, the Canadian aid experts who have been general and operational managers of Swaziland Railways have resigned in protest and have been replaced by South Africans.¹³ Clearly, the conservative regime of King Sobhuza openly prefers even stronger links with the RSA to increasing its links to the socialist Republic of Mozambique.

The basic problem facing development aid strategy to Swaziland is clearly one of justifying aid programmes given these features of the political economy of the state.

Scandinavian aid to the BLS States

The explicit aims of Scandinavian development assistance to the BLS states can be formulated in two ways. One formulation is in terms of the general principles under which Scandinavia assists third world countries generally. The most common official formulation of these principles is to promote economic growth, social justice and to concentrate aid on the poorest sections of the population.

A second formulation of Scandinavian aid policy to the BLS states is in terms of the specific needs of these states. Here one can isolate certain common elements in official aid policy: –

1. Aid is designed to promote the efforts of the governments of the BLS states to achieve greater "independence" from the Republic of South Africa and, in the case of Botswana, from the white regime in Rhodesia.

2. Humanitarian purposes, i.e. to combat intense poverty, malnutrition and disease.

3. Aid is designed to give political and economic support to "anti-apartheid" states, i.e. to states whose official diplomatic policy is opposed to apartheid.

4. Aid is designed to assist those forces and authorities in the BLS countries whose aims are compatible with a type of non-violent transition of the RSA to liberal capitalism, i.e. a version of neo-colonialism.

The implicit aims of development assistance to BLS, and to Southern Africa generally, can seldom be found in official policy statements. There is little direct relationship of Scandinavian aid to economic and business interests within Scandinavia. There is however, an indirect, and often paradoxical relationship between economic interests and aid policy. Thus, for example, Sweden has the most extensive trade and capital interests in the heart of the region, the RSA, and simultaneously pursues the most radical and progressive aid profile both in relationship to the BLS states and in its political and material support to the struggle against apartheid. Such ideological interests play an important and, as we will indicate, often conflicting role in aid policy.

Botswana

It would be beyond the scope of this paper to attempt a total evaluation of Scandinavian aid to Botswana. Instead the transport and communication sector has been singled out for attention whereas aid to education, health and agriculture is not treated. The result is clearly not a balanced picture but balance is not the object of this paper. Rather it is designed to illustrate the problems involved in developed assistance to the BLS states. We can however sketch the extent of Scandinavian development assistance to Botswana.

Norwegian aid. Together with the African states of Tanzania, Kenya, Zambia and (as of 1977) Mozambique, Botswana is a priority country for Norwegian Development Assistance. The explicit aim of Norwegian aid is to support governments which pursue development-oriented policies and which promote social justice for the benefit of all classes of the population. Aid is administered by NORAD, the directorate of development assistance of the Norwegian government. In 1976 NORADs bilateral assistance programme to Botswana amounted to over 38 million Norwegian crowns. As of 31.12.76 Norway had 54 volunteers and experts working in Botswana. By far the largest share of this sum, some 27,543,000 crowns was in the transport and coummunications sector. The other major sector for Norwegian aid is in public health. Here Norway is assisting in the construction and equipment of 50 rural health clinics at an estimated total cost of 30 million crowns over a five-year period.[14]

Turning to *Swedish aid* to Botswana, the stated objective of Swedish development assistance to Botswana – administered by the Swedish International Development Agency (SIDA) – is to support the country's efforts to achieve economic and political independence from RSA and Rhodesia (1976/1977). However, since then Botswana's position as a front-line state and involvement in the liberation struggle in Zimbabwe through diplomatic support for the Patriotic Front has led to a certain shift in SIDA's policy. SIDA's budget request to Parliament for 1978 motivates an increase in aid to Botswana by the direct pressure of the Smith regime, including armed attacks, and to the increasing refugee flow.

SIDA's development assistance for 1975/76 was 45 million crowns making Botswana the highest per capita recipient of Swedish aid and representing some 17% of Botswana's development budget.[15] SIDA's aid to Botswana takes three main forms:

1. Financial aid to the development of the north-south road (see below).

2. Assistance in the development and equipment of primary schools (in all, some 35 million crowns based on a 5-year programme)

3. Aid to a water supply programme which includes feasibility studies of the Okavango delta as a source of water supply.

DANIDA – the *Danish government's development agency* – has two major projects in Botswana. One is the north-south road (see below) to which DANIDA has guaranteed 30 million crowns out of a total cost for the Francistown-Nata stretch of the road of 104.5 million Danish crowns. DANIDA's other main project is the construction and equipment of a secondary school at Selebi-Pikwe to which DANIDA has supplied over 17 million Danish crowns.[16]

We will here single out for attention two development aid projects in Botswana:

1. NORAD's rural roads programme.
2. The north-south road project.

In 1974 Norway and Botswana signed an agreement for the construction of rural roads at a cost of 32 million Norwegian crowns over four years. The project has many interesting aspects. It emphasizes labour-intensive construction, the employment of rural poor who would otherwise be forced to seek work in the RSA and it has concentrated, especially after a somewhat critical report in 1976, on the training of local staff. The primary aim of the project is to provide a type of feder road that will link relatively isolated villages with larger townships. So far, work has been completed on a number of stretches. The first phase of the project involved establishing two construction camps – each of 270 men. Since then two additional work camps have been constructed.

A recent evaluation of this project, which had the purpose of a bench-mark evaluation, indicated a number of problems.[1] A major purpose of the scheme was to promote economic activity in hitherto "isolated" areas. Surveying one village to which the road had been completed, the survey could not discover a single effect, positive or negative, on the economic life of the community. A major economic activity of this area is selling cattle to the abattoir at Lobaste. Before the road was built cattle were transported on the hoof. Cattle are still transported on the hoof. Registering the attitudes of the villagers towards the new road, the survey indicates a clear correlation between income and "positive attitudes" to the project. 70% of the villagers in the lowest standard-of-living category had "no idea" what future effects the road would have on their standard of living.

There are also indications that the original aims of the project – the use of labour-intensive methods and the provision of rural employment – are being diluted. In 1974 the Botswana government raised the minimum wage for all workers in the country from 0.80 Pula (1 Pula= 1 Rand) per day to 2.00 Pula. This increase in labour costs, together with unbudgeted increases in the cost of machinery and spare parts has led to a reduction in the size of the labour gangs and a decision to increase the degree of capital intensity in the use of equipment (which is bought in RSA).

The type of problems that the rural road programme has encountered is not unique to NORAD nor to Botswana – such problems are generic in the literature of development assistance. But they highlight a certain naivety about the possibilities of internal development in Botswana, its class structure and the nature of the political economy of Botswana and southern Africa.

The largest single aid project in Botswana which involves all three Scandinavian governments and the Federal Government of Canada is the Botswana governments project to develop and upgrade the north-south road. The road, which links Botswana with RSA to the south and the Caprivi Strip at the Kazungula river crossing in the north, is in essence a prestige project. It is financed by three types of aid cartel:

1. The southern section of the road, from the southern border to Francistown, is

financed by the International Development Fund, Britain, Sweden and West Germany.

2. The middle section of the road, from Francistown to Nata, is financed by the governments of Canada, Denmark and Norway.

3. The northern section of the road, from Gata to Kazangulu, is financed by the USA.

It is this northern section of the road, where Botswana shares a common border with the Caprivi Strip, Rhodesia and Zambia that is the most revealing. But it should be borne in mind that the three sections of the road cannot be separated and serve common purposes.

Work on the US-financed section is being carried out by the (US) Construction firm, Grove International Construction, and the engineering consultancy work by the (US) firm Tamm, Tibbets & McCarthy. The consultants have recently recommended that the road be tarmaced and the Botswana government has accepted this recommendation.

The official view of the Botswana government is that the road will help Botswana liberate itself from a transport and communication system that chains it to the RSA and the Smith regime and will help develop new markets in Zambia. In practice it is difficult to see that the road will bring these benefits to Botswana. First of all, there is no bridge across the river which links Zambia and Botswana and little prospect of a bridge being built as long as South Africa claims the rivercourse and is in a position to enforce their claim by virtue of their military bases in the Caprivi Strip. Even with a good-quality road and bridge, the project will not give Botswana a transport system that can compete with existing transport facilities to Rhodesia and South Africa. Nor are there any indications that road-building in Botswana stimulates economic activity. Road-building is a good example of the "technical" approach to development that was discussed in section one.

There are also some more alarming indications. The purpose of the road might well be the exact opposite to stated intentions. The same construction company responsible for the upgrading of the northern section of the road – Grove International Construction – is simultaneously involved in the construction of a road through the game park and over a bridge into the Caprivi Strip. Work on this road is apparently well advanced. Exactly whose interests is such a road, linking the Caprivi Strip with a yet-to-be-tarmaced north road designed to serve? Clearly such a road would well serve South Africa's military and strategic interests in the area. It would enable the South African army, from their bases in the Caprivi Strip, to totally control the northern road and prevent guerilla incursion from the north.

All the Scandinavian governments are assisting in this project – a project whose economic potential is highly dubious and whose military and strategic interests might be precisely contrary to official and public policy.

As has been discussed in section one, certain key features of Botswana's political economy – a stagnant traditional rural sector with widespread poverty, a political system weighted strongly in favour of traditional chiefs and growing disparities of wealth, lead one to question whether development aid programmes of a largely technocratic character can contribute to economic growth and social justice. This brief examination of Scandinavia's contribution to the transport sector in Botswana has revealed a number of problems. Botswana's fundamental problem is not a shortage of roads. Indeed, it could be argued that the lack of internal communications and Botswana's relative isolation has, historically, been the cause of her marginal status as regards the requirements of white capital. An aid policy which attempts to break down with isolation will, at best, be a waste of money in terms of overall aid objectives and, at worst, contribute to a more thorough welding of the historical links to the apartheid state.

Lesotho

Lesotho is not an aid priority country for any of the three Scandinavian countries. But there is a considerable Scandinavian stake in Lesotho, particularly Danish. In 1975, following a state visit of Lesotho's Prime Minister, Chief Leabua Jonathon, the Danish Government agreed on a state loan of 20 million Danish crowns, primarily to finance an abattoir. The Danish commitment to Jonathon's regime seems to have been made without prior consultation with the other Scandinavian governments, especially Sweden which has good reasons for a more critical attitude towards the Lesotho government.

The Danish state loan to Lesotho is given under "especially favourable" conditions with a thirty-five year amortization and no capital repayments in the first ten years. In addition, 40% of the loan can be used to cover local expenses. The abattoir project has run into certain difficulties and, as of 30.6.77 only 0.9 million crowns of the state loan had been project-approved.

Another major project, administered by UNESO, is the financing of the development of the Teacher Training College in Maseru to which DANIDA is contributing 11.4 million crowns in the period 1973–78.[18]

An interesting project is the building and equipping of the African Hall of Residence at Lesotho's National University at Roma, to which DANIDA has contributed 3,260,000 crowns. The Hall is designed to provide accommodation for 100 political exiles from South Africa, Namibia and Zimbabwe. It is administered by the Danish branch of the World University Service (WUS). Architects and engineers attached to the Danish WUS have designed the building free of charge. The buildings have been constructed at low cost using local contractors and a considerable extension is planned.[19] Another project, still at the drawing board stage, is the development of an Institute of Labour Studies attached to the extra-mural department of the National University. The aim is to promote research on labour and to help in the task of trade union organization of migrants. Denmark has also developed a considerable volunteer programme in Lesotho. As of 1.7.77 there were 22 Danish volunteers stationed in Lesotho.

Sweden and Norway have relatively small stakes in Lesotho. SIDA's aid is mostly chanelled through UN agencies – UNDP, ILO & FAO – and amounted in 1975/76 to 8 million Swedish crowns. SIDA has concentrated on assisting projects that will diminish Lesotho's dependence on South Africa – especially in local energy supply, government administration and communications. SIDA has assisted in financing a direct telecommunication link between Lesotho and the outside world, linking Lesotho with Nairobi. SIDA has, however, in the past – especially before Jonathon's coup in 1970 – had a much larger stake in Lesotho partly because of the 1970 coup, partly because of the lethargy of the government bureaucracy and partly because of their appraisal of the reactionary character of the BNP regime.

NORAD, in 1976, contributed in all 239,000 Norwegian crowns to multilateral development assistance projects in Lesotho.

In section one, the political economy of Lesotho was described as that of the labour reserve par excellence. The scope and extent of the integration of Lesotho's labour force into the economy of South Africa has so greatly affected the political economy of Lesotho that development assistance can do little except ameliorate certain of the worst features of poverty and neglect and to give a type of diplomatic assistance to the efforts of the regime to oppose the apartheid system.

Danish aid to the building and equipping of the African Hall of Residence at the National University is an example of this second type of assistance which reflects on and comes to terms with the real interdependence of Lesotho's exploitation and the exploitation of the non-white peoples of South Africa. Swedish aid to the development of a direct telecommunication link is another example of this type of assistance. But there are severe limitations to this type of development assistance. The total integration of the Basotho labour force into the South African labour market means that a fundamental change in the living standards of Basotho is dependent on fundamental change is South Africa itself. In the early seventies, when in the key mining industry the bulk of non-white labour was foreign labour there was much talk of labour-cartel strategy under which the governments that supplied labour to South Africa would form a common bargaining front on such issues as wages, conditions of work, accident insurance, pensions etc. However this strategy has lost influence with the decline of South African recruitment of foreign labour. The key factor in Lesotho's development strategy must hinge on the relationship of Basotho to the black working class of South Africa and their struggle to overthrow apartheid. In this context, aid to Lesotho is inseparable from other elements in Scandinavian policy towards southern Africa, in particular aid to the liberation movements and to the victims of apartheid.

Swaziland

Swaziland, like Lesotho, is not a priority country for Scandinavian aid. Nor, given the average per capita income can Swaziland qualify for special UNDP aid. The total development aid of Scandinavia to Swaziland is small.

Swaziland has received two state loans from Denmark to a total value of 25 million crowns. In addition, DANIDA has one major bilateral project – financing the development of a correspondence college, the Swaziland International Education Project to which DANIDA has granted 11.56 million crowns.

NORAD has no bilateral aid programmes in Swaziland. Norway assists multilaterally-administered projects with 1,045,000 crowns (1976) and, in the same year, provided technical assistance to the value of 363,000 Norwegian crowns.

SIDA has, in aggregate terms, the largest stake in Swaziland which, in 1976/77 amounted to 8 million Swedish crowns. Swedish aid is concentrated on rural development on Swazi national land – especially in the development of cooperatives and small-scale industries. SIDA's aid is mostly channelled through UNDP, UNESCO and FAO.

While Scandinavian aid to Swaziland is relatively small the total contribution of western aid to Swaziland is large. In all, over 500 foreign experts are employed in Swaziland financed by multilateral and bilateral aid programmes. Given the trajectory of Swaziland's development strategy which has ignored the rural areas in the Swazi Nation land and has concentrated development on the foreign-owned plantations, industrial enclaves and in tourism the reluctance of Scandinavian states to support Swaziland is understandable. Furthermore, as we have indicated in section one, Swaziland has deliberately cultivated her links with South Africa at the expense of her links with socialist Mozambique.

Scandinavian policy towards southern Africa

In the appendix to this section, the extent of Scandinavian governmental assistance to victims of apartheid and white minority rule in southern Africa is documented. The evaluation of Scandinavian aid to the victims of apartheid is beyond the scope of this paper. This section has the more modest objective of attempting to raise some questions about overall Scandinavian policy vis-á-vis southern Africa.

For the purposes of discussion we can isolate four aspects of Scandinavian policy in southern Africa: –

1. Scandinavian trade and investment in South Africa and in the sub-imperialist region.

2. Scandinavian aid to such progressive regimes as Mozambique and Angola: states that are taking active steps to break out of the sub-imperialist region and to develop socialist modes of production.

3. Scandinavian assistance to the victims of apartheid, including direct material assistance to liberation movements and, indirectly, a degree of moral and political support.

4. Scandinavian aid to the BLS countries.

The contradictions between trade and investment in the RSA and aid to socialist states and victims of apartheid are fairly clear and the subject of considerable public debate within Scandinavia. But despite a number of restrictions recently imposed on trade and investment with RSA (Norway, for example, has imposed a stop on new investment and Denmark has recently announced the withdrawal of their trade consultant in Johannesburg) there is little evidence that Scandinavian states will break off these links and hence support the "isolationist" strategy advocated by the liberation movements. Indeed the volume of Scandinavian trade with RSA increased considerably in the period up to 1975. Nor, despite the considerable increase in Scandinavian development assistance to Mozambique and Angola (particularly the former) is this assistance viewed as incompatible with trade and investment links with socialism's "direct enemy" in southern Africa. Nor, and this we shall return to, is aid to BLS publically regarded as incompatible with aid to progressive forces in southern Africa.

That these four strands of Scandinavian policy can remain in a kind of unstable equilibrium is the product of a number of factors. Not the least of these is the bureaucratic compartmentalization of the strands. Aid and trade are administered by different government organizations with different objectives and policies. But a more important factor is that the various stands cater to different ideological needs and functions in the donor states. Aid to the liberation movements, although couched in liberal and humanitarian terms, appeals to the left-wing parties and to the left-wing of the social democrats. A laisser-faire policy on trade and investment in RSA appeals to business interests. And the voices of business interests are increasingly being heard in government aid bureaucracies.[20]

This paper has been largely concerned with Scandinavian aid to the BLS states. In section two we have pointed to certain ambiguities and inconsistencies in the relationship between the stated aims of Scandinavian aid to BLS and, by way of illustration, the actual results. In section one, we have related these inconsistencies to certain key features in the political economy of the BLS states, features that are largely ignored by donor organizations.

A wider problem is the consistency of these aid policies with material and diplomatic support to the southern African liberation movements. At the diplomatic level, there is no evidence that liberation movements regard aid to Botswana, Lesotho and Swaziland as incompatible with their objectives. This is particularly true of Botswana which, as a Front Line State has strong diplomatic links with the liberation movements, harbours refugees from RSA, Namibia and Zimbabwe and permits limited operations within the country. But it is also true of Lesotho and Swaziland. The liberation movements maintain links with the government of Lesotho and there has recently been talk of rapprochement between the African National Congress of South Africa and King Sobuzha of Swaziland who, until recently, supported the Pan African Congress. Clearly, liberation movements, with long and vulnerable lines of communication, are keen to keep good diplomatic relations with the rand states. And, on their side, the rand states are interested in the progressive image that association with the liberation movements can give.

There are however, certain limits to the degree of cooperation. Not the least of these are the historically forged links between BLS opposition parties – particularly in Lesotho and Swaziland – and the liberation movements. To the extent that, historically, liberation movements have embraced and represented all oppressed and exploited groups within the region, there will be forces that restrain them from close cooperation with the conservative regimes in the BLS states. And as the process of polarization advances and class struggle intensifies in southern Africa it will be increasingly difficult to maintain these types of diplomatic tie.

The same is true, *pari passu,* for Scandinavian aid strategy in southern Africa. In the present situation, the inconsistencies and disappointments attending Scandinavian aid to the BLS states can be dismissed as no different in kind to similar problems facing aid programmes in other parts of the third world. But the intensification of the conflict in southern Africa will undoubtedly bring these inconsistencies and contradictions into the open.

Notes

1. Finland and Iceland are omitted from the documentation and analysis.
2. See, for example, P. Selwyn *Industries in the Southern African Periphery,* London, 1975.
3. *National Development Plan 1973–1978,* Republic of Botswana, Ministry of Finance and Development Planning.
4. R. Chambers and D. Feldman *Rural Development in Botswana,* 1973.
5. John D. Holm "Rural Development in Botswana: three basic political trends", *Rural Africana* 18, Fall, 1972.
6. Alan Osborne "Rural Development in Botswana" *Journal of Southern African Studies* Vol 2 No. 2, April 1976.
7. *Lesotho, Second Five Year Development Plan 1975/76 – 1979/80.*
8. Lesotho, Development Plan, Ibid.
9. D.G. Clarke "Some determinants of demand for foreign labour in South Africa" World Employment Programme, Working paper, International Labour Organization, Geneva, 1977.
10. W.J.A. McArtney "The general elections in Lesotho 1970", *Government and Opposition* No. 4, October, 1973.
11. *Second National Development Plan 1973–1978,* Government of Swaziland.
12. *Annual Report for the Financial Year 1975–76* Monetary Authority of Swaziland.
13. "Swaziland – choosing the SA link", *To the Point,* 26 August, 1977: "SA aid for rail link", *The Times of Swaziland* August 5, 1977.
14. *Norges Samarbejd med Utviklingslandene i 1976,* NORAD, Oslo, 1977.
15. *SIDA om u-samarbetet. Anslagsframställning 1976/77* och *verksamhetsberättelse,* Styrelsen för internationell utveckling, Stockholm.
16. *Danmarks deltagelse i det internationale udviklingssamarbejde 1976/77,* DANIDA, Foreign Ministry, Copenhagen.
17. *Evaluation of Rural Roads in Botswana: a socio-economic survey,* Department of Geography, University of Oslo, February, 1977.
18. See note 16.
19. *Report on our work during the period 1.4.1974 – 31.3.1976* Danish National Committee for World University Service, Copenhagen.
20. See, for example, Tore Linné Eriksen "Norsk bistandspolitikk, Staten og næringslivet", *Internasjonal Politik* Oct–Dec 1977, N. Arnfred et. al. *Hvem Hjælder Hvem?* Blytmanns Forlag, Copenhagen, 1977; K. Hermele & K·A. Larsson *Solidaritet eller Imperialisme* Liber Förlag, Stockholm, 1977.

Appendix

Scandinavian Aid to the "Victims of Apartheid"

Sweden

Table 1. *Swedish official support to liberation movements and refugees: disbursements 1975/76 – 1976/77* (millions of Swedish crowns)

	1975/76	1976/77
Liberation Movements in Africa	*3.63*	*9.9*
Namibia, SWAPO	1.3	5.4
South Africa, ANC	0.8	4.2
Zimbabwe, ANC/ZANU	0.025	0.3
Zimbabwe, OAU	0.2	–
Refugees in Africa		
UN Commission for Refugees UNHCR	12.0[1]	13.0[1]
UN Relief Prog. for Refugees, UNRWA	20.0[1]	25.0[1]
UN refugee educational prog. for southern Africa UNETPSA	0.6	0.6
UN Fund for the victims of apartheid UNTF	0.7[2]	1.0[2]
UN Namibia Fund	0.2[2]	1.5[2]
International Defence and Aid Fund IDAF	2.8[3]	4.2[3]
International University Exchange Fund IUEF	2.1	4.2
World University Service	1.5	3.1
Amnesty International	–	0.46[4]
African Educational Trust AET	0.5	0.65
African Bureau X-Ray	–	0.03
SACTU/OATUU Solidarity Conference	–	0.1
Angola Committee Facts Reports	–	0.03
Rhodesia Conference	–	0.15
Swedish Ecumenical Council	0.2	0.15
Swedish Church Mission (Svenska Kyrkans Mission)	0.1	0.16
Lutheran Help (Lutherhjälpen)	–	0.5[2]
Methodist Church Mission Abroad (Methodistkyrkans Mission)	0.2	–
Swedish Trade Union Movement (LO/TCO) Educ. in sn. Africa	–	0.06
Scandinavian Institute of African Studies (Nordiska afrikainstitut)	–	0.01
Refugee Programme in Kenya	0.1	0.1
Angola Refugees in Zaire	0.2	0.1
School for refugees in Congo (Brazzaville)	1.5	1.2
Tundura School, Tanzania	–	4.0
School clothes etc.	0.3	0.15
Totals	46.7	71.3

1. Disbursed by the Ministry of Foreign Affairs
2. Disbursed by the Ministry of Foreign Affairs
3. of which 1.7 and 3.2 million crowns, respectively, disbursed by the Ministry of Foreign Affairs
4. of which 0.45 million crowns disbursed by the Ministry of Foreign Affairs

Source: Bistånd genom SIDA, Anslagsframställning 1978/79, Stockholm 1978 page 185.

In 1969, the Swedish Parliament (Riksdagen) formulated a general policy under aid and material support could be given to the "victims of apartheid". In terms of this policy, Swedish aid must be shown to be compatible with the principle of non-interference in the internal affairs of other states. However, since the UN had declared, unambiguously, that support to the victims of apartheid is not in conflict with the UN charter there is, according to this formulation, no violation of the principle on non-interference involved in rendering assistance to apartheid's victims.

This general formulation is very similar to that of Norway and Denmark as is Swedish practice. Aid is given, primarily, to support refugees, to finance educational and educationally-related activities and to support, as far as possible, detainees and victims of political repression within the Republic. This is mainly channelled through UN and voluntary agencies with these states purposes. But, and increasingly so, aid is given to liberation movements for implementing these purposes — primarily, south of the Limpopo, to SWAPO and ANC.

In terms of the limited scope of this paper, this aid can only be documented in summary and incomplete form and the documentation excludes non-governmental assistance (including political and material support of solidarity organizations).

A considerable increase in Swedish aid to liberation movements is planned for 1977/78: —

Table 2. *Aid to refugee and liberation movements in Africa* (in millions of Swedish crowns)

	1977/78 (preliminary)
ZANU	
ZAPU	20
SWAPO	10
ANC (South Africa)	8
Refugee Educational Programme	15
Anti-apartheid activities	7
Totals	60

Source: Bistånd genom SIDA, Anslagsframställning 1978/79, Ibid page 118.

Norway

In 1977, for the first time, the Norwegian Parliament (Storting) gave the green light to direct support to liberation movements in southern Africa. Previously, such support had been regarded as interference in internal affairs (i.e. inconsistent with the principle of non-interference). Initially, the African National Congress was recognised as the sole recipient of direct support to liberation movements in South Africa but, after pressure, the Pan African Congress has also received support.

For 1978, the Norwegian parliament has approved a budget of 22 million crowns to be distributed between South Africa, Namibia and Zimbabwe. The exact distribution as between organizations and projects has yet to be decided. Funds can be distributed to liberation movements, UN refugee programmes etc. All aid is tied to humanitarian purposes.

Table 3. *Norwegian state aid to Southern Africa* (in millions of Norwegian crowns)

	1976	1977
UN Educational and Training Programme for sn. Africa	1.7	2.5
International University Exchange Fund IUEF	1.7	1.8
SAIM and Norwegian Church Council (Mellemkirkelig Råd for den norske kirke)	0.35	0.6
UN Trust Fund for South Africa	0.75	0.9
International Defence and Aid Fund IDAF	1.0	2.5
UN Trust Fund for information against apartheid	0.11	0.15
Liberation movements		
ANC (South Africa)	–	2.0
PAC	–	0.65
Black Trade Union Movement	–	1.25
SWAPO	1.5[1]	4.2[2]
ZANU	–	2.0
ZAPU	–	1.0
ANC (Zimbabwe)	1.5[1]	0.45

1. Aid was not disbursed in 1976, presumably due to internal splits within SWAPO and ANC (Zimbabwe)
2. circa

Source: Information supplied by comrades in the Norwegian Council for Southern Africa (Fællesråd for det sørlige Afrika), January 1978.

Denmark

It is no secret that, in Denmark, the relative weakness of Danish social democratic movement in relation to the bourgeois parties has resulted in a relatively feeble articulation of support to liberation movements in Southern Africa. As a result, official Danish policy is formulated in guarded terms. Policy tends to cling to the UN and the OAU rather than establish an independent profile.

Since the mid-sixties, a special post has been allocated in the national budget for support to victims of apartheid and oppression in southern Africa. Between 1964/65 and 1971/72 this post grew from 225,000 Danish crowns to 1.5 million. In the budget for 1972/73 a new post was created for funds for humanitarian and educational purposes and for 1977/78 this amounted to 14.2 million crowns.

Table 4. *Special Funds for humanitarian and educational aid to Oppressed Peoples* (in millions of Danish crowns)

	disbursed 1976/77	proposed 1977/78
UN Fund for southern Africa	0.75	0.78
UN Educational funds for southern Africa	1.0	1.04
UN Namibian Institute	0.7	0.8
International Defence and Aid Fund IDAF	2.5	1.0
International University Exchange Fund IUEF	3.675	3.883
World University Service WUS	2.489	3.227
World Council of Churches	0.5	0.6
Lutheran World Council	0.6	0.4
Church Relief Help (Folkekirkens Nødhjælp)	0.165	0.13
Danish Trade Union Congress (LO)	0.52	0.7
Luthuli Memorial Foundation	0.05	–
International Peace Centre for Namibia	0.075	–
International League for Peace and Freedom	0.075	–
Totals	13.099	12.560

Source: Danmarks Deltagelse i det internationale udviklingssamarbejde 1976/77 Report from the Board for International Development Cooperation, DANIDA, Foreign Ministry and information supplied by DANIDA, January, 1978.

For 1977/78 Denmark has also supplied 200,000 Danish crowns to ANC (South Africa) and 35,000 crowns to PAC. Denmark has also supplied 1.04 million crowns to SWAPO and plans to give 500,000 crowns to ZANU for support to Zimbabwe refugees in Mozambique and the same amount to ZAPU for support to Zimbabwe refugees in Zambia. In addition, Denmark has supplied 500,000 crowns through the World Council of Churches for humanitarian purposes inside Zimbabwe.

Linda Freeman

Canada and the Front-Line States

During the past two decades, attention to Canadian involvement in Southern Africa has centered on the problems and prospects for change in the systems of white minority rule. However, during this period, Canada and other Western countries have steadily increased their association with the independent black states in the region, a phenomenon that has gone on almost unnoticed. Since the late 1960s, Canada has felt it to be in its interest to develop closer ties mainly through programmes of development assistance, but also through the cultivation of friendly political relations at international gatherings. In the contemporary period, Canada forms part of the Western presence in the deepening Great Power struggle for influence in the region. This study is an examination of Canadian interests in four of these states – two 'frontier' countries, Tanzania and Zambia, and two states inside the region, Malawi and Botswana – from the early 1960s to the present.[1]

Canada's involvement in the four countries in the regional periphery has operated at two levels as both an expression of explicit Canadian interests – political strategic, commercial and philanthropic – and in the context of underlying political and economic relationships in Southern Africa. Each form of involvement – normal political and commercial relations, military assistance, and, above all, programmes of official and non-governmental development assistance – has been examined in the context of the recipient country's internal development strategy and its policy on Southern Africa. The long-term implications of the former for the latter have formed one of the core themes of the study – that, inescapably, major aspects of these Canadian interests add force to the undercurrents pulling these countries into dependent relationships with white Southern Africa. In making this case, therefore, it is argued that, whatever the explicit intention behind Canadian development assistance and cordial relations with the black states, it is open to serious question whether they have, in fact, provided a "balance" for Canadian commercial interests in South Africa and Namibia.

The inevitability of this process arises out of the nature of the political economy in Canada. For the fact that Canadian political and commercial self-interest has often acted at cross purposes with humanitarian objectives in Africa simply reflects, on an external stage, the contradictions at the heart of liberal democratic societies

[1] This paper represents the major conclusions of research for a PhD thesis prepared for the Department of Political Economy at the University of Toronto.

and the capitalist market system. Just as a commitment to individual rights at home is undermined by a system whose value on competition and acquisition of property ends in class inequality; so, too, has commitment to individual rights of the poor in the Third World suffered in competition with the export and investment interests and political alliances which have emerged as the external logic of the domestic system.

Tanzania

In Tanzania, Canada's programmes of military and economic assistance and its political and commercial relations were studied in the context of Tanzania's strong commitment to the liberation of Southern Africa from white minority rule and its internal efforts to develop a form of African socialism based on rural communes. In the case of the military assistance programme, Canada's fundamental political alignment with the West and with NATO emerged as the key consideration both in the Canadian government's defence of the programme at home and in the limitations which it set on its terms of reference. The original incentive for Canadian participation had been to cultivate trust and friendship with Tanzania at a time when China's growing influence was causing concern in the West. The programme was also an expression of Canada's desire to offset the forces for racial polarization in the region and to "moderate" Tanzania's militant stance on Southern Africa. But Canada's strict adherence to the concept of training an apolitical army and air force to provide aid to the civil power meant that its programme became steadily less relevant to Tanzanian needs as these evolved with changes in Sothern Africa in the late 1960s. As the pace of wars of liberation quickened, Tanzania had to turn to China for the jet fighters, artillery pieces, training and logistical support which Canada would not provide for Tanzania's defence against white Southern Africa and for the liberation movements based in the southern part of the country. Within Canada's own terms of reference, it had produced a professional corps as promised; within the Southern African context, its fundamental alliances took priority over support for African nationalist interests, leaving the field to China.

Canada's foreign aid programmes have been used in Tanzania not only for philanthropic purposes, but also to serve commercial interests and, most important of all, the same political interests as in the military assistance programme. Although Tanzania is in the process of creating a socialist society, its commitment to non-alignment has opened the way for the involvement of Western capitalist countries like Canada in its social and economic development. For Tanzania, programmes of development assistance have provided extra capital and personnel to speed the process of economic growth and to ensure sufficient material benefit to keep the nation united behind its objectives. There, it has been prepared to accept the risks accompanying major dependence on foreign aid from the West. However, the costs and dangers have been subtle – less outright attempts to purchase friendships than the export of an influence which is antithetical in outlook and experience to the main thrust of Tanzania's development strategy. Without a cadre of leaders forged in the painful process of protracted guerrilla warfare as in the case of China or, hopefully, Mozambique, popular mobilization for revolutionary change in Tanzania has been problematic. For there is a lack of unanimity within Tanzania about the government's fundamental goals and approaches, particularly within the civil service and parastatal sectors, but also in some parts of the countryside. Without unity, discipline and a clear perspective on strategies to put socialist principles into practise, Tanzania is vulnerable to offers of assistance and alternátive approaches which imply a total shift in development strategy. Importing groups of Western experts has injected not only supposedly neutral techniques for economic development but also support for one side of the domestic debate – the side which favours elite consumer tastes, high-level technology, urban development and the fundamental approaches to development in the Western experience.

Therefore, while some Canadian technical assistance has been helpful in 'housekeeping' at a level of high technology – for example, in the provision of a 'trouble-shooter' when the foreign-aided Kidatu hydroelectric project got into difficulty or technical support for negotiations on international shipping rates – the major part has been working in sectors where broader issues of national development are involved. By and large, the perspectives of Canadian bankers, planners and economists have been formed in Canadian institutions where questions of social side effects, of ownership and control or of the process of popular participation in national development have been less important than short-term economic considerations or "sound" commercial banking principles. While there is no barrier to ultimate adjustment to these other factors, Canadian technical assistance personnel at least operate at a disadvantage from the start and, in many cases, have not been prepared to abandon the pre-dispositions which they have brought with them. Equally important is the fact that, as most postings have taken them to urban centers, usually Dar es Salaam, few of the Canadian 'experts' in Tanzania have had a close living contact with the majority of rural Tanzanians or with the process of building ujamaa villages, the two areas where Tanzania is committed, in principle if not in practise, to concentrating its development efforts. Therefore in the practical experience, expertise and attitudes which most Canadians bring with them and in their living experience in Tanzania, most Canadian technical assistance personnel tend to reinforce an urban bias in Tanzanian development programmes and to reproduce capitalist values and assumptions about economic development.

This general orientation has also been demonstrated in the sectoral distribution of Canadian development assistance. The major part has gone towards large infrastructural projects – electrical power, a water supply for Dar es Salaam, road design, major assistance for railways, harbours and air traffic control both in Tanzania and in the now defunct East African Community. Generally, these projects have been of great benefit for Tanzanian development. However, while there is some indirect long-term benefit for the whole country, CIDA has provided little direct assistance to productive projects at the grass roots level in the rural areas. CIDA's major input in this sector has been the development of wheat varieties for use on large state farms which have also been operated with assistance from CIDA. While these farms may help Tanzania meet some of its domestic food requirements, they incorporate several factors which are at odds with its commitment to equitable balanced development. The wheat is to be grown on large farms using a capital intensive sophisticated technology in a country where both capital and skills are in short supply. The project is intended for bread and therefore for elite consumption, bypassing the majority of Tanzanians who grow and use maize as their staple. Wheat farming on this scale is also not intended for ujamaa villages, but will be operated by state farms. Therefore, this project is out of the mainstream of Tanzanian rural development and does not touch the lives of the majority of Tanzanian farmers.

The nature of Canada's aid programme in Tanzania is a product of tying regulations which require that the major part of the funds which Canada provides must be used to purchase Canadian goods and services. Not only does this build in natural orientations through the type of Canadian capital or technical assistance which is available, but also it exports technologies which reflect Canadian, but not Tanzanian conditions. This has been noted above in the case of the wheat farms, but two smaller projects – crop storage research and the infamous semi-automatic bakery – provide other equally telling illustrations of the local costs and distortions which may accompany foreign aid projects. The fact that Tanzania has asked for more bakeries simply highlights the danger of Wstern technological packages for Tanzania in a period when it is still struggling to define its socialist goals in its institutions, policies, and structures of production.

The transfer of certain orientations, technologies and attitudes which have accompanied the tying of Canadian (and Western) development assistance has also tended to strengthen existing dependency ties from the periphery to the center – economically, technolgically and therefore politically. Taken together with the confusion and ambivalence within the Tanzanian leadership, these influences contributed to imbalances and shortcomings in Tanzanian development which left it vulnerable and dependent on international charity for a period in the mid 1970s. Despite its dedication to the principles of equity and balanced development, Tanzania has concentrated its development efforts on agricultural crops for export, on large infrastructural projects with their long term returns and on projects biased towards urban areas, leaving for secondary consideration the crucial area of food production by the majority of Tanzanian farmers and failing to make its ujamaa programme a living reality throughout the country. This set of priorities left Tanzania without basic foodstuffs in 1974 when a combination of external circumstances compounded the costs of its emphases in development. While Canada and other Western aid donors rushed in with emergency food supplies, their assistance (which formed the major part of Tanzania's development budget in the 1970s) is unlikely ever to be capable of providing direct support for grass roots rural development.

The result had been to leave Tanzania both dependent and vulnerable at a time when its attempts to transform its society through socialist development have had symbolic importance for Africa and when it occupied a strategic position as a leader in support for black liberation in Southern Africa. Therefore, there are profound political implications arising from the operation of Canadian and other Western aid programmes. While they have not altered Tanzania's commitment to non-alignment, their presence on the ground has built in influences on the type of development which is pursued. Along with Canada's commercial self-interest, these political influences serve to work against the philanthropic component of Canada's official development assistance programme, a force which has been expressed in Canada's early involvement in Tanzania, in the volume of its aid revenues, and in the enthusiasm of many Canadians for the vision and goals of its leader, Julius Nyerere.

Zambia

Canadian activities have also had implications for Zambia's ability to strengthen its capacity for independent development and to maintain its position as a militant supporter of black liberation in Southern Africa. From the start, Canadian interests in Zambia have had a more unambiguously political character than in Tanzania. Canadian involvement began in support of British efforts to help Zambia re-orient its links with the south following the Rhodesian unilateral declaration of independence. During this period, Canadian Prime Ministers also acted as intermediaries between Britain and African countries, like Tanzania and Zambia, whose leaders wanted tough measures taken to end the white settler rebellion in Rhodesia. Canada continued to provide emergency assistance for Zambia in the 1970s following its border closure with Rhodesia and improved its capacity for independent links when it established a resident mission in Lusaka in 1973.

However, Canada's fundamental alignments and sympathies have placed limitations on its support for Zambia and for African nationalist aspirations generally. At home, Canadian leaders defended emergency assistance for Zambia on the same Cold War grounds as its military assistance programmes in Tanzania: failing to provide help would significantly facilitate Communist influence in these countries. But much further they would not go. Canada's alliance with Britain was more important than African interests in Pearson's mediation efforts in the Commonwealth over action to end the Rhodesian UDI. While he eased Britain's position, he also defused African pressures for considerably stronger measures than economic sanctions against the Smith regime. At the same time, Canada, along with other Western countries refused to make sanctions effective by acting against the other white-ruled states in Southern Africa that had ignored the international economic boycott of Rhodesia. Finally, Canada did not offer military assistance to Zambia despite the fact that it was considerably more vulnerable to attacks and sabotage from the white-ruled states than Tanzania.

Domestic support in Canada for Zambia and the general black African positions on Southern Africa has been even more equivocal. While some Canadians supported the programmes of emergency and development assistance and friendly relations with the black states in the Commonwealth, a vocal segment of the population has been quite unsympathetic. The depth of Canadian feelings was revealed in the public outcry which followed the shooting deaths of two Canadian girls on the Rhodesian side of Victoria Falls by Zambian troops and, to a lesser extent, in Canadian reactions a decade earlier to the breakdown of the Central African Federation. These two sets of responses with their decidedly racialist and paternalist overtones echoed the attitudes which Canadians had adopted towards consular incidents affecting Canadians in Tanzania. They illustrate not only the lack of sympathy for the black African position on Southern African issues, but also the limited understanding among the Canadian public, press and parliament about Southern African affairs and, to some extent, an identification with the white minorities in the region. However, the Canadian government has not given in to these pressures and, in the case of the Victoria Falls episode, maintained its programmes of emergency and development assistance to Zambia despite public calls for their cancellation.

Political interests have also been more important than philanthropic and commercial considerations in determining the size and nature of Canada's development assistance programme in Zambia. Taking the latter first, although Zambia has the most highly developed industrial sector and internal market of all the countries in this study, Canadian commercial interests in Zambia are still relatively small and, with a few exceptions, are either tied to Canada's aid programme or are the offshoot of the promotional efforts of other Canadian government agencies – the Department of Industry Trade and Commerce's trade mission, the Export Development Corporation or the Canadian Commercial Corporation. Although both countries are major exporters of copper, suffering from the same wild fluctuations in the world market price, Canada has shown little interest in the efforts of Third World countries, including Zambia, to form a commodity cartel through CIPEC to moderate these swings and the accompanying vulnerability of economies dependent on copper revenues. As copper forms the major part of Zambia's exports, Canada imports virtually nothing from Zambia.

With revenues from its copper exports keeping it out of the category of least developed countries, Zambia has been less deserving of foreign assistance on the criterion of need than Tanzania and Malawi, although its poverty of trained human resources has been equally acute. As relations with Britain degenerated in the 1960s, Zambia was anxious to secure alternative sources of foreign capital and development assistance and therefore has welcomed Canadian involvement. Like Tanzania, Zambia is non-aligned, but its encouragement of private foreign investment and local capitalism has made it considerably closer in principle as well as in practise to the Canadian experience. Generally, CIDA's programme has supported the main thrust of Zambia's development strategy which has emphasized 'top-down' development, concentration on the urban industrial centers especially on the Copperbelt and neglect of the underdeveloped rural areas, particularly those far from the main railway line.

The major part of Canada's aid programme has been allocated to Zambian infrastructure through capital and technical assistance to Zambia Railways, to the industrial planning process through the provision of senior managerial expertise to INDECO and to the total re-organization of Zambia's system of technical education. In terms of the transfer of high-level technical and managerial skills, Canada's provision of personnel to take over the management of the railway system and then to stay on in an advisory role has increased Zambia's capacity to run a major national institution. Senior Canadian business executives also undoubtedly have passed on their skills acquired in Canadian companies to INDECO. Finally, Canada has helped Zambia develop one of the most sophisticated systems of technical education in Africa.

However, just as in Tanzania, the basic 'givens' in Western technical assistance – the personal lifestyles, attitudes and approaches to development of CIDA-financed 'experts' – have had important effects. The leadership in Zambia has been considerably less restrained in its adoption of Western consumption patterns and living standards and, in the main, is committed to following Western patterns of development. Therefore, although the highly-paid Canadian technical assistance personnel lived in a style which was more compatible with the ethos in Zambia, they reinforced the priority of personal material self-interest over the goal of national development. At the same time, Canadians were far removed from the majority of Zambians in the rural areas or in the peri-urban areas.

This general approach has strengthened certain orientations. Thus, the INDECO managers promoted new industrial projects along the line of rail and in the Copperbelt, generally ignoring the concept of regional balance which would have stimulated development in the far-flung regions. They also supported foreign capital investment in Zambia and short-term economic self-interest in trading with its cheapest suppliers in South Africa and Rhodesia. The Canadians in Zambia Railways also exported the dilemma of choice between free enterprise principles (which put the interests of the institutions first) and national priorities, a fundamental issue which bedevils the Canadian National Railway's relationship with the Canadian government.

The case of Canadian assistance to Zambian technical education illustrates even more clearly the effect of transporting intact certain development formulas which have been created in Canada but which have left Zambia with some serious long-term problems. Canada's attempt to reproduce a high level of technical education was a response to Zambia's need for an indigenous capacity to staff the positions in the industrial and mining centers on the Copperbelt and to undertake research which would lift Zambia out of its state of dependency on Western expertise. Therefore, SIDA was requested by Zambian officials to provide the very best in training and facilities. While copper revenues were still flowing in and domestic support for the programme was strong, the project proceeded swiftly, but when these conditions changed, the programme was in trouble. Once the government was hard-pressed for money and technical education had a lower political priority, its budget was cut and the system was left under utilized at considerable waste. The new Zambian Institute of Technology was extemely expensive with heavy recurrent costs built into the future, the curriculum had not been adequately interpreted to employers who were used to British qualifications, and it totally ignored the need for a lower level of technology in the rest of the country. By concentrating on the requirements of the industries and mines, the system had not made any provision for primary school leavers who would have benefitted from training or for the development of small-scale industries in the rural areas. CIDA's assistance to rural development in Zambia in no way compensated for its other emphases. It consisted of the provision of a few specialists for the Ministry of Rural Development and the development of large wheat farms for a few privileged Zambians – less even than in Tanzania where at least the wheat farms belong to the govenment.

In each of the major programmes which CIDA sponsored, certain biases were expressed. By ignoring the primary school leaver and rural needs for simple technology in the technical education programme, by providing senior personnel at the top of two national institutions and by concentrating its capital assistance on infrastructure which served only a small part of the country, CIDA's programme in Zambia, just as in Tanzania, did not directly assist the poor in either the urban or the rural sectors.

The sectoral distribution of CIDA's assistance strengthened Zambia's own development pattern which has left it vulnerable to external events and pressures with ramifications for its position on Southern African issues. Zambia's own inability to diversify its failure to sustain food production, let alone increase it, and its reliance on pre-independence capitalist structures of production have resulted in a pattern of development characterized by growing inequalities both within and between urban and rural sectors, the development of classes – particularly of an elite in the civil service and parastatal sector – and its dependence on Western and South African commercial links.

Zambia's vulnerability was made painfully clear in the mid 1970s. With the fall in the world price for copper removing the major source of government revenues and with the closure of the Benguela Railway cutting off a main export route during and after the Angolan Civil War, Zambia's options were very limited. It lacked resources to sustain its current lop-sided development pattern and it did not have the conditions necessary for national unity, discipline and self-sacrifice which a more equitable distribution of income and development would have produced. Therefore, it was in this period that Zambia increased its trade with South Africa, is reputed to have accepted South African financial assistance to pay its oil bills and backed Prime Minister Vorster's efforts for detente in Southern Africa. At the same time, Zambia's alliance with Tanzania and Mozambique in support of black liberation in Southern Africa was shaken by Zambia's support of UNITA, the pro-Western liberation movement allied with South Africa and the United States in Angola, and its hunt for a "moderate" solution to decolonization in Zimbabwe and Namibia. Undoubtedly, Zambia's fear of dominance by any great power, including the Soviet Union, played a part in its reactions to events in Angola. However, the underlying economic and political forces which had brought an elite to power in Zambia were more important. For the nature of the government established in Angola with its commitment to *poder popular* (popular participation) and equitable development and the prospect of other militant, radical socialist states emerging in Zimbabwe and Namibia threatened the security of the elite in power in Zambia. For a time, Zambia was considered in the West to be a moderate African state and potential ally, in the same category as Zaire and Kenya, although the adjustment to Zambia's internal economic crisis and changes in Southern Africa have enabled it to ease back into a more militant position, although this stance remains a subject of great controversy within the country.

Seen in this context, Canadian involvement in Zambia, though smaller than in Tanzania, is part of a general Western presence, reinforcing Zambian development patterns which have built in dependence on the West and the industrial metropole in South Africa, and which limits its support for a genuine decolonization in the rest of Southern Africa. The extent of Canadian ties and the size and nature of its development programme will indicate the strength of its political interests in future in easing Zambia out of its position of non-alignment and into the Western camp. For in terms of the strategy guiding Canadian development assistance for the rest of the decade, its comparative wealth would rule out major concentration in the future on philanthropic grounds.

Malawi

Canadian official involvement in Malawi developed later than all the other countries in this study. Until the mid 1970s when events in Southern Africa changed, Malawi was regarded with some apprehension in Canada for its ill treatment of racial, religious and political minorities. In addition, Canada did not want to antagonize the other black states in the region who considered Malawi a renegade state for its development of close relations with white Southern Africa. As black African views on Malawi mellowed in the 1970s, Canada began to increase its involvement, suporting an African state whose views on dialogue with the white states echoed its own and whose pro-Western alignment was considered valuable. This took the form of increased development assistance and the establishment of diplomatic relations in 1974.

Political considerations had been important in keeping Canada out of Malawi, but, once it became more respectable, there were also strong philanthropic reasons for increasing its development assistance. Like Tanzania, Malawi is one of the world's least developed countries and, therefore, it is eligible for top priority in

CIDA's assistance. Commercially, Canada has had even fewer interests in Malawi than in Tanzania and Zambia, and the side-effects of Canada's increased involvement are unlikely to go beyond the goods and equipment supplied under the tying regulations for foreign aid.

As Canada's official development assistance programme was late and concentrated almost entirely on Malawi's transportation sector – with three loans to Malawi Railways – its effect on Malawi's capacity for development and self-reliance in Southern Africa has been mixed. On the one hand, railway loans have been of major assistance both in the development of national infrastructure and Malawi's links with the black states in the region. But, as in Tanzania and Zambia, CIDA has not managed to enter significantly into the priority areas of aid to the poorest people in the rural and peri-urban areas. Part of the problem is related to CIDA's tying regulations and the lack of Canadian personnel or technology relevant to the needs of rural grass-roots development in Africa. In addition, Banda's own priorities have not favoured these groups. Therefore, when foreign aid agencies like CUSO and the Canadian Council of Churches have attempted to become involved in rural development programmes at the village level, they have eventually encountered political difficulties. For Banda's development strategy is at odds with co-operative effort and self-reliance at the local level. Its emphasis has been placed on the individual capitalist farmer or entrepreneur and state involvement in farms and industries.

The result of Malawi's approach to development has been significant growth in production of food crops as well as traditional agricultural exports, but also growing inequalities and dependence. With priority given to short-term economic criteria over social side-effects in development, Malawi has not managed to solve its problems of local unemployment and continues to be dependent on South African mines to employ its labour force. In opting for rapid economic growth, Malawi has also increased its indebtedness through reliance on foreign capital from South Africa and the West.

As long as the Malawi government adopts its present course, its potential for independence in Southern Africa is limited. Banda's decision to ban the recruitment of Malawian workers for South African mines was short-lived. Malawi simply did not have the capacity to withstand domestic pressures for employment and the effects of the loss of foreign exchange which this change entailed. With its emphasis on individual benefit rather than co-operation for development and with strains in both rural and urban areas resulting from internal repression and inequalities, Malawi did not have a secure foundation to call for the sacrifices which would have been necessary to meet its debt obligations, pursue its economic development and re-align itself with black Africa.

Malawi's importance for the West in a region which is becoming the center of Great Power competition may elicit greater Canadian assistance in the future. However, it is unlikely that humanitarian considerations will play a major role in determining the nature of future projects. As long as Banda is in power and as long as Canadian development assistance is governed by its tying regulations, the form of development that each will promote in Malawi will leave it inexorably locked into a dependent peripheral relationship with the developed metropoles in white Southern Africa and in the West.

Botswana

While the other three countries in this study have had some options in determining the extent of their ties with white Southern Africa, Botswana has had to struggle to establish any sovereignty at all. Its economy is part of the greater South African economy and, politically, it has had to walk a tightrope between its growing commitment to black nationalist aspirations and its dependence on the surrounding white-ruled states.

From the start, Canada's long-standing association with South Africa provided the basis for its general approach towards Botswana. Canadian officials conducted relations with Botswana from their resident mission in South Africa, despite Botswana's dislike for this form of double accreditation. With few exceptions, Canadian diplomats have reflected the bias of their white South African surroundings, while Canadian trade officials have advised Canadian suppliers to deal with Botswana through South African agents. Other than the materials and equipment supplied under the tying regulations of Canada's development assistance programmes, Canada's commercial interests are nominal as Botswana's small market is served almost entirely from Rhodesia and South Africa. Not only was Canada's decision to increase its development assistance to Botswana part of its general policy of support for black African states in the region, particularly those suffering from the effects of the Rhodesian impasse, but it also served as a substitute for effective assistance for black liberation movements.

However, there have been definite limits to Canada's political interest even in supporting Botswana's independence from the white-ruled states. These were defined most explicitly in Canada's refusal to countenance a major involvement in Botswana's attempt to take over management and control of its railway system from Rhodesia Railways. CIDA officials decided that the case for Botswana's control was less important than the cost of the project and that it should not attain a high priority in either Botswana's general development programme or CIDA's own choice of projects in Botswana. In dismissing the political and economic reasons for a take-over, CIDA's assessment differed not only from Canada's Department of External Affairs, but also from a team of United Nations experts. In seriously putting forward the suggestion that Botswana should ask South Africa to take over the management of the railways, they were clearly out of step with the times, exhibiting total insensitivity to Botswana's aspirations for independence from the white south. CIDA's position on this project provides a second example, along with its handling of early requests from Tanzania and Zambia for a railway link in the mid 1960s, of the limits of its support for black African interests in the political context of Southern

79

Africa. Both railway projects were of strategic importance to the countries' attempts to lessen their involvement with the white-ruled states, a factor that was not significant in the most recent railway project which has been approved for Malawi.

Other projects in CIDA's development assistance programme have provided greater support for Botswana's efforts to become less dependent on white Southern Africa – most notably Canada's participation in an international project to link Botswana and Zambia with road and ferry facilities and the provision of expertise to Botswana's Department of Mines to the regional university and to the regional Institute of Development Management based in Gaborone. In the first case, Canada and other Western countries expressed their disagreement with the South African contention that no border existed between Botswana and the independent black African countries. In the second, Canadian personnel provided major assistance to Botswana in its negotiations with multinational mining companies and in drafting legislation which would increase Botswana's benefits from its mineral resources. In providing technical assistance for the Institute of Development Management, CIDA was supporting programmes of research, consultancy and training for Botswana's senior and middle level officials.

However, the effect of CIDA's major contribution to Botswana has been considerably more ambiguous on the issue of promoting greater independence in the region. In providing funds for the construction of a thermal power plant for the Shashe Project, CIDA was granting concessional financing for infrastructure for a project owned by two major multinational mining companies and the Botswana government. In the short term, the power project deepened Botwana's dependence on white Southern Africa when the boilers were not able to burn local coal and alternative supplies had to be imported from Rhodesia and South Africa. The preference of Canadian technical assistance personnel for this foreign coal on the grounds of short-term cost considerations revealed their disinterest in the long-term benefits of the development of local coal supplies and, ultimately, the narrowness of their conception of national development. As to the over-all benefits of the Shashe Project for Botswana, the technical difficulties which slowed down production meant that the government received minimal revenues. In addition, the lack of decent wages, living conditions and race relations at Selebi-Pikwe reduced the secondary benefits for local Batswana. Most important of all, the arrangements for financing, management, forward processing facilities and export markets integrated Botswana into the empires of Anglo American and AMAX and tightened its links with South Africa, the United States and Germany.

Just as in its programmes in the other countries in this study, CIDA has concentrated its capital assistance in Botswana on infrastructure and its technical assistance at the top of national institutions in Botswana's urban centres, virtually ignoring direct assistance to the rural sector or the poor in the towns. Partly, this is another illustration of the orientations built into CIDA's programmes by its tying regulations. But also this bias has reinforced the recipient government's own development strategy which, like Zambia, has emphasized mineral exploitation, the development of transportation links and other large physical infrastructural projects, leaving aside questions of regional balance through rural development. In Botswana as in the other countries in this study, rural development has been regarded as a sensitive area for foreign aid agencies, particularly as it has featured the growth of an indigenous rural elite associated with the power structure, the growth of a landless peasantry and the development of a lumpen proletariat which has drifted from the land to the squatter settlements around the towns. While Botwana's capacity to free itself from its dependence on white Southern Africa is related, to some extent, to the discovery and development of its natural resources and to political changes in the region, its inegalitarian pattern of development can only undermine national unity, a pre-requisite for Botswana's continued militancy on Southern African issues. More important still, the external logic of the capitalist system which it has adopted can only serve to keep it as a dependent peripheral outpost of the industrial metropole on South Africa's Rand.

While Botswana's growing mineral wealth and small population have taken it out of the category of least developed countries, and therefore have lessened the philanthropic case for increased attention, there are strong political reasons for Canada and other Western countries to continue providing development assistance. With Botswana's evolution away from a pro-Western stance to a greater emphasis on non-alignment with any Great Power bloc, it has begun to establish closer relations with the Soviet Union, China and the other countries of the Communist bloc. This factor, taken together with Botswana's pivotal geographic location in the region will ensure its importance for the West in the future.

In summary, the nature of Canadian interests in the four countries in this study is primarily political, with humanitarian and commercial interests playing a lesser role. These have been expressed, in the main, through programmes of development assistance although Canada has been prepared to offer military and emergency aid as well. The profiles of Canada's development assistance programmes in each country are remarkably similar, reflecting the restraints put on Canadian assistance by its tying regulations. For, from the outset, Canadian commercial self-interest ensured that the major part of Canadian aid would be used to purchase Canadian goods, equipment and expertise. Throughout, it has been suggested that tying regulations build in direct and indirect costs for the recipient countries. More important, they limit the sectors in which Canada is able to provide assistance – urban, capital intensive, high technology projects, usually with an emphasis on capital assistance to infrastructure and technical assistance to the top of national institutions. At the same time, Canadian philanthropic interests have ensured that Canadian loans have been offered on extremely soft terms and repayment has been forgiven recently for the two countries in this study – Malawi and Tanzania – who belong to the category of 'least developed' countries in the world.

While commercial self-interest has undercut Canada's philanthropic interest in development assistance through its tying regulations, a more indirect expression of commercial interests has also affected Canadian interests in these four African countries. Reforms in trade constitute a fundamental part of the movement by Third World countries to institute a new international economic order, far more significant than programmes of development assistance. Yet in this other sphere, Canada's record has been quite poor. Canada has been reluctant to join with countries like Zambia and Botswana in CIPEC to work for greater control over the world price for copper. In addition, Canada has generally aligned itself with the advanced industrial world in discussions about international commodity price stabilization rather than worked for the sorts of arrangements for tea, coffee and sisal which would help Tanzania and Malawi. Instead, Canada has chosen to express its humanitarian interests through aid programmes, a considerably softer option and one that has a direct political benefit.

Therefore, it has been left to Canadian non-governmental organizations – the churches, the Mennonites, CUSO and other groups – to reduce the commercial self-interest in development assistance through a more genuine expression of help to poorer countries. The location of the majority of CUSO and other NGO personnel in the rural areas has increased their awareness of the sorts of assistance which are most relevant to local needs. In addition, CUSO has attempted to develop criteria which will direct its allocations of financial and technical assistance to the sectors and the countries which CIDA would now like, in principle, to direct its assistance in the future. However, CUSO's experience suggests that this will be difficult. For not only do Canadians lack the relevant experience and expertise to deal with the problems of rural underdevelopment in Africa, but also this sector is politically very sensitive in countries whose emphasis in development has not been on grass roots rural development. With fewer resources, CUSO has been forced to weigh very carefully the alternative benefits of each of its commitments. Therefore, it has been more forthright in withdrawing its programmes from countries like Malawi and Zambia, where it feels it cannot serve its objectives, and in expanding them in Tanzania or establishing them in Mozambique where the governments' development strategies more closely reflect their own concerns. CUSO's greater sophistication in understanding the implications of change in Southern Africa has also been expressed in its greater support for and closer association with African liberation movements.

As has been argued throughout this study, aid programmes serve political ends not only in enabling Canada to establish its presence on the ground in these African countries and in facilitating the development of friendly relations, but also in supporting certain processes in the political economy of the region which are characteristic of metropolitan-periphery relations. Certain objectives are fundamental to the success of peripheral countries resisting the short-term attractiveness and advantages of close ties with the metropoles to the south. Above all, balanced development, equity and participation provide the bases for national unity in the hard struggle for political and economic structural transformation. In each case, therefore, the role of the poor majority in rural and urban areas is crucial.

The question that has been asked throughout this study has been to what extent has Canadian development assistance provided direct support for their development. Clearly, direct assistance has been minimal: The failure of CIDA to put the principles of its Aid Strategy into effect means that Canadian assistance has not provided support for the areas which would make self-reliant development a reality.

However, the question that still remains to be addressed is whether the technical assistance at the top of national institutions and large capital assistance to infrastructural projects, nevertheless, provide indirect benefits which the whole nation, including the poor majority may share. The answer varies from case to case. Clearly, the large infrastructural projects in Tanzania – the Harbours project which is helping all of Central and East Africa expedite its trade, the power and water projects, the mapping and the enormous loans to Tanzania Railways which are crucial for internal communications as well as the delivery of export crops on which Tanzania depends for its foreign exchange – have made an enormous impact on the development of the country. They were each essential projects with a very high foreign cost component. Tanzania could hardly have financed them on her own, at least not as swiftly. Similarly, the large railway loans in Malawi have facilitated the transport of its export crops and have opened up large areas of the central part of the country for development, and aid to Zambia Railways and Botswana's roads has kept their transportation systems running smoothly. The provision of highly qualified Canadians to assist in the operation of senior levels of national institutions also increased the capacity of these countries to function in sophisticated relations both nationally and internationally.

In each of the countries of this study, however, the analysis has gone further to examine the nature of the economic and political structure and its development strategy to determine whether the indirect benefits of these projects ever "trickle down". With the exception of Tanzania, all the countries in this study have pursued variations of state capitalist strategies which have featured an inegalitarian distribution of the benefits from development and therefore increasing disparities in income and power both between urban and rural sectors and within each sector. Therefore, the distribution of the benefits of this indirect assistance from Canada to the majority becomes problematic.

Therefore, in assessing the effect of Canadian development assistance on regional metropole-periphery relations in Southern Africa there are two points to be made: In the short term, large capital assistance for infrastructure or technical assistance at the top of national institutions generally increases the capacity of the recipient countries to counter-act the pull of the south, whatever development strategy they have chosen. However, in the longer term, the concentration of Canada's official development assistance programme in these sectors and its failure to directly aid the poor majority in urban and rural areas has reinforced the pattern of general development in at least three of the countries in this study. Therefore, official Canadian development assistance has made little contribution to solutions for the problems of growing inequalities and imbalances both between and inside urban and rural sectors which have left the countries in question more vulnerable to the economic pull of the white metropoles in the South.

In the context of the larger strategic interests of the Western powers in Southern Africa, it well behooves the West to have Canada represented in these countries through its development assistance programmes. For not only do they strengthen patterns of dependence in the long term, but also they provide a pay-off politically in the short term. In the event that these countries move farther away from the West, friendly ties with Canada, strengthened by strong Canadian statements in the Commonwealth and at the United Nations serve the West's purposes admirably. In the past, Canada has played the role of intermediary with great discretion in Tanzania where it handled a programme of military assistance in a period of escalating warfare in Southern Africa and of growing Chinese influence. In the Commonwealth, Canada eased Britain's position following its ineffectual handling of the Rhodesian crisis. Once again, Canada may be called upon as the most acceptable and innocuous of the Western 'middle powers' to serve larger Western interests in a region of increasing strategic importance. Moreover, as we have seen, Canada, too, has its own interests in keeping Southern Africa friendly to the West. Canadian economic interests in South Africa and Namibia are hostages to the rapidly changing allegiances, fortunes and power ratios in the region.

Paul Ladouceur

Canadian Humanitarian Aid for Southern Africa

During the 1970's, Canada's policy towards Southern Africa has undergone a slow but significant evolution, one aspect of which has been a change in Canadian policy regarding humanitarian assistance for Southern Africa. The decade opened with a publication of the government's White Paper, *Foreign Policy for Canadians.* The White Paper did not deal extensively with Canadian policy in Southern Africa, but it re-states, in the context of relations with the United Nations, the long-standing Canadian policy towards the area, summarised as follows: "Broad revulsion" against racial discrimination and condemnation of *apartheid* and colonial rule; and unrestricted trade in peaceful goods and unlimited investment, because of the "better-than-normal opportunities for trade and investment in the growing economy of the Republic of South Africa".[1] A third element of Canadian policy towards the area was opposition to "violent solutions" and "resistance to the use of sanctions, except where an unmistakable threat to international peace and security exists".[2] In accordance with UN resolutions, Canada applied arms embargoes to sales of military equipment to the Portuguese African territories, ceased providing military assistance to Portugal under NATO mutual aid, and complied with Security Council resolutions calling for a voluntary embargo on the supply of arms to South Africa. In contrast with Canada's vocal opposition to colonial rule and racism, especially in such fora as the Commonwealth and the United Nations, and its implementation of UN resolutions on arms sales, Canada's stand on trade and investment with Southern Africa was characterized by many Canadians as ambivalent and inconsistent, if not outright contradictory.[3] Prime Minister Trudeau himself admitted the inconsistency of the Canadian policy; in March 1970, he was quoted as saying "It is not consistent. We should either stop trading or stop condemning."[4] Canadian trade and investment relations with South Africa, Namibia, and Angola increased substantially throughout the 1960's and up to the mid-1970's.[5]

In contrast with its ambiguous stands on South Africa, Namibia, and the Portuguese territories of Angola, Mozambique and Guinea Bissau, the government's position on Rhodesia was "straightforward and unequivocal".[6] Rhodesia was, of course, in a very different category from the other territories under racial and minority domination in Southern Africa. In 1965, the unilateral declaration of independence by the government of Ian Smith was universally condemned, except by South Africa and Portugal, and the rebel colony incurred the formal wrath of both the Commonwealth and the United Nations. Canada had little difficulty in applying the sanctions imposed by the UN Security Council against Rhodesia, and the government enacted the "United Nations Rhodesia Regulations", which prohibited all official, economic and financial contact with the illegal regime.

The final area of major interest concerning Canadian policy in Southern Africa related to the freedom fighters or liberation movements of various territories. In accordance with the third principle mentioned above, opposition to "violent solutions", the Canadian government did not recognize or have dealings with the liberation movements of Southern Africa, and it was unwilling to extend direct humanitarian assistance to members of liberation movements. The government was, however, prepared to offer some assistance to Southern African refugees, and in fact the White Paper announced the government's intention to increase its contribution to the UN Education and Training Programme for Southern Africans (UNETPSA).' Canada also contributed a small amount annually to the UN Trust Fund for South Africa, which provided legal and social assistance to the victims of *apartheid,* provided some scholarships in Canada for Zimbabweans and Namibians, and contributed to other scholarship programmes such as those of the Commonwealth and the International University Exchange Fund (IUEF). In 1973/74, the total of these contributions was $318,000 (See Table I).

The complacency in Canadian policy towards Southern Africa underlying the White Paper of 1970 produced a strong reaction in the small but vocal community of Canadians concerned about the situation in that region. A conference of Canadians with a major and continuing involvement in Southern Africa, held in Ottawa in May 1970, produced a broad consensus for a stronger and more consistent Canadian policy. At the same time, a group was formed in Toronto called the Committee for a Just Canadian Policy towards Africa, which included among its members academics, officials of voluntary organizations, churchmen, trade unionists etc. The Committee requested four of its members to produce an answer to the government White Paper, and the result was *The Black Paper: An Alternative Policy for Canada towards Southern Africa.* The *Black Paper* was published in September 1970, and served as a broad rallying point for those wishing to influence government policies in the area. The document summarized the situation in Southern Africa and went on to analyze Canadian policy. In general, it called for more consistency between Canadian economic and political stands towards the area, especially in terms of the application of economic restrictions and the reduction of Canadian economic ties with Southern Africa. Specifically, it called for a complete severance of ties between Canadian crown corporations and Southern Africa, the elimination of Commonwealth preferential tariffs accorded to South Africa, and the discouragement of investment by private Canadian companies. The *Black Paper* recommended that "the government publicly recognize the legitimacy of this struggle of the liberation movements", and further suggested that Canada

Table 1. *Official Canadian Humanitarian Assistance for Southern Africa ($000)*

	1972/73	1973/74	1974/75	1975/76	1976/77	1977/78
International Organizations						
UN Education and Training Programme for Southern Africans (UNETPSA)	50	75	175	175	225	250
UN Fund for Namibia – UN Institute for Namibia	–	–	–	100	–	100
UN Trust Fund for South Africa	10	10	10	10	10	20
Commonwealth Rhodesia Scholarship Programme (CRSP)	58	68	73	75	75	150
International University Exchange Fund (IUEF) – Scholarships for refugees	30	40	60	120	80	150
World University Service (WUS) – Scholarships in Rhodesia	–	–	136	140	175	231
UN High Commissoner for Refugees (UNHCR) – Southern African refugees	–	–	–	–	–	700
UN Children's Fund (UNICEF) – African Liberation Movements	–	–	–	–	–	500
International Red Cross – Southern African Refugees	–	–	–	–	–	250
Bilateral						
Scholarships for Zimbabweans and Namibians	99	125	32	12	29	74
Canadian NGOs						
Contributions for various projects	–	–	155	127	116	269
TOTAL:	247	318	641	759	710	2,694

provide "financial, technical, and medical assistance to the liberation movements preferably through the United Nations or the Organization of African Unity".[9] The *Black Paper* also suggested that the Canadian International Development Agency (CIDA) concentrate Canadian development assistance on the principal independent African countries in the area with a record of resistance to domination by South Africa and Rhodesia, namely Tanzania, Zambia, and Botswana.

Canadian assistance to the three countries mentioned was already underway when the *Black Paper* was published. The External Aid Office, CIDA's predecessor, began a programme of assistance in Tanzania in 1966, and in the same year participated in the airlift of oil to Zambia, which was an emergency response to the unilateral declaration of independence of Rhodesia. A more substantial programme in Zambia began in November 1970, and was closely related to a decision to establish a High Commission in Lusaka. Also in 1970, CIDA made a loan agreement with Botswana to supply power generating equipment for Botswana's mining industry. CIDA was already involved in providing technical assistance to the University of Botswana, Lesotho and Swaziland.[10] Subsequently, CIDA's programme in Tanzania, Zambia and Botswana grew substantially, until by the mid-1970's disbursements for these three countries accounted for about $30 million annually, or some 30% of CIDA's total programme in Anglophone Africa.[11] Although this rapid build-up in the level of Canadian assistance was related primarily to developmental considerations, it also reinforced the political objective of providing assistance to the Commonwealth "Front Line" states opposed to continued white domination in Southern Africa.

There was little immediate reaction to the strong challenge to government policy represented by the *Black Paper.* In the early summer of 1971, the House of Commons Committee on External Affairs and National Defence held a series of hearings on the *Foreign Policy for Canadians,* including one major session devoted to Southern Africa.[12] Written briefs were submitted by a number of interested groups, including the Committee for a Just Canadian Policy, Canadian University Service Overseas (CUSO), the New Democratic Party, and the YWCA. Despite the growing body of evidence of widespread support for the alternative policy outlined in the *Black Paper,* the witnesses at the hearing of 1 June 1971 noted both verbally and in supplementary briefs that very little had been done to implement the 21 recommendations contained in the *Black Paper,* and stated that some backward steps had occurred during the year.[13] The Committee hearings did not produce any tangible results and in fact the Committee ignored Southern Africa in its report to Parliament on the *Foreign Policy for Canadians.*

Outside the government, in addition to the policy changes urged by a number of groups and individuals, several Canadian voluntary organizations were in direct contact with liberation movements and were actively assisting them in various ways. The principal organizations involved were OXFAM, CUSO, the United Church of Canada, and liberation support groups such as the Toronto Committee for the Liberation of Portugal's African Colonies (TCPAC), Liberation Support Movement (LSM), and the African Relief Services Committtee. By 1973, the value of contributions in cash and in kind provided by these and other organizations was probably between $150,000 and $200,000 a year.[14] These projects consisted mostly in the provision of supplies and equipment for agricultural, educational and medical purposes. In addition, other organizations, such as the Canadian Catholic Organization for Development and Peace, the Salvation Army and the YWCA, were in contact with counterpart organizations in Southern Africa and provided small amounts for humanitarian and development work. But apart from two minor grants to the United Church of Canada for projects in Angola, CIDA did not assist any projects in Southern Africa or projects involving liberation movements.

The Birth of a New Policy

Beneath the surface of apparent complacency and inaction, there was increasing concern, and it was becoming obvious that something had to be done to reconcile the increasing inconsistencies in Canada's policy towards Southern Africa. The final impetus which produced a change in government policy towards humanitarian assistance and the liberation movements was provided by the Commonwealth Heads of Government Meeting held in Ottawa in August 1973. Prime Minister Trudeau, host of the Conference, wished to ensure that Canada did everything possible to make the Conference a success and even lead to a renewal of the Commonwealth itself. The discussions on Southern Africa were acrimonious, and the final communiqué of the Conference spoke of the "full and frank exchanges of views on changes and developments in Southern Africa", which basically signified the impossibility of reconciling the views of Edward Heath, Conservative Prime Minister of Great Britain, with those of the leading African spokesmen, particularly Presidents Julius Nyerere of Tanzania and Kenneth Kaunda of Zambia. Nevertheless, there were several phrases in the final communiqué which represented significant departures in Canadian policy. In the first place, the Heads of Government "recognized the legitimacy of the struggle to win full human rights and self-determination".[15] Although this did not constitute full recognition of the struggle of the liberation movements for freedom in Southern Africa, it did represent a step forward in recognizing the legitimacy of their basic objectives. Significant too was the mention by Heads of Government of "the efforts of the indigenous people of the territories in Southern Africa to achieve self-determination" and their agreement "on the need to give every humanitarian assistance to all those engaged in such efforts". Unlike Britain, Canada did not reserve its position concerning this particular statement. At a press conference after the Heads of Government Meeting, Prime Minister Trudeau made it clear that the government was prepared to consider offering humanitarian assistance, but not military assistance, through international organizations to the liberation movements of Southern Africa:

Nous serions prêts et nous sommes prêts à venir en aide, par exemple, par l'intermédiare de la Croix Rouge, par l'intermédiaire des Nations-Unies . . . I think the humanitarian assistance we are prepared to give is making more explicit something that we have perhaps done implicitly through some United Nations support . . . We think (it) would have the support of the Canadian people that, if we can support them through humanitarian as opposed to military means, we would do so.[16]

One feature of the Commonwealth Conference which may have influenced the Canadian government to adopt a more forthright attitude with respect to Southern Africa was the holding of a "People's Forum on Southern Africa", sponsored by a number of Canadian organizations, including the Southern Africa Information Group, TCLPAC, LSM, CUSO, OXFAM, the United Nations Association and others. This "counter-conference", held at the University of Ottawa, received extensive coverage in the media because of the presence of speakers from the Zimbabwe liberation movements, as well as a number of high-ranking delegates of African countries. Although the People's Forum was directed at the Commonwealth Conference as a whole, it also served to highlight further the inconsistencies of the Canadian policy with respect to the Zimbabwe liberation movements.[17]

In the autumn of 1973, there were a few public indications that the government was preparing a new policy in respect to humanitarian assistance in Southern Africa. On 25 September 1973, Mr. Mitchell Sharp, Secretary of State for External Affairs, declared at the United Nations General Assembly that "Canada recognizes the legitimacy of the struggle to win full human rights and self-determination in Southern Africa and is studying ways to broaden its humanitarian support for those engaged in these efforts"." But the nature of the new policy only became known some months later.

Shortly after the Commonwealth Heads of Government Meeting, Mr. Sharp instructed his officials to consider what steps could be taken to implement the commitments that Canada had undertaken at the meeting, without prejudicing Canada's traditional policy against use of violence to achieve self-determination. This request sparked a series of intensive discussions and meetings, and resulted in a memorandum to Sharp on Canadian humanitarian assistance for Southern Africa in October 1973.

Even before the stimulus provided by the Commonwealth Meeting and subsequent declarations of the Prime Minister at his press conference, officials in both CIDA and External Affairs had begun to explore in a tentative fashion ways of providing humanitarian assistance to the black population of Rhodesia. Their concern arose partly from the aftermath of the Pearce Commission on Rhodesian Opinion." The Pearce Commission, it will be recalled, was established by the British government to test opinion "from all sections of the population of Rhodesia", concerning the proposals for a settlement of the Rhodesian situation arrived at between Sir Alec Douglas-Home and Ian Smith in November 1971 In May 1972, following extensive hearings in Rhodesia, the Commission found that the great majority of the Rhodesian population rejected the proposed settlement. However, one aspect of the proposed settlement which appeared to offer scope for a modest Canadian initiative was the provision for an increasing African franchise based on educational qualifications and level of income.

In late 1972, it seemed to some officials that the insistence on educational qualifications offered a possibility for Canadian assistance to improve the educational level of Africans in Rhodesia. By providing educational assistance to Rhodesian Africans within Rhodesia, it was thought that Canada could enable them to meet more easily the existing franchise qualifications, and conceivably any future franchise also based on education and level of income. In seeking to provide such assistance, the government was faced with a number of legal questions, since the government's own UN Rhodesia Regulations of 1968 prohibited direct diplomatic and economic assistance in any form to the illegal Rhodesia regime. However, the Regulations specifically excluded assistance for Rhodesians in humanitarian, medical or educational fields and it would therefore be possible to devise a programme which would not run counter to the Rhodesia Regulations. Because assistance through the Rhodesian regime was excluded by the fact of its illegality, attention turned to alternative means of funnelling assistance to the African population. The most obvious candidates were non-governmental agencies operating in Rhodesia, such as Canadian churches and other voluntary agencies. At the same time, CIDA officials were considering the possibility of assisting projects in Rhodesia submitted by various Canadian non-governmental organizations. Through its Non-Governmental Organizations Division, CIDA offers assistance to Canadian organizations involved in development projects overseas on a "matching basis"; that is, CIDA provides financial assistance to the organizations for projects provided that the organizations themselves contributed from their own resources as well. A number of Canadian NGOs, such as the YWCA and the Salvation Army, had submitted projects in Rhodesia for CIDA's consideration; these projects were to be implemented by the local branches of the organizations. Although the projects did not involve the liberation movements in any way, CIDA felt that in the light of the political situation it should obtain clearance from External Affairs before approving grants for any projects in Rhodesia. CIDA was willing to approve grants provided that the projects proposed met normal programming criteria, that it was clear that it was the African population which would benefit from the projects, that groups and institutions that were supported were either African or multiracial, and that the projects were relatively free from direct government interference and control.

However, no specific policy changes resulted from this consideration of the question in 1972 or the first half of 1973. The *Black Paper* and the Parliamentary Committee hearings of June 1971 had not produced significant changes in government policy, and it was only subsequent to the Commonwealth Conference that officials were prepared to consider proposals going beyond those which had been discussed in 1972.

During September and October 1973, a series of intensive discussions and consultations took place, involving a number of divisions in both External Affairs and CIDA. The principal sections involved in External Affairs were the African and Middle Eastern Bureau, which had the prime responsibility for preparing a policy paper for the Minister, the United Nations Bureau, and the Aid and Development Division, which was responsible within External Affairs for coordination of all aspects of aid related questions. On the CIDA side, the principal divisions were the Non-Governmental Organizations (NGO) Division and the Multilateral Programmes Branch. The NGO Division, which was anxious to respond positively to requests presented by Canadian NGOs, would have the prime responsibility for implementing the new policy. The Multilateral Programmes Branch was involved since it was already contributing to several international funds providing educational assistance to Southern African refugees, while the Commonwealth Africa Division of the Bilateral Programmes Branch continued to provide a small number of scholarships for Rhodesian and Namibian refugees in Canada. Thus, the divisions most immediately concerned with the area and with the eventual implementation of a new policy had the largest and most decisive inputs into the final recommendations.[20] An important aspect of the discussions leading to a new policy was the reconciliation of differing points of view among officials. Some

91

reflected a more conservative or "minimal" approach to the prospect of a change in policy, whereas others, especially those most directly exposed to Canadian or international public opinion, pressed for a more forthcoming and progressive point of view.

The main points of controversy revolved around the possibility of assistance, even indirect, to liberation movements, and of assistance to groups within the white-dominated countries and territories other than Rhodesia. There was agreement among all concerned that direct assistance to liberation movements was not within the realm of possibility. The "minimalist" approach favoured continuing to ignore the liberation movements, further studies of assistance in the Portuguese colonies, South Africa and Namibia, and opening the door only to contributions to voluntary agencies for humanitarian activities in Rhodesia. On the other hand, advocates of the "forthcoming" approach argued for a more extensive and meaningful response which would in particular reflect the government's evolving attitude towards the liberation struggle in Southern Africa. In this context, it was argued, a new policy could not avoid assistance in some form to liberation movements. In the end, the "forthcoming" position largely won out; the decisive factor was no doubt the Commonwealth Conference and especially the Prime Minister's remarks at his press conference of 10 August 1973.

In mid-October, External Affairs sent a memorandum on Canadian humanitarian assistance for Southern Africa to Mr. Sharp. The memorandum was endorsed by CIDA and approved by the Minister.[11] Inexplicably, for several months after the memorandum was approved, very little happened. No grants were made for projects covered by the new policy, despite the fact that CIDA had had projects in Rhodesia on hand for some time, and had received a request from the Canadian Council of Churches (CCC) for a contribution for humanitarian assistance to FRELIMO, MPLA AND PAIGC, to be channelled through the World Council of Churches (WCC) in Geneva. Through its Programme to Combat Racism, established in 1971, the WCC provided assistance to a wide range of anti-racist movements, including the principal liberation movements of Southern Africa. The request for a CIDA contribution was a perfect test for the new policy of humanitarian assistance. But before a contribution could be approved, a storm of political controversy erupted over the government's new policy, a storm which caught those concerned by surprise, and which resulted in a year's delay in implementing the most significant aspects of the policy.

The Public Debate of 1974

"Ottawa to give aid to African guerilla groups". So read the headline on the front page of the Toronto *Globe and Mail* on 7 February 1974. The article triggered an extensive public debate on the government's policy towards humanitarian assistance to Southern Africa, a debate which forced the postponement of the implementation of part of the policy, but, more significantly, attracted more public attention to Canada's role in Southern Africa than at any other time in the previous decade.

In truth, the government had not given much publicity to the new policy; the Ottawa officials prefered to keep the issue as low-key as possible. CIDA advised a few of the interested NGOs that it could now consider requests for contributions for projects in the area, and even encouraged some to submit projects most likely to satisfy the criteria. But apart from Mr. Sharp's statement in September 1973 that Canada was "studying ways to broaden its humanitarian support in Southern Africa", the only other public announcement was a brief statement in early December at the Trusteeship Committee of the UN General Assembly to the effect that "the Canadian government has recently undertaken to broaden the scope of its humanitarian assistance in Southern Africa". The statement went on –

Such further aid will be channelled through Canadian non-governmental and international organizations which are assisting the efforts of the peoples of Southern Africa who are involved in the struggle for human dignity and self-determination.[22]

At the same time, Canada announced substantially increased contributions to UNETPSA and the IUEF.

The *Globe and Mail* article of 7 February 1974 was a generally sympathetic and accurate account of the new policy and its background. The article stated that grants would be made by CIDA through intermediary non-governmental groups such as the International Red Cross, the World Council of Churches, OXFAM, World University Service etc. Citing "a senior official" in External Affairs, the article went on to say that the government would need "to be assured that the assistance is used for humanitarian purposes" and would require some form of monitoring or surveillance: "We want to be sure the money goes for blankets, not bullets."[23]

The reaction to the *Globe and Mail* story was immediate. Two days later, on 9 February, a *Globe* editorial entitled "Parliament, not CIDA", questioned whether Canada should be giving aid of any kind to revolutionaries, and criticized the government for using CIDA to circumvent Parliamentary approval of the new policy. "Parliament and the people", argued the *Globe*, "are quite capable of deciding whether they like the road which Mr. Sharp is quietly preparing to have Canada tread". The reference to Parliament raised a particularly delicate point. As a result of the 1972 election, the Liberal government of Pierre Trudeau found itself in a minority position with 109 seats, only two more than the Tories, while the New Democratic Party held the balance of power with 31 seats. The last thing that the government wanted was a popular issue which would unite the opposition parties.

The *Globe* story was picked up by the news services and published by many newspapers. Soon the reactions started to appear. With few exceptions, the initial comments were largely negative:

"Canada gives aid to terror" (Editorial, *The Citizen* (Ottawa), 18 Feb. 1974). "Canada's two-faced policy in Africa" (Editorial, *Toronto Star,* 8 Feb. 1974). "Cash to guerillas interfering (*Journal* (Ottawa), 11 Feb. 1974). "How Canada aids terrorism" (*Toronto Sun,* 25 Feb. 1974). "Financing terror" (Editorial, *Toronto Sun,* 26 Feb. 1974). "Foreign aid is not for terrorism" (Editorial, *Toronto Star,* 15 Mar. 1974).

Among the principal criticisms raised in the media and in letters to the editor were that such assistance constituted interference in the domestic affairs of other countries, that all aid to liberation movements was military aid in the end, that it weakened the security of the West by undermining Portugal, a member of NATO, and that Canada was being hypocritical in supporting opponents of regimes with which it continued to have profitable business connections. References were made to foreign interference in Canadian domestic affairs, to the *Front de libération du Québec;* CIDA was asked if it would assist the Basques, the Palestine Liberation Organization and other terrorist groups; CIDA was accused of organizing a "Canadian Comintern", and, with the WCC, of being "laced with lib-left types". Among the few newspapers which favoured the new policy was *The Gazette* (Montreal), which argued in editorials on 12 February and 21 March that the policy was a natural extension of previous Canadian positions on Southern Africa and of assistance given for the education of refugees, while *The Province* (Vancouver) endorsed the new policy in an editorial entitled "Controversial Charity" on 9 March.

Faced with the vehemence of the media and the public reaction, the government hesitated. On 21 February, External Affairs issued a statement in the name of Mitchell Sharp. The statement outlined briefly the background to the policy and the support Canada was already giving to assist refugees from Southern Africa. Five principal conditions were outlined for the new programme:

1. The projects must be sponsored by reputable Canadian non-governmental and international organizations; 2. The projects must be of a humanitarian or developmental nature; 3. Each project would be evaluated on its own merits; 4. The sponsoring organization would have to demonstrate that strict control of the project would be mainteained; 5. Full accountability would have to be furnished.[14]

The statement went on to say that Parliament would, as urged by the *Globe,* have the last word on assistance to liberation movements:

The Government of Canada does not intend to make funds directly available to liberation movements in Southern Africa. Moreover, no grants to organizations providing humanitarian asistance to such movements in Southern Africa have yet been made and none will be made until the estimates of CIDA for the year 1974/75, which include contributions to non-government organizations, have been approved by Parliament.

Although this represented a retreat for the government, it was far from capitulation to the storm of criticism, and the statement concluded with a re-affirmation of the government's determination to expand its humanitarian assistance to "the indigenous people of Southern Africa who are striving to achieve human dignity and self-determination."

Thus, the focus of the debate on assistance to liberation movements shifted to Parliament, notably to the House of Commons Standing Committee on External Affairs and National Defence, which had the responsibility for the detailed study of CIDA's Estimates. The opening round of the discussion in the Standing Committee was a reference to the matter in a general foreign policy statement by Mitchell Sharp. Sharp again re-affirmed the goverment's commitment to greater humanitarian assistance in Southern Africa, which, he argued, "is one tangible method of demonstrating where we stand on the issues of racist and colonialist injustices".[25] Sharp also revealed more details concerning the policy. First, it covered possible projects in Namibia, Rhodesia, the Portuguese African territories and South Africa. Moreover, projects could also include assistance to peoples in liberated areas and people from white-ruled territories who had taken refuge in adjacent African countries. Finally, to the government it was obvious that "the projects would not be practical without at least the tacit concurrence of the local authorities in the particular regions concerned". The last point caused considerable confusion, but basically it implied that the government recognized that projects in South Africa, for example, had at least to be tolerated by the South African government, while projects in liberated areas could not be carried out without the support of the liberation movement which controlled the area. It did not mean, as some critics implied, that the government required and would seek the formal approval of whatever authorities were in *de facto* control of the area where the project took place.

As the public debate carried on, it was obvious that the new policy enjoyed a considerable measure of support, particularly from individuals and organizations concerned about international development in general or Southern Africa in particular. Indeed, many groups, normally critical of government policy, found themselves in the unaccustomed position of defending the government. The pro-humanitarian assistance forces waged their battle largely through letters to the editor of the major newspapers, letters to Mr. Sharp and to M.P.s, and briefs and statements to the Standing Committee. Among the groups which supported the government were the Canadian Association of African Studies, the Canadian Council for International Cooperation, OXFAM-Canada, OXFAM-Quebec, CUSO etc. There were a few criticisms which belittled the move as too little – notably a widely-reprinted article by James Eayrs, in which he accused the government of timidity, cowardice and failing "to live up to the expectations generated by its previous rhetoric", and an article by Cranford Pratt in *International Perspectives.*[26]

The Standing Committee on External Affairs and National Defence devoted three full sessions to the Southern Africa issue, and the matter was raised at other sessions with Mr. Sharp. On 21 March 1974, Robert Duffy, a journalist with the *Toronto Star,* appeared as a witness opposing the government's policy, arguing that Canada should not be aiding those engaged in violence.[27] He did not receive a particularly sympathetic hearing, in contrast with Mr. Sharp, who appeared before the Committee the following day. At this time, both principal opposition parties declared their support for the government move, notably in statements and questions by Heath Macquarrie of the Conservatives and Andrew Brewin of the NDP.[28] Later, on 4 April, four witnesses favouring the policy appeared before the Committee: Rev. Floyd Honey, representing the Canadian Council of Churches, Romeo Maione, from the Canadian Labour Congress, Clyde Sanger, on behalf of the Southern Africa Information Group, and Cranford Pratt of the University of Toronto and one of the authors of the *Black Paper.* While welcoming the government's move, the witnesses also expressed the hope that it would be the beginning of "a more solid policy of the government in recognizing the legitimacy of the struggle of the people of Southern Africa for their liberation".[29] Cranford Pratt also urged that Canada recognize Guinea Bissau, a step which, as Mr. Sharp explained the following day, Canada was not prepared to take since it was not yet clear to the government "that there is an independent country called Guinea Bissau which has its own independent government."[30]

At the last hearing, on 25 April, representatives of OXFAM-Canada appeared as witnesses, and had invited Dr. Agostino Neto, President of the MPLA, then on a tour of Canada, to accompany them. In a significant step, the Committee invited Dr. Neto to address it on Angola and to respond to questions. In his remarks, Dr. Neto stated that he was seeking political and material support in Canada, and that he hoped that the Canadian government would show its solidarity with the liberation movements and would recognize them as representatives of their people."[31] Neto's appearance at the Parliamentary Committee highlighted the momentous event that had taken place the previous day: on 24 April 1974, the Portuguese military, led by General Antonio de Spinola; brought an end to the government of Marcelo Caetano and 46 years of fascist dictatorship in Portugal. The aftermath of the coup was to have an important bearing on the evolution of Canadian humanitarian assistance in Southern Africa.

Following the hearings before the Parliamentary Committee, it was clear that the humanitarian assistance policy enjoyed all-party support and would receive favourable comment when the Committee reported to the House of Commons. But the Committee never presented its report. On 6 May the government introduced its budget into Parliament and two days later was defeated by the combined weight of the opposition on a no-confidence motion. Parliament was dissolved and elections were held on 8 July. Faced with an election campaign, the government – and the officials – preferred not to press the Southern Africa question, which did not, in any case, become a campaign issue. The question of assistance to liberation movements was shelved pending final approval of CIDA's estimates by the new Parliament – and the government argued that in any case the rapidly changing situation in Portuguese Africa called for a "reassessment".[32]

But not all aspects of the policy were delayed, only the portion dealing with liberation movements. In April 1974, CIDA approved a contribution of $135,000 to the World University Service to support a programme of scholarships at the university and at secondary schools within Rhodesia. Although this contribution was a logical extension of previous support for education of refugees outside Southern Africa, it was significant in that it was the first major grant for a project inside white-ruled Southern Africa.

A second major contribution was made in September 1974, following the July election, which saw the Liberal government returned with a comfortable majority. The situation in Portugal's African territories evolved very rapidly in the months following the military coup in April. On 23 August, the Portuguese government and the PAIGC agreed that Portugal would officially recognize the independence of

Guinea Bissau on 12 September, a year after the National People's Assembly had declared their country an independent and sovereign state. The new republic was quickly recognized by a large number of states, but not immediately by the Western group, including Canada. In fact, it was only in early August 1974, when formal Portuguese agreement to withdraw from Guinea Bissau was only a matter of time, that the Western bloc recognized the PAIGC government. Canadian recognition came on 12 August.[33] In order to show, however belatedly, Canadian support for the newly-independent state, External and CIDA officials agreed that a contribution through an NGO channel would be appropriate; now that the PAIGC was a government party, it was no longer, in the eyes of the Canadian government, a "liberation movement", and hence could be a legitimate recipient of Canadian assistance. This would not compromise Mr. Sharp's undertaking that Parliament would decide on Canadian assistance to liberation movements. Accordingly, on 23 September, CIDA announced that it would contribute $100,000 to the Canadian Council of Churches to provide educational, medical and agricultural assistance to the newly-independent republic; the funds would be administered by the WCC.[34]

But the question of the liberation movements remained for resolution by the new Parliament, which did not meet until October. It was an anti-climax for both the proponents and the opponents of humanitarian aid for Southern Africa. When CIDA's Estimates once again came up for discussion in the Standing Committee, not one word was said on the subject, and the Estimates were approved by Parliament shortly afterwards. The new External Affairs Minister, Allan MacEachen, said that this cleared the way for approval of humanitarian assistance.[35] By January 1975, CIDA had approved about $200,000 in assistance, including $100,000 for assistance to MPLA and FRELIMO through the CCC/WCC.[36]

Conclusion: An Assessment

The acceptance of an expanded programme of Canadian humanitarian assistance in Southern Africa, including aid to liberation movements, required nearly a year and a half of discussion and controversy before it was finally approved. Was it worth it? What were the practical results of the new policy? For one thing, the conditions attached to the expanded policy acted as a restraint on the amounts involved – this had been foreseen by observers and was reflected in Paul Gérin-Lajoie's remark about the sums likely to be involved: "You can bet it will not be in the millions." Since the policy was largely a reactive one, the government limited itself to responding to requests presented by international bodies and Canadian non-governmental organizations. No budget was assigned specifically to the programme, but rather requests were to be met from amounts approved for regular programmes, especially from CIDA's allocations for multilateral institutions and non-governmental organizations.

Nevertheless, the new policy did result in an increase in humanitarian assistance in Southern Africa, as shown in Table 1. Assistance for Southern Africa, including all assistance in the white minority countries, aid to liberation movements and to Southern African refugees, doubled between 1973/74 and 1974/75, the first year of the new policy, from $318,000 to $641,000. Most of the increase was accounted for by a substantially increased contribution to UNETPSA, the grant to WUS for scholarships in Rhodesia, and contributions to Canadian NGOs for various projects. On the other hand, there was a sharp decline in bilateral assistance for scholarships in Canada for Rhodesians and Namibians. In 1975/76, CIDA made a first contribution to the UN Fund for Namibia, earmarked for the newly-established UN Institute for Namibia in Lusaka. In the years since 1974, support for the on-going programmes of international organizations (UNETPSA, UN Fund for Namibia, CRSP, IUEF and WUS) has increased steadily, reaching some $831,000 in 1977/78. It should be noted, however, that without exception these are scholarship and training programmes. Total contributions increased substantially in 1977/78, reaching $2,649,000. The principal reason for this sudden increase is that CIDA made several special contributions to international organizations, largely in response to appeals for humanitarian assistance on behalf of the growing numbers of refugees: $700,000 to the UN High Commissioner for Refugees for emergency humanitarian assistance to Southern African refugees in Zambia and Mozambique; $500,000 to UNICEF for a programme of special assistance for mothers and children under the care of liberation movements in Southern Africa; and $250,000 to the International Red Cross for refugees in Botswana.

The most controversial aspect of the new policy, assistance to liberation movements, has turned out to be minor in terms of disbursements, less than $100,000 a year between 1974/75 and 1876/77, but increased substantially in 1977/78 as a result of the $500,000 grant to UNICEF. Three of the liberation movements did of course become the governments of Angola, Mozambique and Guinea Bissau, and Table 1 does not include post-independence assistance. Post-independence assistace, including amounts channelled through Canadian and international NGOs, is noted in Table 2. None of the former Portuguese territories in Africa became an eligible country for official Canadian bilateral assistance, although they received other forms of assistance, both direct and indirect. In 1975, CIDA contributed $500,000 to the UN High Commissioner for Refugees for the repatriation of refugees who fled from Guinea Bissau, Cape Verde and Mozambique during the years of struggle. In 1976 and 1977, CIDA contributed $2,637,500 to the UN and the International Red Cross for the relief of victims of the civil war in Angola. After Mozambique's declaration of sanctions against Rhodesia in March 1976, Canada agreed to provide assistance to help Mozambique overcome the effect of sanctions on its own economy. This took the form of food aid, valued at $2,800,000 in 1976/77 and $2,000,000 in 1977/8, and a contribution of $400,000 to the Commonwealth Fund for Technical Assistance to Mozambique, established by the Commonwealth Secretariat. These and other smaller amounts are included in Table 2.

The government's decision to broaden the scope of its humanitarian assistance

Table 2. *Official Canadian Assistance to Former Portugese Territories in Africa ($000)*

	1974/75	1975/76	1976/77	1977/78
Angola				
UNHCR / UNICEF –				
Humanitarian assistance	–	–	2,000.0	–
ICRC –				
Medical and protective services	–	637.5	–	–
ICRC – Assistance for Zairois				
refugees	–	–	–	200.0
NGO projects	–	–	15.6	6.9
Cape-Verde				
ICRC·Relief for repatriates from				
Angola and Mozambique	–	45.0	–	–
UNHCR – Repatriation of refugees	–	50.0	–	–
UNICEF – Water Supply project	–	–	50.2	129.2
NGO projects	–	–	57.4	283.2
Guinea Bissau				
World Council of Churches –				
humanitarian assistance	50.0	50.0	–	–
UNHCR – Repatriation of refugees	–	100.0	–	–
NGO projects	–	5.0	128.7	119.0
Mozambique				
Food Aid	–	–	2,810.0	2,000.0
Commo..wealth Fund for				
Mozambique	–	–	200.0	200.0
UNHCR – Repatriation of refugees	–	350.0	–	–
UNICEF·Clean water supplies	–	100.0	100.0	–
NGO projects	–	20.0	31.0	52.2
Sao Tomé				
ICRC–Relief for repatriates from				
Angola and Mozambique	–	25.0	–	–
NGO projects	–	–	–	33.8
General				
IUEF·Scholarships	–	–	50.0	–

in Southern Africa was not associated with a wider change of policy with respect to the liberation movements. The humanitarian assistance policy itself called for an "arm's length" relationship, although implicit was a recognition of the legitimacy of the basic objectives of the liberation movements, if not of their methods. The government refused to recognize the liberation movements as representatives of the peoples under majority rule, and only subsequently did it deal with the leaders of liberation movements as men who could eventually govern their countries. Thus in April 1975, Mr. Sharp refused to see Dr. Agostino Neto of the MPLA on the grounds that Dr. Neto was not "a government representative".[38] Neto did, however, meet with officials of both External Affairs and CIDA, including Mr. Paul Gérin-Lajoie, President of CIDA. As Professor Cranford Pratt pointed out to the Standing Committee on External Affairs and National Defence in 1974, the government had dissociated humanitarian assistance from support for the liberation movements in their struggle for majority rule in Southern Africa.[39]

The government's attitude in this respect was very different from that of the Canadian voluntary organizations which provided assistance to the liberation movements. For the Canadian NGOs, the act of assistance was far more than a humanitarian gesture; it was an act of solidarity which implied recognition of the legitimacy and representativity of the movements – even though not all the NGOs necessarily endorsed the recourse to violence.

Despite the government's unwillingness to move further in 1974, the humanitarian aid policy signified a more open attitude towards liberation movements, and opened the door to closer contact. Although the government had missed the opportunity to befriend the future rulers of the Portuguese territories prior to independence, a few years later it was more willing to meet the leasers of the Zimbabwe liberation movements, especially Joshua Nkomo, and the leaders of SWAPO. In June 1977, Prime Minister Trudeau met Joshua Nkomo at the Commonwealth Heads of Government Meeting in London, and Nkomo subsequently met the External Affairs Minister and senior officials of CIDA and External Affairs during a visit to Ottawa in October. The contacts with SWAPO were primarily in the context of the mediation undertaken by the five Western members of the UN Security Council to find a resolution to the Namibian question.

But perhaps the most beneficial aspect of the events of 1974 was the extensive public exposure of the Southern Africa situation, and the major debate in the press and in the Parliamentary Committee on at least one facet of Canadian policy. The public debate showed that feelings ran strong on both sides of the issue, and that the government could count on a large measure of support from informed segments of the Canadian public, including major voluntary organizations such as churches, labour unions and development groups, for a more progressive policy towards Southern Africa. Even though, as Robert Matthews and Cranford Pratt point out elsewhere in this volume,[40] these groups have far less influence on policy than Canadian business interests involved in Southern Africa, their support for the government during the public debate of 1974 was crucial.

The humanitarian aid policy also marked another waystation in the continuing evolution of Canadian policy towards a more coherent approach in favour of majority rule in Southern Africa. Government policy towards Southern Africa has been far from static, but has moved steadily, if slowly, in this direction. In this respect, the government is probably in tune with the great majority of the Canadian population who know little about Southern Africa, but, nurtured in a broad humanitarian and liberal ethic, find institutionalized racism and racial oppression abhorrent. This majority has accepted the slow progression of government policy towards Southern Africa, but has tended to recoil when more direct, immediate interests and beliefs were involved, such as support for violence and economic self-interest; negotiation, compromise and peaceful change are as much a part of the Canadian ethic as humanitarianism.

Notes

1. Department of External Affairs, *Foreign Policy for Canadians (United Nations)*, Ottawa, 1970, p. 19.

2. Robert O. Matthews, "Canada's relations with Africa", *International Journal*, XXX, 3 (1975), p. 543.

3. See for example, Matthews, *op. cit.*, pp. 544–548; Cranford Pratt, "Canadian attitudes towards Southern Africa", *International Perspectives*, Nov.–Dec. 1974; John Saul, "Both sides of the street", *The Canadian Forum*, March 1973, and *Canada and Mozambique*, Toronto, 1974, and Toronto Committee for the Liberation of Southern Africa, *Words and Deeds: Canada, Portugal and Africa*, Toronto, 1976.

4. *The Telegram* (Toronto), 25 February 1970.

5. For a discussion of Canadian-South African trade and investment linkages, see Steven Langdon, "The Canadian economy and Southern Africa", in this volume.

6. Matthews, *op. cit.*, p. 543.

7. *Foreign Policy for Canadians (United Nations)*, p. 20.

8. Garth Legge, Cranford Pratt, Richard Williams, Hugh Winsor, *The Black Paper: An Alternative Policy for Canada towards Southern Africa*, Toronto, 1970.

9. *The Black Paper*, p. 15.

10. Canadian International Development Agency (CIDA), *Canada and the Developing World: CIDA Annual Review 1970–1971*, p. 34.

11. CIDA, *Canada and Development Cooperation: CIDA Annual Review 1976–1977*, pp. 46–47.

12. House of Commons, Standing Committee on External Affairs and National Defence, *Minutes of Proceedings and Evidence*, no. 30, 1 June 1971.

13. *Ibid*, especially Appendix W·2, pp. 78–81.

14. Cf. Southern Africa Information Group, "Aid from Canadians to the liberation movements of Southern Africa", Ottawa, 1974.

15. *Final Communiqué*, Commonwealth Heads of Government Meeting, Ottawa, 2–10 August 1973, para. 23.

16. "Transcript of the Press Conference by Prime Minister P.E. Trudeau and Commonwealth Secretary General Arnold Smith, Ottawa, 10 August 1973".

17. *Globe and Mail* (Toronto), 6 Aug. 1973, 8 Aug. 1973 etc,; also Southern Africa Information Group Group, "The Missing Leasers of Zimbabwe", Ottawa, August 1973.

18. External Affairs, Speech by the Hon. Mitchell, "United Nations – need for a collective sense of urgency", 25 Sept. 1973.

19. United Kingdom, *Rhodesia: Report of the Commission on Rhodesian Opinion under the Chairmanship of the Rt. Hon. the Lord Pearce*, London, 1972.

20. On the other hand, the policy groups of both CIDA and External Affairs were only minimally involved in the formulation of the new policy. Cf. Daniel Madar and Denis Stairs, "The Policy Analysis Group and the Department of External Affairs", *International Journal*, XXXII, 4 (1977), esp. pp. 745 and 752.

21. Southern Africa Information Group, *Southern Africa Newsclippings*, II, 7 (Dec. 1973), pp. 14–15.

22. External Affairs,Press Release, "Canadian Contribution to the UNETPSA and the IUEF", 3 Dec. 1973.

23. *Globe and Mail* (Toronto), 7 Feb. 1974. Ironically, the journalist who "broke" the story was Hugh Winsor, a former CUSO volunteer and one of the authors of the *Black Paper*.

24. External Affairs, Statement by the Hon. Mitchell Sharp, "Canadian Humanitarian Aid for Southern Africa", 21 Feb. 1974.

25. External Affairs, "Statement by the Hon. Mitchell Sharp to the Standing Committee on External Affairs and National Defence", 19 March 1974.

26. James Eayrs, "Canada's 'copping out' in Africa", *The Citizen* (Ottawa), 26 March 1974; Cranford Pratt, *op. cit.;* See also a letter by Judith Marshall, *Globe and Mail*, 14 Feb. 1974.

27. *Minutes of Proceedings and Evidence*, no. 4, 21 March 1974.

28. *Ibid*, no. 5, 22 March 1974.

29. *Ibid.*, no. 9, 4 April 1974, p. 22.

30. *Ibid.*, no. 10, 5 April 1974, p. 9.

31. *Ibid,* no. 12, 25 April 1974, p. 8.

32. "Canada holds back aid to African nationalists", *The Citizen* (Ottawa), 8 June 1974.

33. External Affairs, Communiqué no. 52, "Recognition of Guinea Bissau", 12 Aug. 1974. For a discussion of the issue of Canadian recognition of Guinea Bissau, see TCLSAC, *Words and Deeds,* pp. 85–89.

34. CIDA, News Release 74–48, 23 Sept. 1974.

35. *The Citizen* (Ottawa), 29 Oct. 1974.

36. *The Citizen* (Ottawa), 8 Jan. 1975.

37. Cf. Cranford Pratt, *op. cit.,* p. 40.

38. *The Gazette* (Montreal), 26 Apr. 1974.

39. *Minutes of Proceedings and Evidence,* no. 9, 4 April 1974, p. 10.

40. Robert Matthews and Cranford Pratt, "Canadian policy towards Southern Africa".

III. Scandinavian Policy Options

Thorvald Stoltenberg

Nordic Opportunities and Responsibilities in Southern Africa

The problem of Southern Africa is one of the most important international questions today. The problems of Rhodesia and Namibia – though separate – cannot be considered in isolation from South Africa. It is the apartheid system in South Africa which presents a grave threat to international peace and security. South Africa is the key to a lasting solution of the problems of Southern Africa. South Africa represents the power in the area. South Africa is by far the most difficult problem to solve. – I am going to speak about policy towards the Republic.

My intention is not to describe the problems and the tragedy of the peoples of South Africa, or to speak about the moral basis of what should be done. Many of you are in a far better position to do that. However, it may be useful for me to go into the following aspects:

– why is there a credibility gap between what many politicians say and what they are finally able to do?

– how can small countries – such as the Nordic countries – influence international developments?

– and finally, to examine present policies and what further measures can be expected from the Nordic countries.

Any responsible politician is faced with the eternal tug-of-war between the long-term perspective and the day-to-day limitations imposed by the reality of political power.

Firstly, there is no disagreement among responsible Nordic politicians about the nature and character of the apartheid regime in South Africa.

Secondly, we agree that action must be taken against a regime which grossly violates basic principles of humanity and imposes a racist system of dominance over its majority population. In other words – the situation in South Africa is not an internal matter – it is one of international concern.

Thirdly, we recognize that the more strength and effectiveness of the peaceful measures applied by the international community the less armed struggle will be necessary. Since 1910 the African people has tried peaceful resistance. Now the armed struggle has started and is continuing. Time is not working for a peaceful solution. How do we then react to make our contribution to bring about a more peaceful solution which we so actively advocate in, among other places, the UN?

Thorvald Stoltenberg

The challenge to our credibility is symbolized in the following question: Why has more drastic economic action not been taken against South Africa? After all the South African economy is not that important – relatively speaking – to the Western industrialized countries.

The answer is obvious. The power of the economic ties is strong. This fact should not be disguised if our ambition is to formulate and execute an effective and concrete policy against South Africa.

The economic power is not only the interest of the large corporation. It is also a question – the job for the individual woman and man.

Let's be frank.

I have seen not tendency in any country to sacrifice jobs in order to contribute to a possible effective economic boycott of South Africa.

And I do not think this attitude will be changed.

Even with a deep and genuine understanding of the tragedy in South Africa – and of our own interest in a peaceful solution of the problem it is not easy to tell any individual that in the interest of all of us – *you* must sacrifice your work – your job.

By facing reality I am not saying that an international boycott of South Africa is not realistic. What I am saying is that a boycott needs long-term planning. Arrangements have to be made for alternative markets in order to avoid that a sudden suspension of trade with South Africa results in increased unemployment.

Is an alternative market policy possible? I think so. Let me mention two examples indicating the same tendency: Firstly, a recent edition of Newsweek contained this short notice: "South African Borrowing Problems. Political unrest in South Africa is making it increasingly difficult for that country to raise foreign loans. Even though the nation is considered a sound credit risk, foreign bankers often pay more attention to the potential for adverse publicity surrounding loans to South Africa's apartheid government. Johannesburg banking sources now estimate that South Africa needs to borrow at least $1 billion abroad this year, but they consider it unlikely that they can achieve even a quarter of their goal. In the past few weeks, public corporations such as Escom, South Africa's state electricity agency, have managed to raise $40.5 million in Switzerland – but interest rates are relatively high and the credit is extended on a short-term basis only. The South African Government faces other problems as well. Since the Soweto riots of 1976, the country has suffered a net outflow of foreign funds."

Secondly, Nigeria and other African countries are beginning to adopt trade policies based on not having dealings with companies which have interests in South Africa. The example of Nigeria shows us that African countries provide a much larger market for most of the major Western countries than does South Africa, and it is important that this fact be recognised when we consider the possible unemployment in our countries arising out of sanctions against South Africa. Interests in South Africa now have to be balanced with interests in the rest of the world.

The importance of African markets was emphasized by the Nigerian Head of

State in his opening statement at the anti-apartheid conference in Lagos last August. He there announced that firms that want to deal with Nigeria in the future would have to make a choice between his country and South Africa.

I will not discuss the effectiveness of economic boycott. I certainly see the dangers and short-comings of economic sanctions. At the same time I see no other measures, short of armed struggle, that could contribute to a change in the South African society.

As small countries without much significant importance' individually or collectively, how can *we* influence international developments?

There are basically two roles the Nordic countries can play in this regard:

1. As the initiator of new measures and policies and create a precedent which is likely to be followed by others. In other words the role of trying to influence international public opinion.

2. To act as a mediator or a go-between to help resolve conflicts.

It goes without saying that rarely can the two roles be played at the same time.

The urgency on the one hand to move towards more meaningful action in South Africa and on the other the tendency up to last year in the Western countries to be virtually inactive, has made it natural for the Nordic countries to take certain initiatives and try to mould public and international opinion to facilitate better policies.

Through initiatives as regards a voluntary arms embargo against South Africa in 1963, the mandatory economic sanctions against Southern Rhodesia, the question of an investment stop against the apartheid regime etc., we have tried to inspire an action-oriented policy. Another example in this area has been our consistent and increasing assistance over the past decade to the liberation movements in Southern Africa. This policy has subsequently been supported by various non-governmental organizations in the Western countries – but not by many governments. For quite a few years we were strongly adviced against supporting the liberation movements in the Portuguese colonies. When the Norwegian Foreign Minister raised that question during the NATO meeting in Lisbon in 1971 he certainly did so against the advice of many governments. Today few doubt the wisdom of a strong stand against Portuguese colonialism in the 60's and early 70's.

Have we learnt from experience in the 50's and 60's for actions in the 70's and 80's? One thing is sure. We cannot go on talking about peaceful measures without implementing any of them. So far Western countries have been advocating peaceful solutions, warning against the armed struggle, and continuing to maintain their links with the apartheid economy. That policy in effect means that the Vorster regime will go on as before.

Let us not forget that South African leaders such as the late Chief Albert Luthuli since 1959 have called for international economic and other boycotts against South Africa. Chief Luthuli repeated this appeal in his Nobel Peace Prize lecture in Oslo in 1961. No major government has so far adopted it as its policy.

The Nordic governments have gone some way in this direction by recognizing the need for sanctions against South Africa to be adopted by the UN Security Council. There has also been some movement in ending export credit guarantees imposing a freeze on new investments. The Netherlands has taken some similar measures. Canada has acted firmly to discourage trade relations with South Africa. But this is a late beginning.

These initiatives, though important, cannot make a major impact on the apartheid system. It is therefore crucial for all nations to examine the nature and extent of their economic and other relations with South Africa, with a view to implementing a policy of disengagement. In the near future it will become even more important for governments to realise the degree of their own involvement in the apartheid economy.

First, we will need to increase international pressure against apartheid by a policy of systematic disengagement. Second, governments will have to stand ready to implement more decisive economic measures at short notice.

These actions will have a direct impact on the domestic economies of the Western countries, (depending, of course, on the extent of their bilateral economic relations with South Africa). It is therefore important, as I already have said, to plan in advance for such measures.

With regard to specific concrete measures it is easier to say what *should* be done rather than what *can* be done. Our objective must be to implement those measures which are capable of having the greatest effect on South Africa.

What has so far been done – and what remains to be done?

The international arms embargo is perhaps the most important action taken so far by the UN. It has been operated by the Security Council since 1963 as a voluntary embargo and South Africa has therefore managed to secure substantial quantities of weapons and military equipment from various sources despite the embargo. In November 1977 the Security Council imposed a mandatory embargo. This too has limited value because South Africa now makes a wide variety of wepons itself. But it is vital that the embargo is strengthened and applied strictly, so as to prohibit all forms of military co-operation with the apartheid regime.

The Nordic countries are committed to the UN embargo on arms, ammunition, military vehicles, paramilitary police equipment and spare parts. We are now in the process of enacting legislation to formalise the decisions made mandatory by the Security Council last November. However, there are serious loopholes in the embargo; South Africa must be denied all forms of technological assistance to facilitate its domestic arms production. All transfer of patents, licences, sub-licences, know-how and other similar arrangements must be ended. The arms embargo must be implemented strictly and followed up by more meaningful action.

Secondly, there should be a total prohibition of all sales or transfers of nuclear material or technology to South Africa, including manpower assistance. The Nordic countries have refused co-operation with South Africa in this field and we believe that the Security Council should prohibit all forms of nuclear co-operation with South Africa.

Thirdly, there should be a ban on all future investments in South Africa. Norway, for its part, has refused to grant licences for the transfer of currency for investments in South Africa since 1976. The flow of foreign investments to South Africa has also allowed the Vorster regime to build up its tremendous military capability. If there is delay in the Security Council in deciding on a binding prohibition of new investments then individual governments should take this initial measure on a unilateral basis. All loans to South Africa, whether by private or national banks, should also be prohibited.

Fourthly, Nordic companies operating in South Africa should not be permitted to increase their activities. All efforts should be made to ensure that such companies pay their black workers a living wage and grant them full trade union rights. They must also provide adequate legal defence for those workers who fall victim to the maze of apartheid laws and restrictions.

I am aware of the efforts made by certain countries to encourage their subsidiaries in South Africa to operate a voluntary code of conduct for African workers. So far these efforts have shown no significant results and some companies merely refer to the code to legitimise their investments in South Africa. If international pressure against companies operating in South Africa is to be effective it will require firm action on the part of overseas governments. It may be necessary to implement specific penalties and sanctions in order to enforce decisions. However, it has to be faced that these subsidiaries are not likely to respond positively to codes or rules initiated abroad as long as they operate in South Africa and accept the customs and laws of the apartheid system.

That is why the fifth point, regarding Nordic support for mandatory economic sanctions to be adopted by the Security Council, under Chapter VII of the UN Charter, becomes a matter of primary importance. The General Assembly has already called on the Security Council to impose a freeze on new investments in South Africa. But this is not enough. We need to follow up an investments ban with total sanctions in some specific area such as South Africa's import of oil and oil products.

All governments should terminate support for trade with South Africa. Since 1976 Norway has stopped granting export credit guarantees. Similar action has been taken by other Nordic countries. I am certain that the clear Canadian initiative in this area will be followed by other Western countries.

Sixthly, we should continue and increase our support for the liberation movements of South Africa. But equally we should recognize the role played by the frontline states and the tremendous sacrifices made by the peoples of those countries. It is our duty to give these peoples assistance.

Seventhly, we recognize the importance of the Canadian decision in imposing visa restrictions on South African citizens and we in the Nordic countries should do the same. Equally, we should ensure that South African refugees and exiles are provided with easy entry and settlement facilities in our countries.

Canada and the Nordic countries are in a unique position to take joint initiatives for a common programme of action against South Africa which likeminded countries can also support. We should promote the widest possible measure of international co-ordination among most of the Western countries in relation to South Africa. In saying this I do not underestimate the difficulties and problems faced by some countries, but in view of the grave danger to international peace and security posed by the *apartheid* system we have to do everything possible to counteract it.

We should recognize that our contribution to a peaceful solution in Southern Africa is a contribution to our own future – and a better future. It is in our own interest that the doctrine and system of race supremacy is destroyed and mankind is freed from the scourge of *apartheid.*

Anders Thunborg

Nordic Policy Trends Towards Southern Africa

"Nordic" is today a well-known concept. For a variety of reasons, a close cooperation has developed between the five Nordic countries Denmark, Finland, Iceland, Norway and Sweden in many fields of their societies. The Nordic countries have always been close to one another because of the common background of their languages and culture, a heritage which has to a great extent been subject to and formed by the same internal and external influences. At the same time, each Nordic country has kept – and is very keen on continuing to develop – its own individual and national characteristics.

This "similar but individual" – character also applies to our foreign policies.

Each Nordic country is totally sovereign in its choice of such policies. And because of different geographical situation, historical experiences, and political, strategic and economic considerations, each Nordic country has developed an individual and separate profile in its relations with the rest of the world.

Sweden and Finland pursue a policy of neutrality. Norway, Denmark and Iceland are members of the Atlantic Pact. Denmark is also a member of the European Community.

However, to mention only these differences in foreign policy orientation would give a very inadequate picture of the position of the Nordic countries in the world. The picture has to be filled out with some additional observations.

First, we have reason to stress the fact that the foreign policies of the Nordic countries, each in is own way, make important contributions to the stable situation in the Nordic region. These policies have been an essential factor in making "Norden" a quiet corner of the globe, also in times when crises and long periods of tension have marked the postwar period in other parts of the world, not least in Central Europe.

Secondly, it is equally important to point out that our different foreign policies have not hampered us from developing a very close co-operation in the economic, social and cultural fields. For instance, in some areas the laws of the Nordic countries have been almost completely harmonized. We have established a common Nordic labour market which enables Nordic nationals to work and to settle down in another Nordic country without a work permit or a permanent residence permit. Nordic citizens can travel across Nordic frontiers without presenting passports. Intra-Nordic trade today amounts to 25% of our total foreign trade. A close and expanding cooperation has developed between private industrial enterprises across national borders. Cooperation in the industrial and energy sectors have been stimulated by the establishment of a joint Nordic Investment Bank. Communications is another traditional field for collaboration between our countries.

The reason for this development is not only what I referred to above as our common heritage, but also the fact that we have been able to keep the Nordic area stable and free from international tensions. Besides giving us economic and other benefits, this intra-Nordic cooperation gives us all greater security and is therefore in itself an important element in the stability which has given the Nordic area the calm which serves the interests of the whole of Europe.

Thirdly, since we share basic views on world affairs, it has seemed natural to us to cooperate in various international fora and, whenever possible and appropriate, to converge our positions and express a common Nordic policy.

The formulation of such a common Nordic policy requires frequent contacts between our governments, parliaments and other institutions of interest in this context. We have in fact established a whole machinery of formal and informal contacts to consult with each other. Since the UN is the most important forum for the presentation and performance of our foreign policy, we obviously have a very close cooperation between our delegations there. In more or less daily contacts, we exchange views on current international events and discuss the coordination of our stands and actions to the extent this is deemed possible and appropriate.

By acting as a group in the United Nations we add extra weight to our own views and have greater possibilities to influence the views of other countries.

Fourthly, this common policy, a "Nordic policy", with regard to specific events and situations in world affairs has gradually got a character of its own. Various circumstances have contributed to the formation of such an identity. Obviously, our own experience in the Nordic region has influenced our attitudes. I have already elaborated on our belief in the benefits of regional cooperation between neighbours. We also firmly believe in the benefits of peaceful solutions in international conflicts. We tend ourselves to take a pragmatic and action-oriented view on various problems and situations. Our policies have also been heavily influenced by our support for human rights, democratic values, and economic and social progress and justice. During the whole period of decolonization we have ardently supported the principles of independence and self-determination. You might say that our policies have contained strong elements of idealism, which we have been able and felt inclined to express in view of our own positive experience of the application of such principles and values in our own societies.

I venture to say that this policy has become appreciated not least by nations in the Third World and by peoples who still are struggling for their freedom and independence. We realize that these countries and peoples do not look to the Nordic countries only because their systems might contain some commendable elements. It is more likely that they find us interesting because we form some kind of alternative as equal partners with which they can establish a fair and mutually prosperous cooperation. The fact that we are small countries, without any possibilities or ambitions to exert the kind of influence that has often prenominated in the policies of the big powers, might be a reason for a special feeling of trust in our relations with the Third World countries.

To conclude, in spite of limited power and wealth, the Nordic countries feel they can play a useful role in international relations, sometimes as providing examples of some models of modern societies, sometimes as a bridge-builder between ideological differences and systems, and sometimes as an initiator, "prodder" and mediator in international negotiations, often with the view to create margins of maneuvre for others who are more intimately involved in such dealings. This is how we consider that the Nordic countries can best serve not only their own national interests but also the concomitant interests of international peace and security, the prosperity of the nations and the well-being of the peoples.

Our relation to the problems prevailing in Southern Africa has long formed an important part of the foreign policy of each Nordic country.

The basis for our Southern Africa policy is the fact that the principles of self-determination and independence have not yet become reality in this part of the world. It is also the fact that fundamental human rights are being constantly violated in societies whose structure is based on racial discrimination.

With regard to the problems in Southern Africa it is particularly true to say that we share identical basic views. Without having taken any specific decisions to elaborate a common, comprehensive policy with regard to Southern Africa, we nevertheless can note that in few other fields has our UN-policy been so concordant. During the General Assembly of last year, we had to take a stand 25 times on resolutions regarding Southern Africa. On 22 occasions all the Nordic countries took the same line and in none of the remaining three cases did we demonstrate any great difference of opinion. And these differences only demonstrate that political strategy and diplomatic tactics always can be a matter of discussion when exerting common efforts to reach a goal that everyone is in accord with. From an academic point of view, it could be interesting to analyse such differences of approach and performance. I do not think such an analysis would serve the best purpose of this seminar, however. I would prefer to concentrate on the basic and common features of our policies and rather deal with the present situation than making historical reflections. It should be noted, however, that I do this primarily on the basis of my own country's policy as reflected during the General Assembly session last year. A similar presentation by one of my Nordic colleagues would for obvious reasons have been based upon his country's specific views and experience and consequently have had a different emphasis and accentuation in various questions. The basic facts and assessments, I am sure, would have been the same, however.

South Africa is crucial in every respect for developments in the whole of Southern Africa. Its regime bears a heavy responsibility for conducting a policy which is objectionable for a number of reasons:

– South Africa practices racial discrimination in its most abominable forms by using the unique apartheid system to suppress and exploit the majority of the South African population;

– South Africa uses its strong military and economic power to illegitimately occupy the territory of Namibia and to exhaust its natural resources to the detriment of present and future generations of the Namibian People;

– South Africa constantly violates decisions adopted by the Security Council with regard to international sanctions against Southern Rhodesia, thus enabling the white minority regime there to continue its illegal rule. This can only delay the inevitable process towards the establishment of a free and independent Zimbabwe and cause further suffering to the Zimbabwean people;

– South Africa has used its military power on several occasions to perpetrate acts of aggression against neighbouring countries.

Therefore, the policy of South Africa constitutes a threat to international peace and security. To eliminate this threat radical changes must take place in all parts of Southern Africa. Free and independent nations must be established in Zimbabwe and Namibia, the apartheid system must be eliminated in South Africa. The goal for the change must be democratic societies which allow all citizens full and equal participation in the political life of the countries and a just and effective sharing of their economic and social development. The goal must be the creation of nations in the region whichcan live in peace and harmony with each other, with other countries in Africa and with the rest of the world. We in the Nordic countries know by experience the great importance of trust and confidence between neighbours in the same region. Our history has certainly had its share of violence and subjugation, but we share today the conviction that a close cooperation between us is the best guarantee for the security and prosperity of our region.

History also proves, however – and developments in recent years in Southern Africa demonstrate this point clearly – that those who are in power will not voluntarily yield to demands for a more equitable and just sharing of this power. The rulers will change the system only when confronted with pressure which becomes too unpleasant or costly to bear.

For years, the South African regime has been totally insensitive to the peaceful and modest forms of pressure that the non-white population has put on the rulers by demanding an orderly change of the system. They have also turned a deaf ear to all kinds of appeals by the international community to change their system. Gradually, as the situation in South Africa has deteriorated as a consequence of the apartheid policy, the black population in the country has taken to more desperate ways to express their frustration. Also within the international community this sense of growing frustration has become very noticeable.

The massacre of Soweto, the killing of Steve Biko, and the wave of repression that followed these tragic events, finally convinced all the members of the Security Council that they had to take strong action against South Africa.

Thus, the increasing threat to international peace and security caused by South

Africa's military build-up spurred the Security Council to adopt its resolution 418 of 4 November, 1977, by which a mandatory arms embargo against South Africa was unanimously decided upon. This was an important break-through. It was the first time that all the members of the Security Council accepted the principle that sanctions under Chapter VII should be applied to the situation in South Africa. Although not as comprehensive as we would have liked it to be, this step constituted a major political set-back for the leaders of South Africa and should be a clear sign to them that all countries are finally prepared to go from verbal condemnation and harsh criticism to effective action.

We believe, however, that it is important not only to secure the full implementation of resolution 418, but also to complement it with other measures. There are, for instance, many compelling reasons why the Security Council should consider steps with regard to foreign investments in South Africa.

During the autumn of 1976, Sweden initiated a proposal in the General Assembly to urge the Security Council to take steps to achieve the cessation of further foreign investments in South Africa. On 9 November, the General Assembly adopted a resolution to this effect by 124 votes for, none against and 16 abstentions. A similar recommendation was made to the Security Council in a General Assembly's resolution of 16 December last year. This resolution was adopted by 120 votes for, none against and only 5 abstentions this time.

This development shows an increasing support among the UN-members to this kind of united action against South Africa. In view of the importance we attach to this way of increasing the pressure against South Africa, I wish to enumerate some of the arguments for our position as I presented them in a Swedish intervention to the Security Council during its debate on South Africa a few weeks ago.

First: The decision by the Security Council on a mandatory arms embargo against South Africa was an important step. But it was not enough. South Africa is making great efforts to achieve a high degree of self-sufficiency in its arms production. The aim is to make the local production, based to quite some extent upon licenses, adequate to fullfil immediate needs and keep the South African military forces reasonably well stocked. However, this capacity for domestic military production is very much dependent on and enhanced by the inflow of foreign capital to South Africa in the form of new investments, be they channelled directly to defence-related industries or used to prop up the South African economy in general. A cessation of further foreign investment would therefore be a necessary complement to the arms embargo and would forestall some of South Africa's efforts to evade it and erode it by increasing its own military production.

Secondly: Such measures to curb the flow of capital to South Africa would also have an impact on the South African economy in general. It would, in other words, hit the most sensitive nerve in the South African society. Since its economy is heavily dependent upon access to new capital from the Western World to develop and expand the South African economy, for instance in the energy field, such a step is likely to have quite a noticeable effect on the South African economy. The decrease

115

of investments in the various economic sectors of the country that would follow must therefore be taken seriously by those who are responsible for the economic stability and welfare of the country.

Thirdly: The psychological impact of such a cut-off of new investments would probably be as important. So far, the white establishment in South Africa has felt that it was part and parcel of the Western political and economic world and linked to it through heavy flows of trade, investments and loans and all kinds of business contacts. This economic interdependence has always made the leaders in Pretoria feel convinced that they could continue as before, since the important Western countries were not supposed to endanger their economic interests in South Africa. The lack of effective action by the Western world so far has therefore no doubt helped the South African regime in its efforts to sustain an aura of respectability and legitimacy. That unjustified complacency would most likely be shaken, if the Western countries were to demonstrate that they would be prepared to sacrifice some of these short-term economic interests. Such a determination by the Western world would be in the longterm interest not only of the oppressed people in South Africa but also of the industrialized Western countries from a political as well as an economic point of view. We noted that certain important African countries have adopted a policy of non-cooperation with firms which have heavy investments in South Africa.

Fourthly: In this context we must also remember the crucial role of apartheid in the functioning of the South African economy. The repressive laws of apartheid and the methods used by the police in upholding these laws offer the investor a source of cheap labour and a virtual guarantee against strikes and unrest among the workers. Therefore, any calculation of the profitability of investments in South Africa should also include a human and moral consideration of the reasons for the high returns.

In this context let me also refute the argument sometimes advanced that economic development in South Africa, particularly if managed by international firms pursuing progressive employment policies, will erode the apartheid system. This is an illusion because all commercial and economic enterprises will have to work within the apartheid framework decided upon by the political leadership in South Africa. A change of this policy will come as a result of pressure, not of appeals to good-will.

Fifthly: A resolution on investments by the Security Council would undoubtedly also be a great encouragement for those people from all strata of the South African society who are now bearing the brunt of the oppressive system. They would know that their struggle for a just and humane South Africa is not being carried out in isolation, that their important internal efforts to change the apartheid society are supported by effective actions by the outside world to achieve this goal. The regime that upholds this abominable system is now devoting a great deal of its resources to extinguishing these hopes for a change. Determined and effective Security Council action would prove to the South African leaders that they cannot count on any further respite or to have been given a "carte blanche" for continued consolidation of the apartheid system.

Finally, the action we propose is in fact quite modest. It would, however, present a clear warning to the South African government that the outside world is determined and prepared to go further in its efforts to put pressure on and isolate South Africa. It should leave South Africa in no doubt that a stubborn continuation of the apartheid policy can only result in even stronger decisions and recommendations taken by the Security Council.

The lesson that has to be brought home to the South African regime should be clear: the pressure will continue inexorably and increasingly until the apartheid system is eradicated.

As you will remember, the session with the Security Council in January regarding South Africa ended without the adoption of any resolutions. The African members of the Council – Gabon, Mauritius and Nigeria – tabled two draft resolutions but they did not press for a vote on any of them, being aware that at least the one on investments most likely would have been vetoed by the Western members of the Council. In this draft resolution the African members even went beyond the recommendations in the special resolution on investments adopted by the General Assembly a couple of months previously, since it contained the following requirements in its operative paragraphs:

"1. *Decides* that all States including non-member States of the United Nations shall:
(a) Prohibit any loans to, or investments in, South Africa, or guarantees for such loans or investments;
(b) Take effective steps to prohibit any loans or investments by corporations and financial institutions in their countries to South Africa; and
(c) terminate all incentives for investments in, or trade with, South Africa;
2. *Urges* all States to review all their existing economic and other relations with South Africa."

Thus, the African draft contains elements which go beyond the problems of investments only and also cover loans, guarantees for investments or loans and also require a review of all existing economic and other relations with South Africa. This indicates what the next steps of economic pressure against South Africa might be if the regime there continues to demonstrate its contempt for actions decided so far by the Security Council.

As to the General Assembly's resolutions on South Africa from last year, they contain also other elements which have been discussed in this context. They include, among other things, a total cessation of not only all kinds of military collaboration with South Africa but also all kinds of cooperation that contribute to the nuclear development of that country. Furthermore, in another resolution the General Assembly requests the Security Council to consider urgently mandatory economic sanctions against South Africa and requests all States to cease economic collaboration with that country. Among specific measures mentioned in this context, I wish to single out particularly the request to all states to apply an embargo on the supply of petroleum and petroleum products to South Africa and to deny facilities to airlines and shipping companies providing services to and from South Africa.

What is then the position of the Nordic countries to this wide range of other possible measures to be taken against South Africa?

In an explanation of vote in the General Assembly on 14 December last year on behalf of all the Nordic countries, I emphasized that the Nordic countries had always taken a firm stand against the apartheid system and the many illegal, repressive and aggressive acts perpetrated by the Pretoria-regime both inside and outside of South Africa. Against the background of recent developments in South Africa, I said, it was now more important than ever that the United Nations was unrelenting in its efforts to bring the apartheid system to an end. For that purpose, the international community had to apply an ever-increasing pressure against the regime in Pretoria. The Nordic countries had therefore voted in favour of most of the General Assembly resolutions pertaining to South Africa.

The Nordic countries had some reservations on certain points, however. For instance, we supported the general objections and goals in the resolutions concerning military and nuclear collaboration with South Africa, but would have liked to see a clearer recognition of the important decision taken by the Security Council to impose a mandatory embargo against South Africa. Besides, we considered it essential to point out that some operative paragraphs in the resolution failed to take into full account that the basic charter of the UN makes it abundantly clear that only the Security Council has the competence to decide on sanctions in this respect. In view of this, three of the Nordic countries (Norway, Denmark and Iceland) had to abstain on this resolution, whereas Finland and Sweden still found it possible to vote for it.

Because of similar difficulties with the text of the resolution on economic cooperation with South Africa all Nordic countries abstained on that one.

We did the same with regard to the resolution concerning assistance to the national liberation movement of South Africa. In spite of our strong and long-standing support for the liberation struggle, which has been demonstrated not least through a humanitarian and educational assistance to the liberation movement in South Africa, we had to abstain on this resolution since it contained paragraphs expressing explicit support for the use of armed force. Although we find it understandable that the liberation movements, in their despair, finally have seen no alternative to armed struggle, we cannot condone that the United Nations, an organization that was created to solve international problems by peaceful means, adopts resolutions containing paragraphs which explicitly support the use of armed force.

The Nordic countries also had to abstain on a resolution concerning the situation in South Africa, since it undermined the principle of universality that we steadfastly support and contained certain generalizations that we could not endorse.

Finally, the Nordic countries voted against one single resolution on South Africa, namely the one on the relations between Israel and South Africa, the reason being that we considered it inappropriate to single out one country in this context.

Our hesitation to vote for these few resolutions does not mean that we would be against various forms of further sanctions decided by the Security Council. To be really effective, however, such sanctions must have the full approval also of those Western countries which have a dominant influence on South Africa's economy. If not, such sanctions would lose much of their meaning or, at worst, even be counter-productive.

The Nordic countries do not rule out the possibility of taking certain unilateral actions, however. The Nordic foreign ministers, at their meeting in Helsinki in September last year, decided to set up a Nordic working group to investigate in what respects the Nordic countries would be prepared to work out a joint program for widened economic measures against South Africa. The result of these deliberations will be considered by the Nordic Foreign Ministers when they meet in Oslo at the beginning of March this year.

South Africa is also the crucial country with regard to developments in *Namibia.*

Here, we are still awaiting the firm commitment that is due from South Africa to comply with the resolutions of the United Nations, enabling the people of Namibia to achieve self-determination, freedom and independence. Instead, South Africa has continued its illegal occupation of the Namibian territory, had continued its massive build-up of troops and military installations, has continued its repression and persecution of members of the leading political organization SWAPO, has continued to use its overwhelming economic and military power to dominate and exploit the Namibian people and the natural resources of their country, has continued to make arrangements for illusory solutions aiming only at the perpetuation of South African domination, has continued to pose a threat against neighboring countries from the South African military bases in Namibia.

In view of this massive list of violations and offences, the world community has emphasized the direct responsibility of the United Nations to ensure the immediate restorations of the inalienable rights of the Namibian people.

On January 30, 1976, the Security Council adopted resolution 385, which contains the basis for a solution of the Namibian problem. In this resolution the Security Council declares, inter alia, that it is imperative that free elections under the supervision and control of the United Nations be held for the whole of Namibia as one political entity. The Council also demands that South Africa take the necessary steps to effect the withdrawal of its illegal administration maintained in Namibia. It also demands that all Namibian political prisoners be released, that all racially discriminatory and politically repressive laws and practices be abolished and that all Namibians currently in exile for political reasons be unconditionally accorded full facilities for return to their country without any personal risks.

In expressing the Swedish Government's support for a negotiated settlement in conformity with Security Council resolution 385, my Foreign Minister stated in the General Debate of the assembly in September last year that "the Pretoria regime

119

must realize that the only alternative to giving up control through a negotiated settlement is international sanctions and an escalation of the armed liberation struggle. SWAPO is playing a leading part in the efforts to secure an independent and unified Namibia, and any agreement must be supported by that movement. SWAPO must also be given full opportunities to work freely in the country and to mobilize its extensive popular following there".

In this context it must be emphasized that a condition for a peaceful transition period is a strong UN presence in Namibia coupled with a rapid phasing out of the South African military presence in all its forms. Only in this way will the political movements of Namibia and especially SWAPO, which has hitherto been banned from political expression and participation, be able to do the political campaigning necessary in preparation for the elections and only in such a way will the parties concerned get the opportunity to communicate freely with the electorate and to rally their supporters. The release of the political prisoners from South African prisons and the permission for those in exile for political reasons to return and participate freely in the political process is obviously also a sine quo non for the holding of fair and democratic elections. Furthermore the UN must be involved in all stages of the transition period and the election process to ensure that procedures are correct and democratic for all and that no doubt can be cast on the authenticity of the election results.

At the Nordic Foreign Ministers' meeting in Helsinki in September last year, the Nordic states expressed their readiness to offer their services within the framework of the United Nations with a view to facilitating a peaceful transition. For our part this means that if the political situation so warrants and the Security Council so decides we would be ready to assist the UN in its effort to carry through a peaceful transition in Namibia.

After Security resolution 385 was adopted, the five Western members of the Council have carried out discussions on their own with South Africa and SWAPO. The Nordic Governments have expressed their support for the purpose of this initiative, which is to find a negotiated settlement in conformity with Security Council resolution 385. It is in this perspective that we express our hope that the talks under way will soon come to a successful conclusion.

Recently, the ongoing negotiations entered a very active phase in the form of the "proximity talks" in New York. It is not yet possible to judge what effect these talks will have for the future process, but it seems obvious that it is now up to the South Africans to give further proof of their willingness to end their occupation of Namibia. The Special General Assembly on Namibia that is scheduled for 24 April–3 May this year will, of course, provide us with a valuable opportunity to make an overall and thorough penetration of the various aspects of the Namibia problem. The Special General Assembly is likely to reiterate and strengthen the resolutions on Namibia adopted by the General Assembly last year. In one of them the Assembly urged the Security Council to take up again the question of Namibia, which is still on its agenda, and to consider the application of sanctions against South

Africa in accordance with Chapter VII of the Charter.

In *Southern Rhodesia,* finally, the role played by South Africa is less direct than in Namibia, but also here we find that the support of the Pretoria regime is decisive for Ian Smith's efforts to prolong his illegal regime. The Rhodesian situation contains a number of intricate components, but there are certain basic principles that need to be stressed as preconditions for an internationally accepted solution. Such a solution, evidently, must lead to the establishment of a free and genuinely independent state of Zimbabwe with a social and economic system created in accordance with the wishes and aspirations of the majority of its people.

The very first precondition is the principle of no independence before majority rule, a condition which has repeatedly been endorsed by the United Nations ever since UDI was declared by the illegal regime in 1965.

The second precondition is, that a lasting solution to the question of Southern Rhodesia leading up to genuine independence must be worked out with the full participation of the people of Zimbabwe represented by their national liberation movement, which, in accordance with the Maputo-declaration, includes all the progressive forces engaged in the struggle.

Such a solution requires the surrender of power by the illegal regime. Its possibilites to exert power must be effectively neutralized. The structure of the army and the police must be totally changed. A government representing the majority of the people must be established. Elections must be held in such a way that the wishes of the people are truly reflected. The elections must be open to all, both to those presently living inside Southern Rhodesia and to those that have taken their refuge outside of its borders.

The national liberation movements that have been banned from political participation must be given the time and opportunity to do the political campaigning necessary in preparation of the elections. Elections must be free and fair, based on universal adult suffrage without franchise restrictions. Should the vote in any way be limited to exclude parts of the people of Zimbabwe living either inside or outside of its border, there can be no true acceptance of the elected government by the totality of the people with the ensuring risks for civil strife, upheavals and continuing instability in Southern Africa.

Sweden supports the national liberation movement of Zimbabwe and its legitimate struggle for independence and self-determination. The liberation movement has sought to reach a settlement through peaceful means. However, faced with the brutal oppression of the illegal minority regime its racially and politically discriminating system and the persecution of its dissidents, the national liberation movement has seen no alternative but to take up arms against its oppressor and fight for the legitimate rights of the people of freedom and independence. The liberation struggle has been one of the decisive elements in forcing the Smith regime into taking part in negotiations.

The Smith regime has recently announced that it is prepared to accept elections in Southern Rhodesia based on adult suffrage and is presently engaged in talks with some Zimbabwean leaders on the contents of a future settlement. Quite apart from the numerous previous maneuvres of the minority regime to evade a settlement and come to an acceptable solution, we find it very difficult to trust the good intention of a regime that oppresses and persecutes the black majority and repeatedly commits acts of aggression against neighbouring countries, incurring the large loss of life of many innocent refugees, women and children.

These acts of aggression are in our view yet another reason for increasing the international pressure against the Salisbury regime. An increased pressure would also be an important element in the efforts to bring the Smith regime to a settlement that can be internationally accepted. As a member of the Security Council, Sweden proposed that sanctions should be broadened, bringing the maximum pressure to bear on the present rulers in Salisbury. We also support the proposals of bringing added pressure on the regime in Southern Rhodesia through putting an end to the oil supply that in contravention of sanctions reaches it by way of its supporter, South Africa.

I have so far concentrated my description of the Nordic policy on efforts in the diplomatic scene. But Nordic efforts to contribute to a change in Southern Africa have also been made in very concrete forms. I particularly think of our humanitarian aid to liberation movements in Southern Africa, our efforts to help the victims of racial repression, and our development assistance to strengthen the economies of the free and independent countries in Southern Africa to help them disengage from their economic dependence on South Africa. The Nordic countries are, taken together, the biggest contributers of assistance to Southern Africa.

This policy is fully in line with our general foreign policy goals. In her speech to the General Assembly last year, the Swedish Foreign Minister presented the Swedish view in the following way:

In our country we are united in the view that we should use our neutral position to pursue an acive, independent and progressive foreign policy characterized by global solidarity and respect for equal rights of all human beings. These are our guidelines as we face up to such problems as injustice in southern Africa, the unequal relationship between rich and poor countries, or the plundering and misuse of the resources with which nature has provided us.

Solidarity is thus a key-word for our foreign policy with regard to Southern Africa, just as solidarity for so many years has been a major component in relations between the Nordic countries.

These Nordic countries in fact also have a tradition of close co-operation in the field of development assistance. The joint Nordic stand so often taken in the UN and other multilateral bodies gives increased weight to the assistance objectives shared by the Nordic countries. Collaboration is demonstrated by jointly financed Nordic development projects in Tanzania and Kenya. Activities in Mozambique have started during the fiscal year 1977/78 and are intended to take the form of substantial support to the agricultural sector.

It would carry too far to try to make a description of each Nordic country's assistance programme and I will therefore limit myself to some brief-remarks with regard to Sweden and to Southern Africa.

Programmes of assistance for educational assistance to refugees, and for legal and humanitarian assistance to victims of apartheid have been carried out since 1964, whereas our humanitarian aid to liberation movements was initiated in 1968. These programmes have been designed in accordance with the rules of international law and in accordance with recommendations and resolutions adopted by the United Nations. A large part of our assistance is also channelled via the special UN programmes set up for Southern Africa and via the UN High Commissioner. It should be stressed that our aid to the liberation movement is strictly humanitarian, consisting of medical supplies, clothing, food, educational material, etc.

The total amount allocated by the Swedish Government for these various programs was 60 mill. kronor ($ 13 mill.) in 1977/78. For 1978/79 the Government has suggested to the Parliament that a sum of 85 mill. kronor ($ 18 mill.) be allocated. The major reason for this increase is the needs caused by the growing streams of refugees from Rhodesia, Namibia and South Africa.

Previously, humanitarian assistance was given to the liberation movements of Guinea Bissau, Angola and Mozambique. After the independence of these countries, this assistance was turned into long term development cooperation. We have had such cooperation for a long time with the other disadvantaged countries in Southern Africa. In 1977/78 our assistance to the frontline states together with Lesotho and Swaziland amounted to in all 570 million kronor ($ 121 millions). For 1978/79 the suggested figure is 657 million kronor ($ 140 millions).

This assistance is to a great extent intended to ease the burdens that the unnatural situation in Southern Africa puts on these countries. The frontline states have assumed the responsibility for many who have been forced to flee their own country. The frontline states suffer economically from loyally observing the sanctions against Southern Rhodesia and from the economic dominations by South Africa. The frontline states therefore deserve and are entitled to our help.

The goal of the efforts exerted by the Nordic countries though their Southern Africa policy is to create true freedom. And true freedom in Southern Africa, as elsewhere, must mean the development of prosperous, stable and democratic societies, in which social justic, economic equality and the respect for human rights are leading principles.

Mai Palmberg

Present Imperialist Policies in Southern Africa: The Case for Scandinavian Disassociation

Introduction

The aim of this paper[1] is to review the main features of present imperialist policies in southern Africa and discuss the widely held view that there has been a major shift in Western, and notably United States policies. The assumed shift would have been one from a concern for the maintenance of *status quo* in the area to a determination to contribute to democractic development in Zimbabwe, Namibia, and South Africa itself. My thesis is that, far from the evolution and beginning of a radically new policy recognizing the legitimacy of the liberation struggle in southern Africa, we find an increasingly desperate double play, clearly seen as such by the liberation movements themselves. Western policies in southern Africa, for which the United States has set the tune for some years, are based on cooperation with the racist regimes, on attempts to make them yield concessions in order to end the armed liberation struggle, and to save the Western interests in the area.

If the Scandinavian governments want to achieve full credibility with the liberation movements of southern Africa – the future governments in the area – they should cease any association with U.S. attempts at steering developments, and listen to the liberation movements themselves, not to Washington, as the author of the strategy of liberation.

What has really changed in U.S. Southern Africa policies?

President Carter has, since his election to U.S. President in 1976, succeeded in creating an image of standing for a new, morally based Southern Africa policy. This is a fallacious location of the change both in time, space, and quality. Whatever change there was in basic premises took place already during Ford-Kissinger, the source of the change was not in Washington but in Southern Africa itself, nor was the change one of morality but rather one of necessary adaptions to carry on "business as usual".

The Kissinger policy had become identified with the National Security Study Memorandum (NSSM) 39 of 1969 whose option 2, the one adopted by the government, was based on the premise that "the whites are here to stay and the only way that constructive change can come about is through them."[2] The option was further outlined:

We would take present Portuguese policies as suggesting further changes in the Portuguese territories. At the same time we would take diplomatic steps to convince the black states of the area that their current liberation and majority rule aspiration in the south are not attainable by violence and that their only hope for a peaceful and prosperous future lies in closer relations with white-dominated states.

There certainly were "further changes in the Portuguese territories", but not because of "present Portuguese policies" supported by the United States. When first Mozambique became independent in June, 1975, and then Angola independent in November 1975, and liberated from interventionist forces from U.S.-backed Zaire and South Africa in March the following year, the Kissinger strategy for the protection of Western interests was in shambles. At this point an effort was made to pick up the pieces and give foreign policy priority to southern Africa.

It is not without importance that the major declaration on this new posture came one month after South Africa in March 1976 had to pull back its invasion troops from the People's Republic of Angola, defeated by the forces of MPLA, aided by Cuban soldiers and Soviet military equipment. In Lusaka on April 27, 1976 Secretary of State in the Ford administration, Henry Kissinger, held his "wind of change" speech, where he said "We support self-determination, majority rule, equal rights and human dignity for all the peoples of southern Africa." He also outlined a ten-point program for "a rapid, just and African solution to the issue of Rhodesia", promising that Smith would get no support until a negotiated settlement was reached on the basis of the Callaghan proposal that independence must be preceded by majority rule, and also promising measures to repeal the Byrd amendment,[3] which had been the "legal" basis for U.S. purchase of Rhodesian chrome in defiance of UN mandatory sanctions.

In the election campaign Carter promised a more active Africa policy after "15 years or more of neglect"[4], but he had no other criticism of Kissinger's initiatives than that they should have come sooner. But the lines laid down by Kissinger were the ones to follow, Carter said in an interview with *Africa Report:*[5]

The United States should move immediately toward using leverage on South Africa to encourage the independence of Namibia and the beginning of majority rule in Rhodesia. There is no question that independence will come in the near future. The only question is whether it comes through armed struggle sponsored by the Soviet Union or through an aggressive diplomacy of peace encouraged by the United States.

The reasons why this sense of commitment suddenly dawned upon the Western leaders cannot be explained by an introduction of a moral element as the bearing principle in U.S. foreign policies. The following are more likely the real causes behind the high priority given to southern Africa at this specific time of turbulent political changes in southern Africa:

1. Southern Africa is the source of a considerable share of Western needs for minerals such as gold, chrome, and diamonds. This is illustrated in the following table:[6]

South African Share of Strategic Minerals in	% of World Reserves	% of Western Reserves
Gold	65	72
Chromium	72	75
Platinum	60	70
Manganese	50	72
Vanadium	50	73
Uranium	25	30
Diamonds	50	60

2. Western investment in the racist-controlled states is bigger than in all of the rest of Africa together.

3. The liberation of Mozambique and Angola under consistently antiimperialist liberation movements move Namibia, Zimbabwe and South Africa closer to their liberation, and increase the risk that not only anti-colonial but also anti-imperialist goals are sought.

4. The massive support of socialist countries make a military victory over the liberation movements improbable.

5. The installation and stabilization of progressive governments in southern Africa will inspire and aid progressive forces in the shaky neo-colonial states like Zaire.

Kissinger had set out the basis of his new initiatives in an interview to the Hearst press on his return from the Africa tour in April 1976:[7]

The situation in Africa was drifting. War in southern Africa had already started. The radical elements were gaining the upper hand. The Soviet Union was appearing from outside as a champion; the moderate regimes were coming under increasing pressures, and therefore all the moderate governments were in danger and all the Western interests in jeopardy.

Similarly, the british Foreign Secretary Anthony Crosland, in an address to the NATO Foreign Minister meeting in Brussels in December 1976, spelled out the motives behind the Geneva conference on Rhodesia:[8]

... if the British Government gave up hope, there would be no doubt over who would eventually win on the battlefield. But if the issue were settled on the battlefield it would seriously lessen the chance of bringing about a moderate African regime in Rhodesia and would open the way for more radical solutions and external intervention on the part of others . . . .

Carter expressed the basis for "the new Africa policy" thus (my emphasis):[9]

There is no question that Africa has been ignored since the days of John F. Kennedy. Africa should become, and will become, one of the major foreign policy issues of the coming decade. *Many of our domestic and international problems will be determined by the direction of our policies in Africa.*

– The only basis of relationships between the United States and any part of the world must be that of self-interest. There is an amazing congruity between the interests and needs of the United States and Africa. Africa needs development assistance and technological advances which only the United States can supply, and the *United States need both the resources and markets of an emerging Africa.*

In the spring 1977 a Carter review of the southern Africa policies had been completed. The policy guidelines as summed up in the presidential directive:[10]

– attaches great urgency to southern Africa's problems;

– reaffirms the U.S. commitment to peaceful solutions, saying that escalating guerrilla warfare allows the Soviets to gain influence they otherwise won't have in the region;

– declares the necessity of working with European allies and African states to find solutions;

– states that a continued American failure to speak out against white rule in South Africa will jeopardize relations with the rest of Africa and much of the Third World;

– determines that the administration will have to take "visible steps" to downgrade relations with South Africa, unless the whites begin to move towards power-sharing with the black majority.

Here we find a substantial difference in tactics between Kissinger and Carter. According to Carter the problem of South Africa cannot wait until solutions are found in Namibia and Zimbabwe. But the strategy is still to work *through* the white minority regimes, in a policy of persuasion, not one of confrontation.

The policy of working through influence with others, rather than through the Kissinger-type shuttle diplomacy, is another difference in style:[11]

America alone cannot have much influence throughout the entire Southern African region. We must work in concert with other relevant powers, such as Britain, which has real influence in Rhodesia, and in those nations such as Zaire and South Africa where we have some clout of our own.

This is a far cry from a program for co-operating with the national liberation movements. It is a program for the manipulation of developments in southern Africa, the intentions of which are clear, but the successes are still wanting.

When we turn to a discussion on the Western policies area by area it is not enough to register the official pronouncements on "support for solutions", "democracy", "majority rule" etc.

We must ask the following questions:

– Are the liberation movements recognized as the legitimate representatives of their peoples?

– Are the initiatives designed to undermine the liberation movements or are they to exercise full sovereignty? Most clearly this comes out in the question of who exercises military control during the envisaged transition.

– What effects are the Western policies intended to have on the liberation struggle?

– How do the Western policies relate to the economic interests they possess in the area?

Angola, Mozambique and Zaire: U.S. choice of allies
It is worthwhile remembering the whole southern African context, before letting ourselves be impressed by the diplomatic maneuvers for "African solutions" in Zimbabwe, Namibia, and South Africa.

The United States hopes to engineer its solutions in southern Africa through the cooperation of African states in the area, particularly among those that would favour moderate as opposed to radical policies. Among the Front line states (Zambia, Botswana, Tanzania, Mozambique, Angola) Tanzania and Zambia are seen as key states in this operation. Surely, both President Julius Nyerere – who exclaimed that "we want the two greatest sources of power on our side – God and Kissinger"[12],

127

and President Kenneth Kaunda who, overwhelmed, embraced Kissinger after his Lusaka speech, welcomed the U.S interest and turn to Washington for solutions. But the hunch is that these states no longer hold the keys to the external support for the liberation struggle. With Mozambique the main base-area for the armed struggle in Zimbabwe, and Angola the base area for the struggle in Namibia, it is Mozambique and Angola who could exert a prohibitive influence on a radical development. And this is precisely what they do not intend to do.

The crux then for the United States is what to do about Angola and Mozambique, both of which in 1977 took one step further in a political consolidation that must be perceived as a major threat to Western interests, by transforming the liberation movements into Marxist-Leninist vanguard parties and reaffirming the principle of proletarian internationalism.

William Minter, in a perceptive article on U.S. policies in Mozambique and Angola, outlines what he calls a hypothetical "destablization" option, "on which the United States might get effective cooperation from South Africa, Rhodesia, disgruntled Portuguese exsettlers and ex-PIDE agents from Angola and Mozambique, and perhaps the Portuguese government as well":[13]

Objectives
Maximum: replacement of regimes in Angola and Mozambique by suitably non-revolutionary pro-western governments;
Minimum: discrediting of the results of liberation struggles in Angola and Mozambique; aggravation of economic and political difficulties so as to prevent effective aid to Nambibian and Zimbabwean guerrillas.

Means
1. Angola –
(a) Maintain low level of guerrilla warfare against People's Republic;
(b) hinder establishment of normal relations with Zaire and Zambia;
(c) stimulate to the maximum political divisions within MPLA;
(d) hinder normal relations with Portugal;
(e) focus propaganda on Soviet and Cuban role in Angola.

2. Mozambique –
(a) mount propaganda campaign against Mozambique, aimed at portraying it as extremist, chaotic, collapsing;
(b) attempt to mobilize people in Mozambique against FRELIMO by identifying new government as cause of economic difficulties;
(c) attempt to isolate Mozambique from the other "front-line" countries (Zambia, Botswana, Tanzania) especially on issues of the Zimbabwean struggle.

The maximum objectives have not been reached. In Mozambique the FRELIMO government is much too firmly established for a policy of betting on discredited traitor organizations. In Angola, although the abortive coup d'etat did have its internal roots in the long and difficultly coordinated liberation struggle, a success for the putschites would have been welcome for the West.

In May, 1978 U.S. newspapers could report that the Carter administration was considering a resumption of the funding of UNITA military and terrorist activities against MPLA. The administration had expressed its irritation with the so called

Clark amendment from December 1975, which explicitly forbids covert assistance to any group carrying out military activities in Angola. The idea was to circumvent this law, and channel funds to UNITA through a third country. France and Zaire were mentioned.[14]

In the meantime, the propaganda war goes on – Allen Isaacman's article on how "U.S. Press Smears Mozambique"[15] with the effect of a redefinition of "the legitimate struggle for majority rule and self-determination in Southern Africa in global Cold War terms" is well worth reading, and would deserve a parallel study of the press campaigns against Anglola.

The U.S. Congress in the summer of 1977 passed an amendment prohibiting any appropriated funds from going "directly or indirectly" to Marxist African states, an action directed clearly against Mozambique and Angola.[16] Congress also directed the administration to vote against Angola and Mozambique in international financial institutions, such as the World Bank. When the foreign aid bill for 1969 was discussed in the summer of 1978, similar prohibitions were put forward.[17]

The use of mercenaries, particularly in Rhodesia, is another method of de-stabilization. According to some estimates, about a third of the regular forces are made up of foreign "volunteers" in Rhodesia.[18]

The recruitment of at least 2 000 mercenaries, most of them from Britain, with U.S. as second supplier, could not take place without the knowledge of the U.S. and British governments. The continued acquiescence in the use of mercenaries cannot be interpreted as anything else than a support for Smith's attempts at beating the Patriotic Front out of the political map by military means. The war against the Patriotic Front has involved numerous incursions into Mozambique and is seriously hindering the normal development of the country (see Bertil Egerö's paper in the companion volume). There are also persistent reports about the continued recruitment of mercenaries for action in Angola.

Despite the promises in Carter's election campaign, and despite the expressed will of the Angolan government, the United States has so far refused to recognize Angola. Some contacts between a representative of the U.S. government and the Angolan authorities in June, 1978 have been interpreted as the first step towards the normalization of relations. But in a speech Carter himself assured a businessmen's audience that he was not at all seeking diplomatic relations with Angola, but that contacts were necessary in order to achieve results in Namibia.[19]

Zaire, on the other hand, was estimated to get $57.5 million in economic and military aid from the United States.[20] As we saw earlier, Carter saw Zaire as one of the partners in his new Africa policy. It is well known that the share of Mobutu's government in southern African liberation has been that of a base for any reactionary groups combatting the liberation forces, particularly in the case of Angola. Today, Mobutu's support is still essential for the "low level guerilla warfare" against the People's Republic of Angola, both in Cabinda, where Mobutu-supported FLEC groups operate, and in northern Angola, where Mobutu-supported FNLA remnants make occasional incursions to disrupt the civil reconstruction.

Zaire is one of the states whose pro-Western position would be seriously put in question with a consolidation and extension of the successes of the liberation struggle. It is one of the richest African states, holds a central position geographically, is second only to South Africa as a site for U.S. investment in Africa[21], yet governed by an utterly corrupt regime which despite an army of 65,000 soldiers is hardly able to defend itself against serious opposition to the government, because of the low morale of the soldiers, fostered by the virtual bankruptcy of the economy. No wonder the U.S. stepped in, together with France and Belgium to rescue Mobutu when in March, 1977 the regime was threatened with sudden collapse after the insurrection by the Congolese National Liberation Front (FNLC) in the Shaba province. The U.S. government refused to go in directly, and advocated an "African solution", with Moroccan troops providing the back-bone.[22]

A year later, when the FNLC launched a new campaign in Shaba and took hold of the important mining town of Kolwezi, the United States contributed directly to a military intervention in support of Mobutu. The Carter administration claimed that it had been a case of aggression from abroad, of which Angola was part, and where Cuban soldiers were involved, but failed to produce a shred of evidence. They were not even able to produce an exile Cuban from Miami, something Castro warned that might be their reply to demands from Cuba that the accusations be documented.

In the Western press the Shaba II intervention was depicted as a humanitarian rescue mission tó save the whites in the area. But when the French legion was shipped in by U.S. aeroplanes from Corsica (and possibly Djibouti) they started a violent recapture of Kolwezi, which had been quiet until the saviours came. "Rescued" Europeans told the press in Europe that the rebels had behaved with discipline, whereas most of the killings were done by Mobutu's own soldiers.[23]

The Shaba II operation was the first military cooperation in action between France and the United States since the Vietnam war, and the biggest military operation undertaken by the Carter administration. It not only shipped in the soldiers by an air-lift, but also provided military communications personnel, fuel, jeeps etc.

After the second revolt in Shaba, France called for a permanent inter-African commando force to go in, with the aid of the French, wherever an uprising threatened to upset the political map of Africa. It was coldly received by many African states, but the French puppet states of Senegal, the Ivory Coast, Gabon, the Central African Republic, and Morocco in actual fact are going on with the scheme. In June, Moroccan troops again were sent to Zaire, to maintain order in Shaba, and apparently to replace the French and Belgians.[24] The stand taken by the United States on the issue of the continental commando force was that it had to be decided by the Organization of African Unity.

Zimbabwe

The first priority in the new Africa policy, as outlined by Kissinger, was Rhodesia. Rhodesia is not insignificant in Western economy. Rhodesia, South Africa, and the USSR are the major exporters of chrome in the world. It can be reasonably well expected that a nationalist African government will raise prices for its chrome. Even a modest price rise for chrome in turn increases production costs for steel. The outcome of political developments in Zimbabwe will thus touch the core of Western capitalism.

The economic aspect is not the only explanation behind Western initiatives on Zimbabwe. A progressive Zimbabwe would be a source of greater consolidation for Mozambique, and it would move both Tanzania and Zambia closer to a socialist path. A regional grouping containing Mozambique, Zimbabwe, Tanzania, Zambia, Angola, and perhaps Namibia would constitute a strong material basis for a coordinated socialist reconstruction on the African continent, and be a blow to the visions of South Africa as "the banker and industrialist" dominating the sub-continent.

Out of the Kissinger initiative came the Anglo-American proposals, based on the idea that Ian Smith could be pressured to at least share power with the nationalists through South African backing of the proposals.

What role the Patriotic Front?

When Kissinger started his shuttle diplomacy on Zimbabwe, the nationalist scene was still unclear, and there was room for speculation on what African grouping could be picked to guarantee a neo-colonial solution. The tactical alliance between ZANU under Robert Mugabe and ZAPU under Joshua Nkomo anounced in October 1976, and followed by an agreement on a platform in January 1977, under the name of the Patriotic Front, has made it impossible to bypass these experienced nationalist organisations, who command the armed forces in the intensified armed struggle. A further set-back to efforts at bypassing ZANU/ZAPU came with the recognition by the OAU in 1977 of the Patriotic Front as the sole representative of the people of Zimbabwe.

The Patriotic Front forces of ZAPU and ZANU are flooded with new young recruits fleeing their country to join the armed struggle, and the problem is that more training is demanded than can be offered. At the same time, the morale of the soldiers in the rebel colony army is at a low ebb, and the sources of new recruits are drying up. Reg. Cowper, Smith's defense minister, said as he had to resign in February 1977 after protests from the business commuity against the call up of men between 38 and 50 for military service; "My principal concern is the morale of Rhodesians who have, unfortunately, been subjected to public debate on the country's ability or otherwise to win the terrorist war."[25]

The total number of men in the Rhodesian armed forces is about 50,000. The budget expenditure for the war in 1976/77 was 34% higher than the previous year (now £122 mn).[26]

The white-minority regime admitted in April, 1977 that more than 36,000 school pupils have quit to join the guerilla forces.[27] In September, 1978 a figure of 700 closed African schools was mentioned. In some areas the schools have been reopened by the guerilla forces.

The Front Line States decided in November 1976 to recognize the Patriotic Front as the political voice of the freedom fighters in Zimbabwe.

Realities have forced the U.S. and the British governments to recognize a role for the Patriotic Front in any settlement. It is a response to the pressures of the situation, but far from recognizing the legitimacy and representativity of the liberation movements. The rationale of expediency is illustrated in the following statement by Owen:

An internal settlement which excludes one of the leading nationalist groups cannot bring about a ceasefire during the elections or give peace and stability to a newly independent Zimbabwe. (Owen in the British Parliament, Jan 25, 1978.)[28]

And Young, while acknowledging a leading role for the Patriotic Front, said:[29]

That does not mean everybody else will have to be excluded. But if then you are trying to stop killings, you have got to talk with the people who have the guns and who are doing the killings, and right now that is the Patriotic Front and Ian Smith.

When Smith announced his plan for an internal settlement with Muzorewa of United African National Council, Chief Chirau of the newly created ZUPO (Zimbabwe United People's Organization), and Sithole with his remnants of ZANU, Young said:

We've seen what happened to South Vietnam whenever they tried to hold elections without the participation of the Vietcong.[30]

While this is one of Young's flashes of realism, it also shows the limits of his view. The national liberation forces is just one of several factors which must be brought into a settlement, while the principal collaborator still is the regime in power:

Any solution has to be worked out with the people in power, and I do not see the United States role as one of upsetting the indigenous leadership of any country, whether it be Smith in Rhodesia or any other nation in Africa.[31]

The complete lack of understanding of the nature of the struggle, and of its current phase, was shown by the U.S. performance at the UN sponsored conference in Maputo in May 1977, where Andrew Young was trying to sell a civil rights boycott strategy to the Zimbabwean nationalists. He suggested that people should buy nothing but food and medicine for six months to force a settlement. Robert Mugabe, ZANU chairman and co-leader of the Patriotic Front, noted that the intervention ignored Zimbabwean history: "/We/ used strikes, sit-ins, and passive resistance. We tried these methods and our people got shot . . . we came to the conclusion that what remained to be tried was the armed struggle."[32]

To the disappointment of the Washington and London architects of change, Ian Smith concluded an agreement with Muzorewa, Sithole, and Chirau in April, 1978. It gave the Europeans 28 of 100 Parliament seats (a veto on constitutional changes), and guaranteed that whites could not be fired from the state apparatus during the next ten years. Little in the way of satisfying majority demands has been made, except a release of some hundreds of political prisoners, but further arrests of several more.

The reason why this internal settlement was not satisfactory to the West had little to do with the political content or achievements. It had to with the failure of obtaining a cease-fire and an end to the armed struggle. The chief, the bishop, and the minister failed to "bring in the terrorists", as the Smith regime openly claimed it would.[33]

The war continued after the internal settlement, and actually was intensified. In September 1978 Ian Smith finally had to admit that there was no possibility of holding the envisaged elections for a "majority" parliament, which was to take over from the settler parliament at the end of the year. The position at the time of writing is that England and the United States are eagerly trying to call a conference on the future constitutiuon where all parties would be represented (the Patriotic Front, Smith's Rhodesian Front, and his three partners in the internal settlement). The Patriotic Front has insisted that both Smith and his African partners could only be part of a British delegation.

The Zimbabwe Development Fund

Kissinger's rounds on Rhodesia were accompanied by unusual activity among business circles.

Meetings were held between the U.S. administration and some 20 corporations including Chase Manhattan Bank, Citybank, Union Carbide, Foote Mineral, and Mobil Oil, to organise large-scale U.S. investment into Rhodesia during an envisioned transitional period, when, it is hoped, sanctions would be lifted.[34]

Reports also circulated about a U.S. – British – South African plan for a large-scale development fund to ensure the stability of independent Zimbabwe under black rule. Details of the proposal were revealed only in the spring of 1977, when it was confirmed that the Carter administration had continued with the scheme. For the sub-committee on Africa of the House International Relations Committee, deputy assistant secretary of state for African affairs, Talcott Seelye, revealed that:[35]

– 18 nations have been asked to contribute to the Fund over a five year period. Great Britain has pledged 75 million pounds but other countries have not yet responded. The U.S. share will be 40 percent of the total, or $520 million, out of a projected total of $1.–$1.5 billion.

– The Fund is to be administered by the World Bank, which would respond to requests for project funding by an independent Zimbabwe government, only after independence.

– If independence comes by military victory, rather than through negotiation, the Fund would become a "dead letter" and would not be made available to the new government.

The British contribution to the plans for the fund was based on the experience from Kenya, where a compensation fund had been set up for white farmers, but integrated in the development plan of the country.

The Byrd Amendment was repealed in the spring of 1977, putting an end to a 6-year old defiance by the U.S. of mandatory sanctions against the buying of chrome from Rhodesia. By the time this repeal was made "even the chrome companies admit they can live without Rhodesian chrome because of stockpiling, new refining processes, and access to other sources, including South Africa."[36] If it gave the impression, during a brief period, that the U.S. was now prepared to put pressure by economic disengagement, the Fund plans clearly revealed that this was just a window-dressing exercise, to make it possible to come back soon, in a big way.

To buy out or not to buy out the whites

When U.S. Vice-President Mondale had met with Vorster in Vienna in May, 1977 he reported:[37]

I explained that our concept of the Zimbabwe development fund is different from that of the previous American administration. Instead of being a fund aimed at buying out the white settlers in Rhodesia, we want to reorient that fund to a development fund; one which will help build a strong economy and one which will encourage the continued participation of the white population in an independent Zimbabwe.

This line taken by the U.S. government can explain the relative silence about the reported plan to transfer 150,000 racists from southern Africa to Latin America, and particularly from Rhodesia and Namibia. At a conference in Costa Rica in November 1976 the West German government had reportedly offered $150 mn to Latin American governments willing to receive white immigrants. The aid was to be given through the Inter-American Development Bank, while the cost of the transport was to be borne by the Inter-governmental Committee in European Emigration (ICEM), based in Geneva. West Germany's special interest in the matter was to avoid to have to take responsibility for the whites with German passport in Namibia (5,000 with only German passport, 10,000 with both South African and German), but it was also assumed that West Germany acted as a mediator for U.S.-Anglo interests. Bolivia responded favourably, and work is apparently underway for the infrastructural preparations. Bolivian consulates in Salisbury, Windhoek, and Johannesburg are actively recruiting prospective immigrants. The plan is viewed with apprehension by the Bolivian opposition, who see it as a way to strengthen the Fascist Forces in the country and to export the system of racist supremacy.[38]

Even if Western policies in southern Africa did not include this organized exodus as a basic element in the strategy, the plan can be realized through the "natural" immigration of whites, which today results in net outflow of whites from both Zimbabwe, Namibia, and South Africa. And although the Bolivian province set aside for immigration seems to be singularly unattractive, this type of plan in itself is an interesting and disconcerting "reserve option", which certainly will reoccur because the present ideas of continued white participation seem based on continued white privileges, something not accpeted by the liberation movements.

Just as the first plans for an organized mass transfer of whites from southern Africa to Latin America was based on the experiences of the mass exodus from Angola in 1975, the apparent hesitation today could be based on that experience. Because, even if the exodus, in the short run, upset and sabotaged the economy in Angola, the exodus of most of the colonial state employees, the managerial and white collar staff in enterprises, and the big and medium landowners, in the long run it also removes many obstacles to a socialist transformation of the state apparatus, industry and labour relations, and agriculture.

Namibia

Namibia is as important as Zimbabwe for future Western interests. A controlled settlement is vital for three reasons: Namibia's riches include vast resources of strategic metals, Namibia has a strategic position between Angola and South Africa, and the liberation of Angola has contributed to a more coherently anti-imperialist line within SWAPO.

Consolidated Diamonds in the south and Tsumeb in the north are old mining companies, the latter exploiting lead, zinc, silver, vanadium, germanium (the only other source for this metal used in electronics is Zaire), and beginning to exploit copper on a large scale. Uranium is the new focus of mining development, and when the Rössing mine near Swakopmund will be developed it will be the largest site in the world. Reports say that "Rössing is just a drop in the bucket compared to the uranium along the treeless sandy coast".[39] Apart from the mining resources the Namibian coastline provides among the world's richest fishing waters.

The armed struggle in Namibia was launched by the South West Africa People's Organization (SWAPO) in August 1966, and in 1967 the UN Council for Namibia was set up to exert authority over Namibia in accordance with the UN mandate provision, ignored by South Africa which has held Namibia as an occupied territory. The armed struggle did start, waged from Zambia, but only the liberation of Angola opened up definite prospects for liberation. It is also from this time that we can date South African maneuvers to fake independence for Namibia in order to retain full control, and Western attempts to produce a guided withdrawal.

From Turnhalle to the mediations by the Western Contact Group

It seems as if Kissinger first thought that the South African charade at a constitutional settlement could provide a basis for the solution of the "Namibian problem". This was the Turnhalle confernce, so named after the old German drillhall in which South Africa on 1 September 1975 gathered 135 "delegates" selected on an ethnic basis. One of the delegates, Chief Charles Kapuuo, (who was murdered in the summer of 1977), had been promoted by a U.S. firm as the future leader of Namibia. But as the unrepresentativity and total lack of international support for the Turnhalle conference became obvious, and SWAPO military and political strength increased, the Turnhalle exercise has turned into a sham. Intensive efforts to encourage a split in SWAPO, by bringing in long-time prisoners like Toivo ja Toivo from Robben Island (who refused), recruiting defectors, and driving a wedge between "internal" (legally and openly working) SWAPO and "external" SWAPO (the armed wing) have failed to produce the image Kissinger hoped for by bringing "at least a part of SWAPO" into the Turnhalle negotiations.

The line taken by the Carter administration is that there must be a "full participation" by SWAPO in the independence process. But as in the case of Zimbabwe, the realization that the liberation movement cannot be excluded is a decision taken out of expediency, and never formulated as a recognition of the legitimacy of the struggle or a recognition of the liberation movement's right to exercise authority in its country.

On 30 January 1976 the Security Council unanimously adopted Resolution 385 which declared that "in order that the people of Namibia be enabled to freely determine their own future, it is imperative that free elections under the supervision and control of the United Nations be held for the whole of Namibia as one political entity." This was also accepted by SWAPO as a workable basis. But in the subsequent diplomatic moves the question of control was dropped by Kissinger, and also by the Carter administration. In April, 1977 the five Western members of the Security Council, U.S., France, Britain, Canada, and West Germany, took upon themselves a self-appointed mandate, formed a "contact group", which outside the U.N. framework opened talks with South Africa on the solution of the Namibian question.

In July, 1978, it finally looked as if the Western initiatives had borne fruit, and that a solution through the cooperation with South Africa could be reached. In the spring of 1978 the Western contact group had put forward their proposal for a process of the transfer of power to the majority in Namibia, whose will would be tested in an election at the end of the year. In June the South African forces had attacked a SWAPO transit camp at Cassinga, killing more than 500 Namibians by paratroopers. Even despite this SWAPO had agreed to certain compromises (on the stationing of S.A. troops in Namibia during the transition period as the most important point), and agreed to give the Western plan a try. Many details remained to be worked out, but at least the Security Council had stated clearly that Walvis Bay (regarded by South Africa as their territory), the only deep sea harbour and Namibia's second town, was part and parcel of Namibia.

In September Vorster announced, just before resigning as Prime Minister, that South Africa was not going to continue with the transition plan. The successes of the armed struggle had forced the Western powers into a much more effective recognition of SWAPO as the legitimate representative than they had really wanted when Kissinger first talked about bringing majority rule to Namibia.

Meanwhile, as in the case of Zimbabwe, efforts are made behind the scene to secure the maintenance of the Western-oriented economic structure. In Namibia's case these efforts are best known in the form of major studies conducted and authorized by the U.S. Agency for International Development on the premise that the present international division of labour and exploitative relations be preserved.[41] Although there has not been talk of a fund as in Zimbabwe, the bait is similar to that promised by Kissinger (August 1976): "Once concrete steps are underway, the U.S. will ease its restrictions on trade and investment in Namibia and provide economic and technical assistance to help that nation consolidate its independence."[40]

South Africa

In mid-May U.S. Vice-President Mondale met with Vorster in Vienna, and explained that there was need for "progressive tranformation" to majority rule, not only in Namibia but also in South Africa.[41] The *Rand Daily Mail* gave a 9-column headline to the report from the meeting: "COLLISION COURSE".[42] An image was created that the United States now had finally given up cooperation with the apartheid regime. A closer scrutiny of the pressures promised, the measures actually taken, and the nature of change sought impel a more cautious view.

'I don't see sanctions'

The most urgently needed change for the United States government is a restoration of its reputation in the Third World, and particularly black Africa. In Nigeria, in early 1977, Andrew Young explained:[43]

I see the United States as likely to have a very aggressive policy to move towards majority rule in Southern Africa. I think when the nations of Africa realise that we are serious about majority rule . . . I think we will get a new measure of cooperation from the Third World that has not been there largely because they felt we did not care.

If the word "aggressive" is changed to "active" we get a more realistic picture of actual policies. When it came to the crucial question of sanctions on South Africa to actually exert pressure, Young continued:[44]

I don't see sanctions. I would see an arms embargo, of course, but sanctions very seldom have worked. I think what we have got to do is find ways to use the tremendous influence we have to move toward majority rule.

Change could come, he said, from private firms. "I think that is to some extent possible. I don't view the South African white community as monolith and I think that there are forces within that country that will respond to efforts and initiatives that might come both publicly and privately from the United States."[45] This belief in corporate change has been a consistent theme in the U.S. view on South Africa, and there have been no changes despite the verbal confrontation on political rights. As late as December 16, 1977, the United States together with the other four members of the "contact group" were alone in voting against a General Assembly resolution calling for an end to new and further investments in South Africa.

The ideology that the corporations will be agents of change in South Africa is an old one, and has been sharply criticised for its premise that removing apartheid is equal to improving the lot for those Africans employed in industry. In fact, no company had and can be expected to break with or do anything about the laws and regulations ruling the black labour market. Exploitation of black labour is the very core of the apartheid system, and the reason why foreign companies are attracted there in the first place.

Civil rights struggle or national liberation?

The idea of corporate change runs parallel to the theme reiterated by Carter and Young that one can view the situation in South Africa in the same terms as the civil rights struggle in the American South, which, as a fringe benefit, would bestow upon the United States the undisputed role of being the most qualified advisor on the process of change. This view contains a message of hope to both blacks and businessmen in South Africa. To the businessmen Young broke the news at a visit in Lesotho:[46]

What the Africans have not realized, I thing, is something we learned in the South (in the U.S): that when we changed our racial situation we created an entirely new economic market. Fuller participation by blacks in society has provided a basis for tremendous economic and business growth.

It was elaborated with an optimistic conviction that surprised even the South African press most closely allied to capitalism during Young's tour to South Africa in May, 1977. Young's message to the businessmen headed by Harry Oppenheimer at a special dinner for their special friend was that South Africa's industrial empire would dominate half Africa if the country acted quickly to give all races a stake in the system.

There is no doubt that the South African struggle will be – as it has been – long and hard, and that there will be Africans, Coloureds, and Indians who will be bought off. But the exteme racial oppression, the long traditions of struggle, and the intransigence of the political leaders make Young's dreams rather remote today.

By the liberation movement the parallel with the civil rights struggle in the United States is seen as an attempt to avoid the real issues of the oppressive system in South Africa. It is a long time since the question could be put as one solely of discrimination and civil rights. According to the leading force in the liberation struggle, the African National Congress, the struggle in South Africa, no less than in Namibia and Zimbabwe is one of national liberation. The president of ANC, Oliver Tambo, said in his address to the UN General Assembly in October 1976:[47]

In as much as the apartheid is a regime product of colonial conquest it is itself an imposition on our people. From the earliest days of their arrival, white settlers, as they did elsewhere in Africa, set themselves the task of subjugating the indigenous population politically and economically. The apartheid system of today is the outcome of a process of historical development which has led to the entrenchment of white settler colonial domination.

As a colonized people, we assert not only our right to rebel against the colonizer, but also our right to determine for ourselves the means and methods to use to liberate ourselves and our country, as well as our right to determine what to do with our liberation.

It is still possible to hear views on South Africa based on the assumption that nothing much is changing there, except the death toll, and that South Africa, in contrast to Namibia and Zimbabwe, experiences no liberation struggle. This is not the view of the South African regime, however. In April this year, the Minister of the Interior admitted that during the past months about 2,500 persons had been detained as insurgents or suspected insurgents, and he also said that "the guerilla cannot be stopped". After Soweto, an intensive underground organizing work has taken place. Those hoping for a "peaceful" alternative had to be disappointed when almost all Black Consciousness organisations were banned in October, 1977.

In the words of the ANC representative in London, this "will have the inevitable effect of drawin the protest movements closer to the underground ANC"[48]. All these developments explain the urgency of the United States to try to steer developments.

The middle class solution – Oppenheimer version

Although pointing at the unique experience of the civil rights struggle in the United States the "civil rights approach" to South Africa is in fact an attempt to resort to an old recipe in Africa: The creation of an African middle class as a cushion to prevent any fundamental structural changes which could endanger economic exploitation.

Among the most-favoured South African partners in Carter's search for a middle-class solution is Harry Oppenheimer, chairman of the Anglo-American Corporation.

Harry Oppenheimer in his message to the shareholders of the Anglo-American Corporation 1976:[49]

Developments in Angola and Mozambique confront South Africa with difficult problems, not only in foreign and defence policies but also in domestic policies. It is not surprising that a large part of our black population has shown sympathies for the peoples of Angola and Mozambique in their struggle to liberate themselves from Portuguese rule. . . In the long run free enterprise cannot successfully be defended and developed if not a large part of the population, especially the part capable of leadership, believes that it gives them more possibilities than today.

Anglo-American is today the largest mining house in the imperialist world, with assets estimated in 1974 at $7.4 billion, discounting rich reserves and hidden assets. 56% of Anglo's shares are held by South African interests, but both interests and activities reach far beyond the South African borders. The Anglo or Oppenheimer empire (so named after its chairman, Harry Oppenheimer, son of the founder Ernest Oppenheimer) includes *de Beers Consolidated,* the largest diamond company in the world where Anglo owns 36%, and the *Charter Consolidated,* based in London which owns 10% of Anglo and is its associate. *The Anglo-American Corporation* itself has a direct ownership influence in about 660 companies.[50]

The Oppenheimer empire has extensive contacts with other giant companies and international finance. One of the close ties are with the U.S firm, *Engelhard Minerals and Chemicals Corporation,* the world's largest refiner and fabricator of precious metals.[51]

Of special interest in this context are the Anglo connections in Canada and Sweden. In 1966 the Anglo-American Corporation of Canada was founded, with 'both direct and indirect investment in copper, zinc, cadmium, gold, silver, potash and uranium mining, chemical, crude oil and natural gas production and prospecting operations'.

AAC Canada owns 34.75% of Hudson Bay Mining and Smelting, 40% of Francana Development Corporation and 10% of Anglo Lake Mines Ltd. Charter has direct interests in Falconbridge Nickel Mines of Canada. Harry Oppenheimer sits on the board of the Canadian Imperial Bank of Commerce.[52]

The Swedish connections include a 50% interest in McCarty Main Holdings, which controls Anglo Illings that together with the Lawson Motor Groups has exclusive sales rights on Volvo vehicles in South Africa; a 90.1% holding in Svenska Bromsbandsfabriken (Swedish Brake Lining Industry) in northern Sweden through Cape Industries; a 10% interest by Avesta Jernverk (iron works) in Transalloys (Pty) Ltd., in South Africa controlled largely by Anglo; and a 100% control of Scandiamant in Sweden held through de Beer controlled but Ireland based Ultra High Pressure Units ltd.[53]

It remains only to be mentioned that the Oppenheimer empire is deeply involved in mining and other fields in the southern African subcontinent. These interests range from interests in iron in Swaziland, diamonds, uranium, and copper in Namibia, nickel, copper and coal in Botswana, fishing, agriculture, and hydro-electric power (Cabora Bassa) in Mozambique, diamonds in Angola, to copper in Zambia and Zaire.

There are two genuine points of opposition from the Oppenheimer and allied business interests: in the first place they see the job reservation clauses as cumbersome obstacles to the recruitment of small groups of blacks to take skilled jobs. This is an acute problem especially in the mining industry, whose resources of black labour from other countries in southern Africa are drying up (or in the case of Mozambique deliberately reduced), and which therefore are embarking on mechanization. In the second place, for economic reasons, they do not believe in the ultimate objective of the bantustan policies. As *Rand Daily Mail* writes:[54]

> They (the blacks) have become inextricably integrated into the economic fabric of South Africa, and there is no way they can be pulled apart without tearing up the whole. Which is why they can never be physically separated into different "nations" . . .

Even if apartheid on these two points is "irrational" for capitalism, those business interests inside and outside the country opposing these features in principle, cannot find it "rational", given the political situation, to upset the system by confrontation. The more and more desperate appeals to abandon these two aspects of apartheid should not be mistaken for mounting forces towards such a confrontation.

The futile hopes for gradual transformation

The whole idea of gradual transformation conceded in response to pressure and the laws of the market forces might have had some credence years ago. But if proof of the futility of such hopes was needed it certainly have been provided during the past two years. Just to mention a few examples:

In the 18 months after the student demonstrations in Soweto and the ensuing general strike of tens of thousands of black workers more than 1,000 blacks have been killed by police bullets.

Out of 48 known cases of political detainees known to have died under interrogation by the police since 1963, as reported in *Anti-Apartheid News*, more than half have died since 1976.[55]

Few black South Africans would be impressed by the British Foreign Secretary's logic that it is the task of the Western nations to make the blacks understand that if the whites are pressured into a "laager mentality" it could lead to "a horribly repressive regime"[56] in South Africa and increase oppression of the blacks.

Nor should the foreign policies of South Africa leave any room for hopes that it can be a partner to "peaceful change". The invasion of Angola, and its forced withdrawal in March, 1976 was a signal both to South African aggression and a blow to the myth of South African invincibility. It was a major factor behind the renewed wave of resistance in South Africa itself, and an inspiration to the liberation forces in Namibia and Zimbabwe.

But the Government of South Africa only increased its military budget after Angola. It rose from 857 million Rand in 1974/75 to 1,350 million Rand for 1976/77.[57] Efforts have also been made to increase the armed forces, which is done in three ways: by admitting Coloured and Indians to military training, by increasing the standing forces, and by giving arms training to women, to include them in the Home Guard.

New interventions beyond the borders were "legalized" when, on March 17, 1976, the Defense Act from 1957 was amended to allow the S.A. army to send conscripts and soldiers "to perform service against an enemy at any place outside the Republic."[58] The initial draft of the bill defined the area included in the Act as that of "Africa south of the Equator", which would have included 11 African states, and parts of a further four, plus Namibia and Zimbabwe. The United Party proposed that no territorial limits be defined, and also received approval for its proposal to include no obligation of consent by the individual conscripts.[59]

The continued unrest in South Africa has resulted in a situation experienced only a brief period after the shooting at Sharpeville, when foreign capital, badly needed for South Africa's economy, is hesitant to come in. In the first quarter of 1977 there was for the first time a net outflow of lon-term capital,[60] and Barclay's South African Chairman warns in his annual statement at the end of the year:

The attraction of fresh capital from overseas to alleviate the Republic's capital account is dependent upon overseas investors being satisfied that evolutionary change, as distinct from revolutionary change, will take place at a reasonable pace.[61]

Emergency aid from IMF

Although rumours are spread that the Carter administration informally encourages moves to isolate apartheid,[62] when it comes to the brink, the United States government is actually stepping in. Carter's National Security Adviser, Zbiegnew Brezesinski, explained in October, 1977:[63]

What we are trying to do is to encourage a process of change which will outpace what otherwise looks like a rather apocalyptical alternative. We're not putting pressure on South Africa to commit suicide. We are trying to get the South Africans to rethink the historical destiny of their country, *so that through change that society can survive. . .*

Whether the apartheid leaders were thinking about the historical destiny or not, immediate rescue was necessary in the balance of payments situation, and the usual artificial respiration for capitalist states had to be used: the International Monetary Fund. IMF is in a key position to provide short-term non-investment funds crucial to alleviate the balance of payments problems. In 1972 the IMF was the source of 60% of these funds for South Africa.[64]

Andrew Young threatened during his southern Africa tour that South Africa could be cut off from international credit sources such as the International Monetary Fund.[65] Yet, behind the scenes, the United States has actually helped Vorster's regime to obtain a $463 million loan. During the past two years IMF's assistance to South Africa has been greater than IMF assistance to all other African countries together. Only Mexico and Britain have been bigger beneficiaries.[66]

Unofficial lobbying for the apartheid regime continues and is growing, with no visible official opposition. For example, on June 20 to 21, 1977 the South African government hosted a conference outside New York for 350 American businessmen, with the purpose to spur U.S. investment in South Africa. This conference was part of a campaign for more support in the U.S. for South Africa's view on Communism in Africa, U.S. investment opportunities, discrimination and apartheid, the homelands policy, Transkei "independence", and sports competition. When, after intensive South African lobbying, the House of Representatives voted on a resolution on the recognition of Transkei it failed by only 23 votes.[67]

In January 1978 Henry Ford visited South Africa, and was received as a state guest by Vorster. He declared that he had no intention at all to withdraw any of his $70 mn investment in the country, and that he knew of no American business corporation of any importance which was prepared to leave.[68]

U.S. interests in South Africa

In fact, the U.S. interests in South Africa are the real key to U.S. policies in the area. In the Kissinger study they were summarised thus:[69]

The U.S. has a significant economic stake in South Africa: investment of about $700 million, (nearly 30% of our investment in all Africa) and a substantial favorable trade balance (over $450 million in U.S. exports and $250 million in 1968). The U.S. provides roughly 17 per cent of South Africa's imports. South Africa produces about 60% of the Free World's gold, and the orderly marketing of this production is of key importance for the maintenance of the two-tier gold pricing system. South Africa is the third largest Free World supplier of uranium. · · · The U.S. has a NASA satellite tracking station and an Air Force missile tracking station in South Africa. · · · U.S. aircraft use South African fields for space support and other missions. Because of the uncertainty of overflight rights in northern and central Africa, there is U.S.

military interest in alternative routes through southern Africa to support contingency operations in the Indian Ocean and the Middle East areas.

According to a U.S. Department of Commerce survey in 1977 of corporate investments in Africa[70] the book value of U.S. investments in Africa as a whole was $4.467 mn, of which 37.3% or $1.665 mn was in South Africa. This was more than double the 1969 figure.

British investments in South Africa are still far more extensive. The British government has the sincerity to frankly admit that it simply cannot afford sanctions against South Africa.

The political alternatives in South Africa

In the long run, black political alternatives must be sought for the U.S. version of necessary changes in South Africa. Like in Namibia and Zimbabwe, U.S. policy-makers are seeking alternatives to the liberation movement recognized by the Organization of African Unity (in South Africa's case ANC, and PAC, the latter, however, not having been able to prove any mass support). The problem is where to find them. The United States Information Service is reportedly pouring out black power material, with the hope that race consciousness will supersede class consciousness and a clear political program, hoping also to cause a split in ANC, an organization assailed before by "black nationalists" for having whites in its ranks. But the links between ANC and the Black Consciousness movement, which could have provided the alternative, have apparently been stronger than expected, nor have the leaders of the Black Consciousness movement been willing to be coaxed into U.S. sponsored leadership roles. When Young visited South Africa, the U.S. Embassy in vain invited the Black People's Convention to an informal meeting – they replied that Young should talk to the authentic leaders of the South African people, who were in jail. Also, Steve Biko refused an invitation by the State Department to the United States in the spring of 1977.

One who came, however, and apparently is one of the cards the U.S. wants to try, was Chief Gatsha Buthelezi, the KwaZulu bantustan leader. His view that South Africa should dismantle some of its racial laws and absorb more blacks into government and thus minimise the scale of impending violence[71] squares fine with the Carter-Young approach, as does his many proposals for reforms intended to pave the way for an emerging black middle class. As long as his constituency was a bantustan he could not really be counted on as leader of an organisational alternative. The creation of his Inkatha movement, and its talks with the (coloured) Labour Party, and the (Indian) Reform Party[72] could take care of that.

The arms embargo

A major victory in the international pressure on the apartheid regime came with the mandatory arms embargo on November 4, 1977. But this came only after attempts to water it down by the Carter administration's suggestion for a six-month moratorium on arms shipments, not invoking the clause on mandatory sanction under chapter VII of the UN charter on threats to international security and peace.[13] South Africa is largely self-sufficient in arms production, thanks to previous Western licensing and aid.[14] Also, the use of third countries for the export of sensitive war material is already a tested device. Israel and Iran are likely partners in such plans to circumvent the arms embargo.

The case for Scandinavian disassociation

The Scandinavian governments have been in the forefront among the capitalist states in giving support to the liberation movements in southern Africa. They have obtained, although not always earned, a reputation for being unequivocally on the side of liberation by a number of initiatives in the United Nations and other international contexts.[15] The Danish, Swedish and Norwegian governments give humanitarian aid to ANC-South Africa, the Patriotic Front (ZANU/ZAPU) and to SWAPO. The Finnish government has assisted SWAPO for some time, in December it took the first decision to support ANC-South Africa, but has not yet decided on Zimbabwe. The most important support for the liberation movements comes from the socialist countries, and from the African states, particularly from those where the liberation movements are allowed to open schools, camps etc. But the Scandinavian support is not insignificant.

The Scandinavian aid to the liberation movements, which is a *de facto* recognition of their legitimacy, should be followed up by a recognition of their right and capacity to determine the terms of the liberation of their own countries. However, we find too often a view that the solution lies in the efforts of the U.S. administration and its allies.

Denmark seems to follow the U.S. line more closely than the other Scandinavian countries. This is probably due to Denmark's foreign policy line in general. Both Norway and Denmark are members of NATO, but Denmark is also a member of the Common Market. The Danish Foreign Minister affirmed in the UN in September 1976 his government's recognition of the efforts of the U.S. government in Zimbabwe.[16] In the speech to the parliament that autumn he also noted as a positive fact the active Africa policy of the U.S. government (then Ford's administration), describing it as being "completely in line with the positive interest for colonial liberation the United States has shown earlier against the background of its own historical development".[17] In the General Assembly in September 1977 the Danish Foreign Minister praised the Angolo-American proposals for "a peaceful solution in Zimbabwe".[18]

South Africa is in the Danish official view "not a colonial problem, but a racist problem" because of the suppression of "fundamental human rights"[19] – a view parallel to Carter's, but contrary to that of ANC. What the Foreign Minister had to say about Namibia in his statement to the Parliament in 1977 was that Denmark supports the activities of the Western five nations "to reach a peaceful negotiated settlement".[80] He also defended Danish aid to liberation movements, taking the example of Angola, by describing Denmark's activities as part of a crusade for the West. "We wanted to see to it", he said, "that in any case we, by default, by what we did not do, did not contribute to giving other political systems and powers behind these, increased possibilities for influence in Africa."[81]

"Thanks to the efforts by the five front-line states and other powers, among them the United States and the United Kingdom, the situation today does not seem totally hopeless" (in Zimbabwe), said the Norwegian representative in the General Assembly in October 1976,[82] expressing the hope that majority rule can still be achieved "by peaceful means". "The alternatives are frightening", he added, probably unconscious of his paraphrasing of Vorster's view that the alternative to a quick "solution" in Zimbabwe is "too ghastly to contemplate". On South Africa he recorded that Norway had "appealed time and again to South African authorities to reverse this inhuman policy"[83] of apartheid. The international efforts to "effect a peaceful transition to an independent Zimbabwe" was hailed as a hopeful sign also by the Swedish representative during the same General Assembly session.

This is no complete review of the Scandinaivan position, nor do I want to say that the Scandinavian countries support the U.S. views on all details. But what is absent in the declarations is an acknowledgement of the role of the liberation movements, not only as victims to be helped for altruistic or anti-communist reasons, but also as the only really hopeful sign of change in the region.

These are some reasons why a belief in and support for the imperialist policies in southern Africa are totally displaced and can only compromise the credibility of the Scandinavian governments:

– The U.S. administration pretends to look for "peaceful" solutions in a situation of an intensive war, as if there was no need to take sides.

– The South African government is treated as a potential liberator of Namibia and Zimbabwe, legitimizing it instead of treating it as the threat to peace and progress in the region.

– Any dialogue with the South African regime is only an attempt to evade pressures for its isolation.

– The U.S. manoeuvres are based on the premise that what is at stake is only white contra black rule, in total disregard of the liberation movements' expressed goals of not only political but also economic independence.

– Not only does the United States have any right to steer developments in southern Africa, but there are no signs, either, that it is able to provide solutions. It is time to give up the illusion that the United States is ruling the world to its liking. The essence of the situation in southern Africa is that events there have drastically changed the balance of forces in favour of socialism. The priority given to southern Africa in U.S. policies is not a sign of its power, but a sign of its desperation at its weakness.

The Scandinavian governments need not look hard to find an alternative to hope placed in veiled U.S. efforts to undermine the liberation struggle. There is strong public support for the support given to the liberation movements and for the programs of action adopted in recent years at broadly based international conferences, beginning with the OAU and Scandinavian sponsored Oslo conference on southern Africa in April, 1973, followed more recently by the world conference against apartheid, racism and colonialism in Lisbon, the conference on Namibia and Zimbabwe in Maputo, and the UN conference in Lagos in August, 1977.

Let me just quote two recent examples of this popular demand for a more consistent policy of full support for the liberation movements. In October 1977, a hearing on South Africa was held in Norway, concluded by a declaration signed by members of a commission of inquiry representing a very broad spectrum of political, religious, trade union, and youth organisations. The declaration (separately presented to the seminar) gave its full support for the UN Programme of Action Against Apartheid passed in November, 1976, and the decisions at the Lagos conference, the main elements of which was a call for a complete isolation of South Africa, and considerably increased assistance to the liberation movements, whose heroic struggle was hailed. A similar hearing on South Africa was held in Denmark in March 1978.

Similarly, demands for the Scandinavian countries not to hesitate on isolation actions against South Africa because of the Western vetoes on mandatory sanctions in the Security Council, is expressed in the revived boycott movement against South Africa in all Scandinavian countries.

The solidarity organisations working for broadened direct political and economical support for the liberation movements gathered in Oslo in January 1978. There they unanimously expressed their demand that the Scandinavian governments pursue their actions against investments in South Africa, not only by stopping new investments but also by withdrawing previous investments, that actions be taken to stop the flights of the Scandinavian Airlines System to South Africa, that the Scandinavian countries should take actions to leave that small group of nations which still maintain diplomatic relations with South Afrca, and that support for the Patriotic Front in Zimbabwe, the ANC in South Africa and SWAPO in Namibia be considerably increased.[84]

When we advocate a disassociation from the imperialist strategy on southern Africa, we are thus not only engaging in and promoting a negative exercise, based on the unmasking of motives and scepticism of measures. The positive alternative policy is already there, formulated and broadly supported.

Notes

1. The paper as presented here is an abbreviated and revised version of the paper I presented at the seminar in Canada in February, 1978. The final revisions have been made at the end of September 1978. I am indebted to Lars Rudebeck for constructive criticism of the first version.

2. *The Kissinger Study of Southern Africa,* London, Spokesman books, 1975, p. 66–67.

3. *The Times,* London, April 28, 1976.

4. *Financial Mail,* November 5, 1976.

5. "Jimmy Carter on Africa", *Africa Report,* May-June 1976.

6. A South African study, quoted in *Southern Africa,* April 1977, p. 16. See also Ann and Neva Seidman, *U.S. Multinationals in Southern Africa,* Tanzania Publishing House, Dar es Salaam 1977, pp. 85–86 for a detailed table on the extent of U.S. dependence on South Africa for strategic minerals.

7. Quoted in R.W. Johnson, *How Long Will South Africa Survive?,* London, the MacMillan Press, 1977, p. 226.

8. Quoted by John Saul, "Transforming the struggle in Zimbabwe", *Southern Africa* (New York), Jan–Feb 1977.

9. *Africa Report,* May–June 1976, p. 20.

10. *Southern Africa* (New York), August 1977, p. 29.

11. *Financial Mail, loc. cit.*

12. Colin Legum, *Southern Africa; the Year of the Whirlwind,* London: Rex Collins, 1977, p. 32.

13. William Minter, "U.S. Policy in Angola and Mozambique", *Africa Today,* Vol. 23, No. 3, July–Sept 1976, pp. 58–59.

14. See for example *Washington Post,* May 19, 1978 and May 26, 1978.

15. Allen Isaacman, "U.S. Press Smears Mozambique", *Southern Africa,* August 1977, pp. 6–9.

16. *Ibid.,* p. 6.

17. *Southern Africa,* June–July 1978, p. 31.

18. Colin Legum, *op. cit.,* pp. 54–55.

19. *Rand Daily Mail,* June 26, 1978, reproduced in *Facts and Reports* item 1372.

20. *Southern Africa,* May 1977, p. 10.

21. Carolyn Fleuhr-Robban, "Zaire: the U.S.-Belgian-French Connection", *Southern Africa,* August 1977, p. 13.

22. *Loc. cit.*

23. See for example *Le Monde* 22.5.1978. The section on Shaba II is a summary of my article "Koppar, kobolt och kontrarevolution" (Copper, cobalt, and counterrevolution) in *Kommentar* (Stockholm), 5–6 1978.

24. "Que font les marocains au Shaba?", *Jeune Afrique* No. 918, 9.8. 1978.

25. *Daily Telegraph* (London), Feb. 14, 1977.

26. *Marchés tropicaux* (Paris), Feb. 4, 1977.

27. *Daily News* (Dar es Salaam), April 2, 1977.

28. *The Times,* Jan. 26, 1978.

29. AFP telegram, Feb. 8, 1977, quoted in *Facts and Reports,* 7th Vol., No. 5, March 9, 1977, item 498.

30. *The Times* (London), Nov. 26, 1977.

31. *International Herald Tribune,* Feb. 8, 1977.

32. *Southern Africa,* June–July 1977, p. 9.

33. See *Anti-Apartheid News* (London), June 1978, which quotes the Defense Minister of Rhodesia as saying that it was important that Sithole and Muzorewa were trying to bring in the terrorists. "Yes, we cannot kill them all off unfortunately," he had said.

34. Robert Manning, "The Transition to Zimbabwe: How U.S. Big Business Plans to Play", *New African Development,* Jan 1977, p. 19. Muzorewa visited U.S. in the summer of 1978 to ask for the repeal of sanctions. The proposal was narrowly defeated in Congress.

35. *Southern Africa,* May 1977, p. 13.

36. Stephen Talbot, "United States Intervention in southern Africa: The New Area", *Socialist Revolution* (San Fransisco), Nr. 34 (Vol. 7, No. 4), July–August 1977, p. 20.

Mai Palmberg

37. *Rand Daily Mail,* May 24, 1977.
38. Documents and summaries of this plan are presented in a "dossier" prepared at the Department of Peace and Conflict Research in Uppsala, Sweden in June 1977: *Documents on Colonialist Export from Southern Africa to Latin America.*
39. See William Johnston, "Namibia: 'A Sacred Trust of Civilization' ", *Africa Today,* Vol. 23, No. 3, July–Sept 1976, pp. 47–54.
40. Quoted in Johnston, *op. cit.,* p. 52.
41. *Rand Daily Mail,* "The Message from Vienna", May 24, 1977.
42. *Ibid.,* May 21, 1977.
43. *Africa Diary* (Quoted from *Daily Times,* Lagos), Jan 29 – Feb 4, 1977, pp. 8322–8323.
44. *Loc. cit.*
45. *Loc. cit.*
46. *International Herald Tribune,* Dec. 2, 1976.
47. Reproduced in *Solidarity* (Cairo), April–May 1977, pp. 32–44.
48. Interview with Reg September, *Anti-Apartheid News,* Dec. 1977.
49. Quoted in *Kommentar* (Stockholm), "Sydafrikansk imperialism, Oppenheimerimperiet – en okänd stormakt" (South African Imperialism, the Oppenheimer Empire, an unknown great power), No. 11, 1977, p. 23.
50. See Ann and Neva Seidman, op. cit. pp. 40–43 and *Kommentar* op. cit. pp. 16–23. Among the main sources for the *Kommentar* documentation are two parts of an unpublished thesis at the University of Essex by Duncan Innes, "The Anglo American Group of Companies" and "Anglo-American, the International Connection".
51. Ann and Neva Seidman, *op. cit.,* pp. 40, 88.
52. *Ibid.,* p. 41, 43.
53. *Kommentar,* No. 11, 1977, p. 19.
54. *Rand Daily Mail,* May 31, 1977.
55. *Anti-Apartheid News,* November 1977, p. 7.
56. *Svenska Dagbladet* (Stockholm), April 10, 1977.
57. *Republic of South Africa, Estimate of the Expenditure to be defrayed from State Revenue Account during the year ending 31 March 1977,* Pretoria 1976, p. 4/1.
58. *Republic of South Africa, Government Gazette,* Vol. 129, No. 5009.
59. "Army's Role Widened; New Threat to Africa", *Focus on Political Repression in southern Africa,* No. 3, March 1976, p. 3.
60. *The Star Weekly,* November 26, 1977.
61. J.M. Barry, Barclays National Bank Limited, Chairman's statement, *Financial Mail,* Dec. 23, 1977.
62. See Robert Manning in *New African Development,* December 1977, p. 1194.
63. *The Times,* Oct. 10, 1977, quoted in *African Communist,* "Imperialist Strategy in southern Africa", No. 72, First quarter 1978, p. 9 (their emphasis).
64. Seidman, *op. cit.,* p. 75.
65. *Rand Daily Mail,* May 25, 1977.
66. *Washington Post/The Guardian Weekly,* Jan. 8, 1978.
67. Sheila Pitterman, "A Fine Face for Apartheid", *Southern Africa* (New York), Sept. 1977.
68. *The Times,* Jan. 20, 1978.
69. *The Kissinger Study, op.cit.,* p. 81–82.
70. *The Financial Mail,* Sept. 30, 1977.
71. *Africa Diary,* April 2–8, 1977, p. 8414 (from the *Patriotic,* New Delhi).
72. *Financial Mail,* January 13, 1978, p. 63.
73. *Anti-Apartheid News* (London), December 1977, p. 3.
74. See Bob Atkinson, "UN arms embargo – will it really bite?", *New African Development,* January 1978, p. 85.
75. Certainly, there is a need for a closer examination of the existing gap and reality. It should be one of the concerns for the Scandinavian Institute of African Studies to encourage research into this. Unfortunately, so far, there has only been a publication on *Nordic Statements on Apartheid.*

76. Again repeated at the Foreign Minister's speech Nov. 16, 1976, to the Danish Parliament (Udenrigsministerens redegørelse i Folketinget den 16, November 1976 om Danmarks Afrika-politik, p. 3.).

77. *Ibid.,* p. 7.

78. *Udenrigsminister K.B. Andersens indlaeg den 27 september 1977 i generaldebatten under FN's 32. generalforsamling.*

79. *Udenrenrigsministernes redegørelse i Folketinget den 18. November 1977* (mimeo),, p. 2.

80. *Ibid.,* p. 3.

81. *Ibid.,* p. 6.

82. Tor Oftedal at the UN October 1976, speech reproduced in *Nordic Statements on Apartheid,* Uppsala, The Scandinavian Institute of African Studies and the United Nations' Centre against Apartheid, 1977, p. 11.

83. *Ibid.,* p. 12.

84. The participating organisations were the Norwegian Council for Southern Africa, The Norwegian Students' International Support Fund, the Norwegian Festival Committee, the Danish section of the World University Service, the Danish League against imperialism, Internationalt Forum (Denmark), the South Africa Committee of Århus (Denmark), The Africa groups of Sweden, and the Finnish Africa committee.

IV. Canadian Policies and Policymaking

Donald C. Jamieson

Canada's Attitude toward Southern Africa

As the Prime Minister indicated in the House some two weeks ago on December 5, Canada, along with a great many other countries, has been re-examining the attitude it ought to take beyond what has already been undertaken in South Africa to which we in Canada take the strongest possible objection, and with which we – and I am sure this extends well beyond the government of Canada – are in major disagreement.

It is true, of course, that in other countries of the world there are clear violations of and disregard for human rights. There, too, Canada is expressing its concern, as are all members of this House. South Africa stands alone. It is the only country which as a basic part of its government structure – whether it is constitutional in the legal sense is beside the point – has a declared and unequvocal policy. It stands apart as a country which makes decisions affecting human beings on the basis of race and colour. Therefore, over time it is not surprising that the attitude of the vast majority of the countries of the world has become harder, particularly during these past months when we have seen an increase in the amount of repression, rioting and especially in the disturbances which followed the still unexplained death of a respectable and respected black leader of South Africa, Steve Biko.

Along with others, Canada has been asking what further steps we ought to take in order to display and to demonstrate our disapproval of the present regime and our disapproval of apartheid. We strongly believe that what must come in South Africa is the destruction of that kind of system, the introduction of the principle of one man, one vote and of the normal democratic process which all of us in this part of the world take for granted.

I am, therefore, announcing today that Canada is phasing out all its government-sponsored, commercially-supported activities in South Africa.

For example, we will as quickly as possible withdraw our commercial counsellors from Johannesburg and close the office of the consulate general in that city. We will also withdraw our commercial officers from Cape Town. We will, of course, maintain our offices in Pretoria for normal business, because we do not feel that the breaking off of diplomatic relations at this time is advisable. We wish to still have an opportunity to do what we can in order to impress upon the government of South Africa the necessity for change. We also want to have an opportunity to talk to respected leaders who are opposed to apartheid in South Africa.

In addition to this phasing out of our commercial activities, we will also withdraw all Export Development Corporation government account support from any transactions relating to South Africa. This involves, for example, export credit insurance and loan insurance, as well as foreign investment type of insurance. This is a step which is not as complete as what may very well come in time. We are examining the implications and the possibilities for other such actions. After consultation with the Canadian companies concerned, we will be publishing a code of conduct and ethics for Canadian companies operating in South Africa, designed to govern their employment and similar practices. This will be done as quickly as possible.

The fourth measure is related to South Africa's former membership in the Commonwealth which we now propose to change. From a date to be announced, we will require non-immigrant visas from all residents of South Africa coming to Canada. We have asked the appropriate officials to examine the impact and the capacity that is open to us to renounce the British preferential tariff. It is still in effect even though the Commonwealth membership of South Africa has long since ceased to exist.

In addition to all of these measures, we are very much concerned about two other aspects of South Africa and South African operations, namely, the activities of Canadian companies in Namibia. Once again, we have asked the officials of the Department of Finance and others to as quickly as possible look into all the implications of possible tax concessions and the like which these companies may be obtaining and which are being provided by what is essentially an illegal regime in Namibia, by our standards and by our demonstrated conduct at the United Nations.

We are also establishing possible codes of conduct for further investment by Canadians in Namibia. It may be asked – I am sure it will be – why these measures are not introduced immediately. There are two reasons: first, we want to be very sure that we do not penalize Canadian companies which may have been active in that country under legitimate and perfectly acceptable processes. Nevertheless, there is unquestionably an incongruity in a situation which permits an illegal regime, by world definition, to be participating with Canadian companies in the manner I have outlined.

There is a second reason why we are withholding, for the time being, any further action. We continue to hope that a means will be found of ensuring that there is a peaceful and satisfactory solution for Namibia, one that will bring about equality – one man, one vote. We hope this can be done through negotiations and the process in which Canada is participating, which relates to the five western members of the Security Council talking with the government of South Africa and the other parties concerned.

In the process of making this statement and of expressing my hope for a peaceful outcome in Namibia, it is also Canada's hope and wish that the black leadership there, as elsewhere in South Africa, will show its own high level of responsibility. We hope it will do everything reasonable and possible to bring about transition by peaceful means, rather than plunge another region on the tragic continent into the kind of bloodshed we have seen repeated over and over again in recent years.

There is one final point. We will keep the whole South African situation under review. We are moving now to make sure that our own embargo against sales of arms to South Africa is on all fours with the recent declaration of the Security Council which placed an international embargo on arms shipments. This is the first time in the history of the United Nations that such an embargo has been imposed on a member state. I believe this is a step in the direction which it is inevitable and appropriate for us to take. I re-emphasize that we will keep the whole South African situation under review.

I could take time to discuss in considerable detail such questions as Rhodesia. I will simply say, in the interest of saving time, that we are very closely in touch and in tune with the efforts now under way, particularly those of the Anglo-American initiative to once again bring about a peaceful transition in Zimbabwe, or Rhodesia, whichever you wish to call it. We are looking with great interest at the most recent steps taken by Prime Minister Ian Smith. We can only hope that he has made fully legitimate commitments and that he is, indeed, prepared to take all the steps necessary to ensure a peaceful transition there. The situation is extremely complex. There are two major factors: Mr. Nkomo's forces located outside of Rhodesia, and the issue as to how they are to be dealt with in any negotiation. That continues to be a serious issue.

In so far as Canada is concerned, we have made no commitments as of this moment with regard to Canadian participation in any possible settlement arrangements for Rhodesia. We have said, provided the circumstances are right – and if, indeed, the provision of a peacekeeping force with a Canadian component in it would serve to bring about this peaceful transition – that we would then be prepared to look at it most sympathetically. Indeed, we would not be the party that would stand in the way of bringing about that resolution. So far no request has been made, no specific proposal has come forward. The same is true in the case of Namibia. (House of Commons December 19, 1977)

Donald C. Jamieson

Appendix

Code of Conduct Concerning the Employment Practices of Canadian Companies Operating in South Africa

In South Africa there are policies, legislation and practices based on the principle of racial discrimination which are repugnant to Canadians, and which the Canadian Government has condemned as contrary to internationally-accepted standards of human rights. Many Canadians are concerned about the extent to which companies identified with Canada are involved in South Africa in an economic system based on racial discrimination.

The Canadian Government has noted that a number of Canadian companies have already shown leadership in establishing programs to improve the working conditions of the non-White employees of their affiliates in South Africa. It strongly hopes that every Canadian company active in that country will promote employment practices which are based on the principle of equal treatment for all its employees, and which are consistent with basic human rights and the general economic welfare of all people in South Africa. While these objectives are applicable to all employees, they have particular relevance to the employment conditions of Black African workers. The Government believes that, by promoting the achievement of these objectives, Canadian companies will be able to make an important contribution towards improving the working conditions generally of Black and other non-White workers in South Africa.

The Government commends to Canadian companies the Declaration adopted unanimously in 1973 by the Executive Committee of the International Organization of Employers. Among its other provisions this declaration "appeals to the Republic of South Africa to fulfill its obligations in respect of human rights and to repeal its discriminatory legislation with the aim of giving equal rights and protection of those rights to all workers and in particular by guaranteeing: –
– equality of opportunity in respect of admission to employment and training;
– equality in conditions of work and respect for the principle of equal pay for equal work; and
– freedom of association and the right to organize and collective bargaining".

The Declaration also appeals "to all employers in South Africa to take urgent measures to promote the conditions necessary for acceptance of the well established standards in the field of human rights approved by the International Labour Organization". The Government believes Canadian companies should implement the above-mentioned principles of the Declaration of the International Organization of Employers, which were reaffirmed by the I.O.E. in June, 1977.

Accordingly, it is the view of the Canadian Government that:

(1) *General Working Conditions*
    – in general companies should improve the overall work situation of Black employees to the fullest extent possible, and ensure that employment practices applicable to any group of workers are equally applicable to all workers.

(2) *Collective Bargaining*
    – companies should ensure that their employees are free to organize collective bargaining units that can effectively represent them, and undertake to engage in collective bargaining with such units in accordance with internationally-accepted principles. As companies are aware, under South African law Black trade unions are not "registered trade unions" officially empowered to negotiate industrial council agreements, but such organizations are not illegal. Companies should extend customary basic rights to such bargaining units, i.e. to organize for the purpose of negotiation, to solicit support among employees, to disseminate trade union information material, and to engage in other traditional trade union activities on company premises.

(3) *Wages*
    – companies should ameliorate the effects of the job reservation and job classification system by implementing the principle of "equal pay for equal work" – i.e. the staffing of and remuneration for a position should be based on the qualifications of an individual and not on his racial origin. They should also strive to provide remuneration sufficient to assist their Black employees in particular to achieve a standard of living significantly above the minimum level required to meet their basic needs. The Canadian Government endorses the widely accepted guideline that the minimum wage should initially exceed this minimum level by at least 50%.

(4) *Fringe Benefits*
    – companies should provide to Black workers improved fringe benefits such as contributory medical and pension plans, disability insurance schemes, sick leave benefits and annual vacations. Companies should ensure that any benefit available to one group of employees is available to all employees. The Canadian Government encourages companies to assist in providing for their staff adequate medical and health facilities for them and their families, transportation to and from their place of work, adequate housing, education for their children, and other social services such as legal assistance and unemployment.

(5) *Training and Promotion*
    – companies should provide training programs and job opportunities to facilitate the movement of Blacks into semi-skilled and skilled positions and introduce Blacks to supervisory positions on an accelerated basis, rather than recruiting expatriate personnel.

Donald C. Jamieson

(6) *Race Relations*
   – companies should, to the fullest extent possible, integrate their working, dining, recreational, educational and training facilities. Companies should seek the advice and assistance of such South African organizations as the Institute of Race Relations and the National Development and Management Foundation which have done extensive studies of the problem of worker productivity and efficiency and which can provide invaluable advice on ways to find solutions which benefit both workers and companies.

The Canadian Government intends to follow developments closely. Canadian companies operating in South Africa should make annual public reports in sufficient detail to permit assessment of their progress in realizing the objectives of the Code of Conduct. (Department of External Affairs, *Communiqué* April 28, 1978.)

Georges Blouin

Canadian Policy Toward Southern Africa: The Decision-Making Process

As you know the Secretary of State for External Affairs announced on December 19, 1977, a series of policy decisions regarding Southern Africa. As you also may know this was the only review which had been made since 1970 about South Africa.

Why was it decided in 1977 to make a review of policy towards Southern Africa? What were the main elements in the decision-making process which we had to consider in making this policy review? And finally what are the prospects for evolution of future policies? I will comment on these three points in sequence.

It was decided to review our policy towards Southern Africa in 1977 because the area had become a major focus of international concern. South Africa's *apartheid* policies were coming under even stronger international attack. The long-stalemated situations in Namibia and Rhodesia were moving towards either negotiated settlements or much increased violence and important shifts were underway in the positions of Western countries, particularly the U.S.A. These shifts became evident when on November 4, 1977, for the first time in the history of the U.N., the Security Council, with the active co-operation of its Western members and acting under Chapter VII of the U.N. Charter, unanimously adopted a mandatory arms embargo against a member state, South Africa. Canada's election to the U.N. Security Council for a two-year term beginning January 1977, also imposed on us special responsibilities and had the effect of giving a higher "profile" to our policies in Africa. Thus we would be required to share in the very serious decision which the Council would make if it ruled that South Africa's policies and acts were "a threat to international peace and security" opening the way to possible mandatory economic sanctions and isolating economically South Africa from the world community. Finally, groups of concerned Canadians, particularly in Church and academic circles, were criticizing the Government more sharply for what they claimed to be a lack of coherence in our Southern African policies. Therefore we had to place ourselves in a position to respond to these new realities.

As you surmise, I am sure, the nature of the review which has been done on our Southern African policies has been a complex undertaking. It involved no less than nine federal government departments – although those principally concerned were External Affairs, Finance and Industry, Trade and Commerce. It was natural that officials often disagreed with each other even within each department – since of course, they frequently represented equally valid, but quite different, interests and points of view. Thus it was not easy to reach a consensus. And, when officials had finally made their recommendations, the whole subject was again very carefully considered by Cabinet.

The main elements which we had to consider, to put in the balance so-to-speak, were, on one hand, the Canadian domestic elements and, on the other, the elements which have international ramifications. The frst ones were:
– the concepts of social justice and of basic human rights;
– the public opinion in Canada
– our economic interests in South Africa
while the second group included:
– our relations with Black African States;
– our relations with the principal Western states and close allies involved in the area (U.S.A., Great Britain, France and West Germany);
– the credibility of the U.N. and particularly the Security Council as effective instruments of peace and justice in the world.

I would now like to analyse and to weigh for you these elements in order to assess the wisdom of our decisions.

On the domestic front, the element which was in the forefront of our considerations was the whole question of social justice and human rights. For 30 years successive Canadian Governments have condemned South Africa's *apartheid* policies as being unacceptable. The events in South Africa last autumn, including the death of Steve Biko and the crackdown on dissenters of October 19, provided further evidence of even more repressive attitude by the Government of that country. Thus it was now necessary to send a clear signal to South Africa that time for peaceful change was running out. What is particularly repugnant to us is that South Africa's political and legal system is explicitly built on social discrimination. No doubt there are gross violations of human rights in many other countries, but in no other state but South Africa does the constitution actually *guarantee* the permanent violation of such rights. This situation is thus unique. Clearly the Canadian Government cannot be indifferent to violations of human rights anywhere. However, if we did nothing against South Africa, how could we justify measures against other countries which violate human rights?

As to public opinion in Canada it is clearly divided on the question of South Africa. In certain quarters – particularly perhaps in Church and academic circles – our policies had been often attacked as being inadequate or incoherent. (How could they be? Our policies are never incoherent!) In other quarters, particularly in the business community, it was thought that we were already being too severe to South Africa. Certain groups particularly concerned with human rights situations elsewhere (for example in the U.S.S.R., Argentina, Chile, etc.) were arguing that the Government should take the kind of action against these countries that it is taking against South Africa. You can readily understand that all these aspects of public opinion had to be analysed before submissions were made.

Another important domestic element was our economic interest in South Africa.

Our exports to South Africa, $96 million in 1976, are larger than to any other African country but have not been growing appreciably over the years. The economic effects of withdrawing the availability of EDC and other Government export promotion facilities, removing the work of two commercial offices in the country, etc., could not be estimated with any certainty. The answer would depend partly on what steps would be taken by our competitors, many of whom have larger trade representation and promotional activities in South Africa than we do. However, it was relevant that 80% of Canadian exports to South Africa are fabricated goods with substantial labour input – a not unimportant consideration in a country such as ours, with a serious unemployment problem. Therefore because of political uncertainties and external pressures, South Africa appeared to be declining in relative economic importance. Nevertheless, it would have been unrealistic to expect that curtailment of our trade with that country would bring countervailing gains in the rest of the continent. It was also necessary to bear in mind the long-established tradition in this country of the Government not interfering in private trade. The only real exception to this rule has been in the case of Rhodesia where the Government imposed an economic boycott because of the mandatory sanctions adopted by the U.N. Security Council under Chapter VII of the Charter.

Let us now examine the elements which had an international factor. As you well know Canada's relationship with the countries of Black Africa is an important aspect of our foreign policy. It is a fact that historical circumstances have combined with certain domestic concerns to create strong Canadian links with many of these countries. Both with African countries of the Commonwealth and with those of *la Francophonie* the past decade, at least, has seen the development of close personal relations with African leaders and important development aid ties, as well as prospects for increased trade and cultural relations. We believe – are we being naive? – that Canada is perceived in Africa as being one of the more progressive of Western nations. We have no colonial past; and it is useful in this context that our two official languages are those which are understood by many Africans. Therefore due concern for African opinion was certainly an important factor in the equation.

It was also clear that, if economic pressure was to have any real impact on South Africa, it would have to be concerted among those Western countries which are South Africa's major trading partners: Britain, France, the U.S.A. and West Germany. It is in Canada's national interest to co-ordinate and move broadly in parallel with these countries, which are at the same time our commercial competitors and our political allies vis-à-vis South Africa. The trend of opinion among the majority of Western Governments is that business-as-usual with South Africa was no longer a sustainable policy; however, the timing and pace of pressures pose problems. Excess pressure, as well as inadequate pressure, could equally have undesirable results. There was no doubt also that the serious negotiations on Namibia and Rhodesia which had been going on for a considerable time had to be taken into account in regard to the timing and the amount of pressure to be exerted on South Africa.

Finally, Southern African questions have been before the U.N. for 30 years. If, due to lack of support at the present crucial juncture, the organization cannot help to bring about peaceful change in the area, the third of its membership which is African will regard it as irrelevant to their problems. Furthermore, as I mentioned earlier, Canada's membership on the Security Council imposed on us special responsibilities.

Those were the main domestic and international elements we had to weigh before making recommendations. There is one element which I have not mentioned specifically although it supports all the others. That is: Canada's national interest. You might say that this goes without saying. However, I think it should be said and quite strongly. After all, practical realities make it imperative that foreign policies have to be based first and foremost on national interest.

Although it is difficult for me to foresee with any degree of reality what the prospects for evolution of future policies are, I believe that they will still be governed by the main issues which concerned us during our review in 1977. It would interest you in this respect to know that the decisions announced on December 19 have been well received in some quarters and not as well in others. You are, of course, aware of the mixed reaction in the House of Commons, with the NDP generally favourable and the Conservatives making the "double standard" argument. In the Senate a pointed question on the "double standard" theme was tabled. From the Canadian public and from Church, civic and labour groups we have received about 150 letters and telegrams. That mail was divided almost evenly. About 50 per cent of our correspondents applauded the new policy and the same number disagreed with it. Many of those who agreed said, however, that it was only a good "first step" and that we should eventually go further. Many who disagreed took the line that we were guilty of a "double standard". They asked why we picked on South Africa when there are violations of human rights in other countries such as Chile, Argentina, the U.S.S.R., etc. Some also said that we were trying to bring down "enlightened White rule" in favour of "Black dictatorship" which would probably be "pro-Communist". Editorial reaction in Canadian newspapers has not been extensive and has been generally confined to the major Ontario and Quebec newspapers. However, editorial reaction was in general more favourable than unfavourable. Therefore this public reaction seems to indicate, on one hand, the degree of interest in Canada about Southern African questions and, on the other, a split practically in the middle between the ones in favour and the ones against our new policy decisions.

Unless therefore there are dramatic changes in South Africa and in Black Africa, and unless there are profound domestic changes in the political climate in Canada, I foreseee no significant changes in the political climate in Canada, I foresee no significant change in our policies but a continuation of practical steps in the direction of the policy announced on December 19. The situation is a developing one and it would be unwise, I think, to be dogmatic.

Let me conclude by saying that I have not sought today to persuade you of the correctness of our decisions but to give you an insight into the various elements we had to take into consideration in the course of this complex and important review. As a group of scholars who by definition look at all the factors in any given problem this is the least you could expect from me. I hope I have succeeded in giving you a clear picture.

Robert Matthews and Cranford Pratt

Canadian Policy Towards Southern Africa

It will be the argument of this paper that the interaction of four factors very largely determined the policies and actions of the Government of Canada in regard to southern Africa. These four factors are: (a) a deeply entrenched and largely unexamined set of ideological perceptions through which the government and the Department of External Affairs understand. Canadian national interest and also the issues relating to Southern Africa; (b) a self-image of Canada as a middle power which is accepted by the Third World as honest, sensitive, and neutral; (c) a particular responsiveness to the interests in southern Africa of Canada's major allies, the United States and Britain, and to what are loosely conceived as the interests of the "West"; and, finally, (d) a greater empathy towards Canadian economic interests which are involved in South Africa than to the much more substantial groups that have called for a more vigorous and just Canadian policy and a decision making process that is largely closed to non-governmental interests, but which is more accessible to business interests.

We are not at all contending that but for the influence of these factors, Canada would have vigorously supported the liberation movements. States do not usually dispense moral judgements concerning internal politics of other states nor do they aid armed efforts to overthrow foreign governments. That Canada has not rushed forward to send military assistance or to train guerillas hardly requires any special explanation. Rather what we are seeking is an explanation of the timid policies followed by Canada, in contrast with those pursued by the Scandinavian states, after African states had made South African internal repression an important issue at the United Nations and in the Commonwealth. We suggest this explanation can be found in the influence and interaction of these four factors. Before looking at each of these in turn we will outline briefly what Canadian policies are, how they have developed over time and the Government's own explanation of these policies.

Canadian Policies Towards Southern Africa 1945–1960

Canada's policies towards southern Africa have evolved since 1945 in response to Ottawa's changing perception of its domestic and international interests in that area. In fact, the evolution of our policy can usefully be divided into two periods, the

164

first lasting from the conclusion of World War Two until roughly 1960 and the second extending from then until the present.

Initially most of southern Africa was dominated by the European colonial powers. In the spirit of its newly enunciated principle of functionalism Ottawa considered that colonialism fell outside its competence. As long as the administering powers accepted in good faith an obligation to promote self-government for their dependent territories, Canadian spokesmen argued that Canada could not and, indeed, should not do anything to upset the slow process of constitutional evolution that would eventually result in independence.[1] Even if there was good reason to question the sincerity of British and French pledges to grant independence to their colonies – the Algerian revolution had begun in 1954 and the Central African Federation was formed in 1955 – Ottawa was simply not prepared to embarrass its allies in the North Atlantic Treaty Organization. The imperatives of the struggle against the Soviet Union weighed more heavily in Canada's calculations at this time than did any interest in accelerating the process of decolonization.

During this period it was only in South Africa that Canada had any direct interests at all. With the establishment of Canadian commercial offices in Cape Town (1907) and Johannesburg (1934) trade between these two countries flourished. Although insignificant by comparison to American and European markets, South Africa has since 1945 become one of Canada's ten most important markets in the world. In addition to this trade Canada and South Africa shared a common interest in fighting against Germany in both world wars and in securing dominion autonomy and independence from London. In the context of the Cold War South Africa's geographical location was viewed as having strategic value for the West.

These specific interests were in part offset by Ottawa's embarrassment at being associated with a country whose policies were increasingly becoming the centre of controversy at both the United Nations and the Commonwealth. However, as long as South Africa was a member of the Commonwealth and the anti-colonial forces remained relatively weak, Ottawa pursued a policy of "disinterested detachment". The United Nations could, it was argued, quite properly discuss South Africa's treatment of Indians, the National Government's policy of *apartheid* and Pretoria's control of South West Africa, but it could not effectively "intervene" in these matters. What this meant was that Ottawa voted for only those bland resolutions that condemned racism in the world or called upon South Africa and India to settle their differences peacefully but abstained on or voted against any stronger or more pointed recommendations.

By 1960, however, the international environment had so changed that such a policy of studied aloofness towards colonial and South African related issues no longer served Canada's interests. The expectations of the early 1950s that decolonization would take place over a period of 40 to 50 years had to be altered as 16 newly independent states were admitted in that year membership in the United Nations. Together with the Soviet bloc the new states of Africa and Asia were to press at the 15th General Assembly of the UN for the passage of a Declaration on the Granting of Independence to Colonial Countries and Peoples, which recognized the right of all peoples to self-determination and the obligation of all colonial powers immediately to transfer power to their dependent peoples, "without conditions or reservations". If Canada and other Western powers failed to move with the changing tide of forces, it was feared in Ottawa that the Soviet Union might employ the colonial issue at the UN as a means of fostering an anti-Western attitude among the new states.

The Portugese Territories since 1961
The outbreak of African revolt in Angola in April 1961 marked a turning point in the struggle against Portuguese colonialism. Canada could no longer hide behind the legal provisions of the UN Charter. For the first time it supported a resolution that openly condemned one of its allies and that recognized the right of the Angolan people to self-determination. In the years that followed Canada found it increasingly difficult not to support resolutions that annually became more severely critical of Portugal and that annually expanded the range of their demands. The intensity and growing influence of the anti-colonial campaign coupled with Portugese intransigence left Canada little alternative but to vote on the side of the angels. To its credit Canada, even before the Security Council recommendation of 1963 suspended shipments of arms to Portugal under the NATO mutual aid program and commercial sales if, in the government's judgement, they "would be used for military purposes in Portugal's overseas territories."

Beyond the use of moral suasion and the imposition of a voluntary arms embargo, however, Ottawa would not move. It rejected the argument that our common membership with Portugal in NATO was inconsistent with our verbal attack on Portugal's colonial policy, even when our military assistance program in Tanzania was compromised by this security arrangement.[1] It consistently opposed the use of diplomatic sanctions on the grounds that this would isolate Portugal from the salutary influence of world opinion and therefore harden rather than soften her stance. It strongly resisted any consideration of economic sanctions, since in all probability they would be ineffective, counterproductive and, thus, unnecessarily costly to Canada. Furthermore, unless the Security Council formally decided that the situation in Portugal's African colonies constituted a threat to international peace and security, Canada was not prepared to break off commercial relations with any country. To do so would set a precedent which the Canadian government regarded as unfortunate and which it felt a country such as Canada could ill afford.

Finally, Ottawa expressed its opposition to "violent solutions" and, for this reason, refused to recognize the legitimacy of the liberation movements and to extend any assistance to them. It was only belatedly (at the Commonwealth Conference held in Ottawa in August 1973) and somewhat half-heartedly (goods rather than funds were to be made available and those only indirectly through Canadian nongovernmental organizations) that the government gave in to external and domestic pressures and agreed to offer "humanitarian assistance" to all those engaged in the struggle for self-determination. By the time Parliament had reviewed this government proposal the Salazar regime had been overthrown and independence for Portugal's African colonies had been assurred.

Rhodesia since 1961
It was not until 1962, when the question of Rhodesia was first placed on the agenda of the UN General Assembly that Ottawa had to adopt an official position. At that point and since then Canada has expressed its support for the objective of ultimate majority rule and for British policy, which Canada publically has regarded as working "faithfully" towards that end. Canada consistently supported the British on Rhodesia, arguing that as long as it was felt that Southern Rhodesia was moving in the right direction, Canada should oppose any action that was likely to upset the delicate negotiations then proceeding between the British government and Rhodesia's white leaders. Ottawa approved the proposal advanced at the Commonwealth Conference in 1964 to threaten Rhodesia with economic sanctions if it unilaterally declared its independence (UDI) and encouraged the British to adopt a menacing military stance in 1965, but both these steps were seen in Ottawa as ways of strengthening London's hand at the bargaining table.

Ian Smith's declaration of independence on November 11, 1965, changed the situation dramatically. Nevertheless Canada has continued to be very supportive of Britain regard to Rhodesia. Canada's initial moves never went beyond what Britain herself was willing to do. Along with almost every member of the UN Canada condemned UDI, announced its intention not to recognize the so-called independent state of Rhodesia, closed its commercial office in Salisbury and gradually broke off all commercial and financial relations. Given the intensity of world outrage at UDI, especially within the Commonwealth, it was virtually inconceivable that Ottawa could have behaved otherwise. In due course, Ottawa supported and applied the economic sanctions which were made mandatory by the Security Council. That action also was entirely in step with British initiatives.

Even the minor fluctuations in Canada's policy on Rhodesia seem to be closely related to British interests. On occasion, for example, Ottawa has backtracked from its original endorsement of the principle of NIBMAR (no independence before majority African rule) and has chosen instead to support successive British governments in their various attempts to reach a settlement with the Smith regime that fell short of this aim – in 1966, 1969 and again in 1971–72. Canada has also refused to entertain the use of force to bring down the white regime. Recognizing that moral suasion would not be sufficient, Ottawa supported the British effort in 1966 and in 1968 to press for economic sanctions as the most effective and least painful way of achieving the desired result. As long as the British were unable and the superpowers unwilling to underwrite the militay invasion of Rhodesia, Canada could (and would) not advocate such a step. This pattern has continued in recent months when Canada has supported the Owen-Young initiatives to bring a settlement in Rhodesia.

South Africa since 1961
During this same period Canada has adjusted its stance on South Africa's racial policy as well as on her control of Namibia. As it became all too obvious that the Nationalist regime in Pretoria was unprepared to make concessions to legitimate black demands and even to permit non-white opposition to voice its dissent through peaceful channels, Ottawa found it difficult to remain aloof, no longer protected by the legal provisions of the UN Charter or the Commonwealth tradition of noninterference in the affairs of a fellow member. Indeed, by the time of the 1961 Commonwealth Conference it had become obvious to even the Canadians that South Africa's policy of apartheid was inconsistent with the multiracial character of the new Commonwealth. South Africa's hasty withdrawal in March 1961 was the inevitable outcome.

Since then successive governments in Ottawa have never hesitated to voice their abhorrence of apartheid and to join with most UN members in calling upon South Africa to reverse its discriminatory policies. Shortly after coming to power in 1963 the Pearson Government carried out the Security Council's request for a ban on the sale and shipment of arms, ammunition and military vehicles to South Africa. In November 1970 Trudeau extended this embargo to include military spare parts.

In a manner exactly paralleling its stance on Portugal's colonial policy Canada has sided with most other Western countries in resisting the use of force and the imposition of economic and financial sanctions against South Africa as well as her diplomatic banishment from the UN and other international organizations. Ottawa's public justification for rejecting such policies closely resembles the arguments advanced in the Portuguese case. For instance, it is suggested that the maintenance of contact with South Africa, whether through diplomatic representatives or trade and other economic relations, is more likely to promote progressive changes within that country than its effective isolation from the world. The isolation of South Africa, so the argument continues, would mean that opponents of the present regime would lose the moral and material support they had previously secured. In addition, the argument concludes, such a policy of deliberately isolating South Africa both economically and diplomatically would affect most adversely the very people it was designed to serve, the non-white majority.

If all these arguments fail to convince the suspicious observer, the responsible ministers and officials in Ottawa then produce another. Even if Canada faithfully carried out the wishes of the UN majority, many others would not. Canadians might therefore pride themselves on their righteous behavior, while others would profit at their expense. Finally, they pull out two farther arguments. As a country so dependent on trade for its well-being, Canada, they argue cannot possibly afford to break off commercial relations with South Africa, even though the latter country's policies are abhorrent and even if trade with South Africa is relatively unimportant. Secondly the claim, that as so many Canadian are recent immigrants from countries that have repressive regimes, the Canadian Government would be overwhelmed with demands for similar actions if it were to take any strong action against South Africa. What matters above all else in each of these 2 final arguments is the precedent; once Pandora's Box is pried open, no one can possibly shut it again.

Namibia since 1961

Canada's position on Namibia has shifted from one of demanding international accountability to that of insisting on self-government and ultimate independence. When the World Court dismissed the South West African cases in the summer of 1966 Canada voted along with the vast majority of other states to declare South Africa's mandate over that territory terminated, as South Africa had, by her actions, forfeited the moral and legal right to continue the mandate. In accordance with the Court's Advisory Opinion of June 21, 1971 Ottawa informed Pretoria one month later that it no longer recognized South Africa's jurisdiction over Namibia and made known to the Canadian business community that it was unwilling to assist or provide advice to companies' that might wish to trade with or invest in that territory.

This shift in government policy on Namibia has, however, been minimal, carried out only to the extent that the moral and legal dictates of the world community absolutely required. Thus a Canadian mining company, Falconbridge, continues to operate in Namibia, to pay taxes to South Africa and to secure tax credits for the payments under Canadian tax laws. Ottawa's attachment to peaceful rather than violent change has meant that it has observed an ambivalent position vis-à-vis groups like SWAPO that have come to the conclusion that liberation can only be won through the barrel of a gun. The position Ottawa has adopted during the recent discussions held between the five Western powers in the Security Council and South Africa has never been made public. Given our past record, however, this participation by Canada must be seen primarily as an effort to manage, in ways compatible with western capitalist interests, the changes in Namibia that are now unavoidable.

Summary Overview

Canada has thus modified its original stance on Southern African issues from a position of disinterest and detachment to one of modest involvement consistent with the consensus as it enfolded with its major allies, the UK and the USA. The federal government, Conservative and Liberal alike, developed a set of arguments to justify its more active involvement in Southern Africa since 1960 as well as its essential timidity. Taken together these arguments provide what we consider a superficial explanation of Canadian policy. They are outlined briefly here in juxtaposition to our explanation offered below.

Simply put, the official position of successive Canadian governments runs as follows: whatever government is in power in Ottawa is obliged by Canada's ethical values to condemn colonialism and the principle of racial domination on which the rule in Rhodesia and South Africa is founded.' However, Canadians cannot endorse and will not support any groups which advocate violent and abrupt change, no matter how desirable their final objective. Only in extreme instances, when the United Nations, including those with the principal responsibility as well as effective power, decides that a situation exists which constitutes a threat to international peace and security, only then will Ottawa accept the necessity of imposing sanctions (economic or military) against another state in the international system. But such a step should not be taken lightly and only after every other possible alternative has been explored. In most situations then, the Government of Canada should not obstruct the flow of peaceful goods and services that normally takes place among states and should avoid offering significant assistance in any violent conflict.

The Factors Determining Canadian Policy

Canadian policies towards Southern Africa cannot be explained in terms of the involvement there of any national interest which is of such importance that it has had a determining influence. No major Canadian economic, strategic or political interest is involved in Southern Africa. Our trade with South Africa is unimportant; our exports to South Africa actually declined in recent years as a proportion of our total exports. There are a few investments that are important to the Corporations involved, but, seen nationally, Canadian investment in South Africa is very nearly negligible. Canadian strategic interests in the security of the Indian Ocean trade routes are insignificant and Canadian ethnic and cultural links with South Africa are tenuous. Nevertheless, the Canadian Government has given closer attention to this component of its foreign policy than to other components that also touch no major interest. It has done so, it is safe to say, very largely because many African states are tending to judge the sincerity of foreign states' commitment to racial equality by their policies towards Southern Africa. The force of this consideration has been increased by the fact that Southern African issues have caused deep divisions in the Commonwealth and Canada has been pressed to define its position in more detail than it would have likely done had the issue not had this Commonwealth dimension.

All this has meant that the Canadian Government has had a wide margin of discretion in the development of its policies towards Southern Africa. No doubt at either end of the spectrum of possible policies there were actions which it could not take without generating strong Canadian reactions. For example, it is hard to imagine that the Canadian Government could have decided to send military advisers or even military assistance to the liberation movements without generating a strong and hostile public reaction. Hopefully also public reaction would also have made it hard for the Government to endorse apartheid. However, within quite wide limits, the Government has been free to develop a policy without much likelihood of any major political reaction.

If this is true, then the policies of the Canadian Government have been the product of the judgement and the political morality of the Department of External Affairs and of the Government, acting very largely on their own, free of any sustained and compelling Canadian pressures. What then has shaped their decisions?

Alan Wolfe has argued recently in his powerful and perceptive *The Limits of Legitimacy* that the ruling elites in late capitalist societies tend "to become more ideological as the basis of their rule becomes more and more pragmatic."[6] There is, he observes a worship of power itself rather than of the ends for which power might be used; a denial of the depth and reality of the injustices that are a consequence of capitalism and a naive utopianism about the technocratic, post-industrial society. His analysis can easily be transposed to illuminate the attitude and belief system of those who have shaped Canadian policy towards southern Africa.

Firstly, there is a central and unquestioned concern to maximize Canadian influence and power within the international community. John Holmes, an excellent and fluent expositor of the foreign policy ideas of our ruling elite, has written that "Canada, as much as older nations, has a national interest in maintaining as strong an international position as it can acquire."[7] This requires that Canada maintains cordial relations with as wide a range of countries as can be done. In a manner paralleling the process observed by Wolfe in regard to pragmatism in internal politics, the emphasis has become much more on the accumulation of a capacity to influence events than on the ends for which that power has been carefully garnered. An impatient hostility is often shown towards those who focus instead on the ends to be served by this Canadian power.[8] Those who are concerned that our foreign policy should reflect the liberal and humanitarian values which, at its best, are features of our culture are dismissed as bleeding hearts.

Nevertheless, Canadian policy has not been devoid of a concern for wider objectives than merely the argumentation of Canadian power and had been influenced by factors that go beyond the dictates of the narrow objective.

It was suggested in the introduction to this paper that there have been four influences which have very largely determined the policies and actions of the Government of Canada in regard to Southern Africa.[9] These four influences are: (a) the ideological perceptions with which the Government and the Department "understand" Canadian national interests and the issues relating to South Africa; (b) the image of Canada's role in international politics which is widely held within the Government and the Department; (c) a particular responsiveness to Canada's major allies, the United States and Britain, and the interests of "the West", and finally, (d) a sense of common cause with Canadian economic interests which are involved in South Africa. We will look at each of these in turn and then test their explanatory powers when considered together.

a) *Ideological influences.* The processes and decision-making that shape Canadian foreign power is an unquestioning commitment to the promotion of Canadian capitalism. The "National interest" indeed is often reduced to the promotion of Canadian economic interests. Wider interests, such as in prompting social justice or a lessening the gap between the levels of prosperity of the North and the South do not seem in fact to be decisive or even important when more specific issues are to be decided. Where important economic interests are involved, our government is unlikely to be responsive to any wider ethical responsibility. Think for example of our position recently in regard to international ownership of the sea beds or to changes in the operation of the international economic system.[10] Concern to promote the interests of Canadian capitalism influences policy even when no great interests are at stake. They fix a style and establish a sense of what is appropriate. They result in a conviction that ethical positions, by and large, are to be avoided even in cases where no great interest is involved as they might aggravate states whose support Canada may want on other issues or they might set a precedent which it would be costly to copy in other issues. Therefore, to avoid such possible adverse secondary consequences, it is best, as a seeming "matter of principle", never to allow foreign policy, particularly in its economic dimensions to be influenced by moral considerations.

The influence of this basic value premise operates in other and subtler ways. Governments often do not like to proclaim that their policies are narrowly selfish and economic in their primary objective. Ideologies therefore emerge, within which the policies and actions that are in fact in the narrow economic self-interest of those who control a country's economy are seen as also serving a wider general good. In this regard as well the pattern in Canada parallels the analysis presented by Wolfe. A naive and utopian view of the operation of capitalism seems widely to be believed within our government. This views serves to hide both the existence of real conflict in South Africa and also the fact that Canadian economic interests are benefiting from exploitation and are directly aiding a very repressive regime.

This ideology has several components to it. Firstly there is a belief in the benefical consequences of international trade and foreign investment to all who are affected by them. Canada is a trading nation, as our government is fond of reminding us. Canadians are also heavily dependent on foreign investment while also being themselves important investors in foreign countries. Our governments for a long time have therefore felt that an open system of international trade and investment was of great importance to Canada. For an equally long time they have been convinced that Canadian trade and investment are as much in the interests of the recipient countries as they are in Canada's interests. Thus Canadian officials and government leaders are able with an easy conscience, to oppose adverse foreign limitations to Canadian trade and investment and to ignore Canadians who argue that trade and investment in specific countries be limited by Canada in the interest of the peoples of those countries. Because of these essentially ideological beliefs, Canadian officials not only see such limitations as damaging to Canada but also as not being in the interest of the peoples of the other countries that would be affected.

This general ideological belief is applied to each individual case as it arises. It certainly is frequently applied in discussions about South Africa. In that context, it becomes a belief that Canadian trade is in the interests of all of the people of South Africa. Three features of this official belief establish that this is essentially an ideological belief rather than a reasoned conclusion. Firstly, it is rarely argued by

Canadian officials in detail. Instead it is presented as a self-evident truth. Secondly, it is held tenaciously in the face of specific arguments and evidence to the contrary. This is not surprising. The basic position, after all, was not developed in the context of the South African relationship. It is a deeprooted element in the Canadian perception of international economic relations. Because a whole belief system would be imperilled if it were undermined, it is not easily abandoned on the strength of arguments relating to South Africa. For more frequently the position is sustained and new arguments are quickly found to justify it.

Finally, this government-held belief in the universality of the advantages of foreign trade, though resistant to arguments that suggest the South African blacks benefit little from western trade and investment, and indeed may directly suffer because of it, is often and easily ignored when it is Canadian interests which might benefit from Canadian interventions to influence the flow of trade.

A second important component in the belief system with which the Canadian Government seeks to understand South Africa is the belief that economic development in South Africa will undermine apartheid and contribute to the liberalization of the social and political policies of the South African regime. This is also much more an ideological statement than a conclusion based on detailed study. It also is rarely, if ever argued in detail by government officials, though, at least until recently, it was frequently affirmed. Moreover, this belief exhibits the key quality of an ideology in that it presents what is in the narrow self-interest of the investor as if it was also in the interests of black South Africans.

In very recent years, reality has pressed in too hard upon this particular belief. However, the result has not been an admission of error. Rather, new rationalizations are produced to protect positions which the now-abandoned arguments had been meant to safeguard. Thus, to illustrate, at a recent session of the United Nations M. Pierre Charpentier, a Canadian delegate, no longer referred to the liberating consequences of economic growth. Neither, however, did he therefore support the imposition of economic sanctions. Instead he suggested that the resolution of South African problems be left to the main protagonists. What has disappeared entirely is that concern for the promotion of social justice which in 1970 was presented as one of the important determinants of Canadian policy. Once that promotion seemed to conflict with Canadian interests as narrowly conceived within the ideology that shapes the Department's reactions, it disappeared as an influence.[11]

A more important illustration of this same process has been the replacement of the utopian capitalist argument that foreign investment will benefit all, by what amounts to a social-engineering type of argument in favour of continued foreign investment in South Africa. This suggests that foreign firms can spearhead important changes in South Africa. They can abolish *de facto* job reservation, they can negotiate labour contracts with black unions, they can introduce equal terms of service for each job category, no matter what the race of the employee involved, they can abolish discriminatory practices within their business. Codes of conduct for foreign investors such as those announced recently by the OECD, by the twelve major American investors whom Andrew Young had urged to take such an initiative and by the South African Council of Churches are not only guides for foreign corporations, they are, or can easily become, a justification for their continued presence. It is an easy step from advocating such guidelines to the argument that foreign investors who follow these guidelines thereby set an example which others will follow and, as a result, are a liberalizing progressive influence.

(b) *The Canadian self-image.* Canada is sensitive to the opinion of Third World countries, not only because Canadian diplomats wish to increase their international influence but also because we have taken pride in an image of ourselves as a nation which is trusted by Third World countries and which deals with them fairly and with a real understanding of the enormity of the problems they face. This factor along with the desire to accumulate influence in international affairs, provides, respectively, emotional and *real politique* reinforcement to the moral argument that Canada ought to be more responsive to the African pressures that Canada take a firm stand against the South African regime.

(c) *The Primacy of Canadian relations with the United States and Britain.* Canada has long had a close association economically, culturally and politically with both Britain and the United States. As both Britain and the United States have major involvements in South Africa, Canada has persistently tended to support the objectives of these her senior allies. These objectives are of course shared by the Canadian Government: the containment of the Soviet and Chinese influence, the maintenance of a political and economic environment receptive to trade with and investment from the developed capitalist world and the support of regimes generally pro-west in their orientation.[12]

This American and British influence upon Canada's policy does not mean that Canada meekly follows the American and British lead. Canada, as an ally, contributes to the development of the overall approaches which it shares with Britain and the United States. However, Canada makes a special contribution to the alliance to the extent that it can keep a measure of distance between Canadian policies on the one hand and U.S. and British policies on the other. Canada is then able to act on the alliance's behalf in situations where British or American action would be impossible or less effective. Canada can also, by supporting American or British positions, suggest that these positions have thus won the backing of an independent minded and neutral middle power.

(d) *The politics of official decision-making regarding South Africa.* We have argued that the government has a wide discretion in setting policy towards South Africa. However Canadians are not totally acquiescent on the subject. There are, we think, three rather separate public influences that seem to have their impact on government policy towards South Africa. First of all there is a substantial but usually subdued body of Canadians which is responsive to pleas of racial solidarity with white South Africans and which harbours prejudice against blacks. This component of Canadian public opinion is sometimes identified as the reason why the Government often does not take a firmer line. We accept the probable truth of the judgement that a backlash of hostility to more forthright policies might well come sooner in Canada than some critics of the government are ready to concede. However it can hardly be claimed that the government has, over the years, pressed her South African policy to that limit. In fact the Government has been able, when it so wished, to ignore the influence of this opinion and to persevere with policies that had generated a racist backlash. Mitchell Sharp's refusal to "get tough" with Zambia after the killing of two Canadian women by Zambian soldiers, firing across the Zambesi, is one example. Another example is Mr. Lalonde's persistence in refusing to support any athletic associations' activities which involve the participation of South African athletes.

The second body of opinion is that expressed by the humanitarian, liberal, Christian and radical groups which have pressed the government towards a more just policy. These include a number of substantial organizations – the major Canadian Churches, C.U.S.O., the Y.W.C.A., and the Canadian Labour Congress, to name the most obvious, and active radical citizen groups in most of the major Canadian cities. Moreover, there has been significant all-party support for a stronger Canadian policy. It is true to say that these groups have not succeeded in making this issue a matter of wide-spread popular concern. As a result this body of opinion is less influential than its Scandinavian counterparts. Nevertheless it is true that these groups are far more substantial than the few organizations that actively and publically advocate Canadian support for white South Africa.

Finally, there are the business interests who trade with South Africa and invest in South Africa. They are neither numerous nor, in themselves particularly powerful. However, they have much easier access to senior government officials than do the spokesmen for the second body of opinion just identified. On certain key organizations, such as the Board of the Export Development Corporation, they are powerful represented. Their representatives often belong to official Canadian delegations to internal and economic conferences. These business leaders share the same belief system as the members of the Government and the Department of External Affairs. They are of a common class. Thus, despite the more widely representative characters of the organizations urging a stronger government policy, the affected business interests tend to receive the more sympathetic reception.

We suspect that the first factor, the ideological factor, could in fact be so presented as to subsume the other three. In particular, we believe it is more important than the final factor, the particular responsiveness of the policy makers to lobbying by Canadian business interests which are active in South Africa. The point we would make is that by and large the Canadian government has not needed to be pushed and prodded into policies which favour Canadian capitalists. We doubt, for example, that Canadian policy would be much different even if no Canadian capitalists were involved with South Africa. We therefore cannot attribute to their direct influence any major influence in policy. The more important influence is the ideology which the policy makers and the businessmen share in common.

Conclusions

Our hypothesis is that the evolution of Canadian policy can be explained in terms of the influence of the four factors discussed in the previous section. We hope that the explanatory power of that hypothesis is obvious from the review of the policy with which we began this paper. That policy has consistently exhibited a concern to maintain a liberal image, a very great reluctance to intervene to lessen trade and investment linkages and a willingness to act on behalf of or in conjunction with Britain and the United States.

As this paper was being written the government announced important changes in Canadian policies towards South Africa. The Canadian Government is withdrawing its trade consultates from Johannesburg and Cape Town, is instructing the Export Development Corporation not to use the Government account for support for activities relating to South Africa and it will be preparing comprehensive guidelines for Canadian firms investing in South Africa. Moreover, Canada is considering such further action as abrogating Commonwealth preferences, denying tax credits to companies operating in Namibia for taxes paid to South Africa on these operations and requiring visas of all South Africans travelling to Canada. These are important policy changes, though largely symbolic. However, they do seem easily explained by the hypothesis in this paper.

The United States and Britain had in the last year or more begun to take positions regarding South Africa which were stronger than those of the Canadian Government. Some action was therefore needed if Canada was to be able still to present herself as a particularly sensitive middle power. Moreover, developments in Southern Africa were making it clear to all but the most short-sighted that without major changes, South Africa is likely to be increasingly insecure and unstable. Moreover, as this happens, any state which wishes also to have good political and trading relations with the independent black states of Africa must anticipate increasing pressure for a stronger policy towards South Africa repression. For these reasons, a new and shrewder perception of the long term interests of western capitalism began to emerge. Western investors and western states would need to apply what pressures they could upon South Africa to secure improvements to the status and welfare of blacks. This, we may hypothesize from Andrew Young's statements, was seen as necessary to help assure order and stability and to provide evidence to both South African blacks and to the independent African states that western capitalism could be a progressive force and that change in South Africa need not require an expulsion of foreign investors. The new Canadian policies are directly in step with this new perception of how the long-term interests of western capitalists can best be safeguarded.

Finally, in the details of the new policies, the influence of the affected Canadian interests can easily be identified. The E.D.C. decision is less than it seems as the government account has not been used for a South African project for 15 years and 90% of E.D.D.-backed projects are supported from its own account, not the government account. Two of the most blatant and serious anomalies of Canadian policy – Commonwealth preferences for South Africa and the granting of tax credits to firms paying taxes to South Africa on their Namibian operations – have long been the subject of informed and forceful pressure from groups of concerned Canadians. Nevertheless, the government has still not corrected these anomalies even though the interests affected are not major interests. Indeed, in all probability, the two most important of the interests that would be affected are sugar importers, amongst whom subsidiaries of the British firm, Tate and Lyle, are dominant, and Falconbridge Mining Corporation which, though legally a Canadian firm, is controlled by Superior Oil, an American Corporation. However, the measures that would touch them have been postponed despite the fact that these measures have long been advocated by organizations which, one might have thought, were politically more important.

We do not, for these reasons, deplore the new policy changes. We welcome them and we think that this shift in western strategies regarding South Africa of which they are a part, are of significance to the on going struggle for majority rule in South Africa. Any movement in the positions of western governments for whatever reason which contributes to the isolation of South Africa and to the international recognition of the moral and political necessity of the rapid and total dismantling of her racist policies is important. As one looks ahead, there is clearly still the possibility of a Vietnam-like struggle in Southern Africa, with the liberation forces, aided by African states and strongly backed by the Soviet Union, engaging in an escalating struggle with South Africa. Should that develop it would be disastrous for countries such as Canada – and even more so for the United States and Britain – to choose, for reasons of economic interests and fear of the Soviet Union to support South Africa. This underlines the importance of as realistic and accurate an assessment as possible of the factors and influences that shape Canadian policies towards South Africa.

Notes

1. Until 1960 Canada in effect endorsed Portugal's argument that her colonies were not colonies at all but overseas territories and thus not subject to any UN supervision.

2. It should be pointed out that Canada followed the widespread practice of qualifying support for a resolution through a series of reservations. In this way Canada managed to convey its sympathy for the African struggle and yet make clear its opposition to the use of force, to economic sanctions and to the recognition of specific groups as authentic representatives of the people of Portugal's African colonies.

3. There were those in Ottawa who saw clearly the contradiction involved in enlisting Portugal as a full member in NATO. See, for instance, Escott Reid, *Time for Fear and Hope, The Making of the North Atlantic Treaty,* 1947–1949, McClelland and Stewart, Toronto, 1977, pp. 198–200.

4. It should be noted that Canada has not always been prepared to condemn South Africa partly because of the embarrassment caused by our own practices and partly because of negotiating tactics. In the 1940s and 1950s, Canada abstained on resolutions that singled out South Africa for criticism. It was only in 1960 that Canada dropped its earlier reservations about criticizing South Africa.

5. We exclude from these four factors the explanation that because of the variety of the national origins of the Canadian population, it would be inviting continuous pressure, that similar action be taken against other governments were the Canadian government to take a stronger stand against South Africa. This certainly is a widely prevalent attitude in Ottawa, but what still needs to be explained is why this concern should be more influential than the commitment to promote social justice and the recognition of the particularly abhorrent form of oppression, both of which are prominent in official statements on the factors that are weighed when Canadian policy to South Africa is considered.

6. Alan Wolfe, *The Limits of Legitimacy: Political Contradictions of Contemporary Capitalism*, New York, Free Press, 1977, p. 318.

7. John Holmes, *Canada: A Middle-Aged Power*, Toronto, McClelland and Stewart, 1976, p. 155.

8. See, for example, the rather colic article by John Holmes on "Morality, Realism and Foreign Affairs", *International Perspectives* October–November 1977.

9. These two examples are particularly appropriate in a paper by University of Toronto professors at a conference at Carleton University as Gerald Helleiner of Toronto had done so much to sensitize Canadians to the continued selfishness of our internal and economic policies and Peyton Lyon of Carleton had done likewise in regard to Canadian policies at the Law of the Sea Conference.

10. Gerald Helleiner has encountered a similar irritated rejection of detailed argument when he and others criticized Canadian opposition to the demands of third world countries for changes in the international economic system. He has characterized the responses of the Canadian Government, in these terms, "First it is argued that the proposal in question will not work. . . If it is demonstrated that it will work it is argued that it will have detrimental side effects. . . and that the proposal is not really in their (the Third World's) interest. . . If it is shown that the scheme will increase third world incomes the next step is to point out that since developed countries are very wise they will immediately perceive what is happening and will cut back foreign aid. . . The gains will therefore not be additional. . . What if it is granted that the proposal might conceivably raise the resource flows from rich countries to poor? The next argument. . . is that the distribution of the gains among countries is unattractive. . . If the intercountry distribution is finally agreed to be not wholly unreasonable, then the argument becomes one of internal distributional equity. . . If all these points are met, if each level of objection is beaten back. . . there comes the moment of truth – when the policy-maker at last declares what it has all been about" "Ah, he says, but this proposal is not in our interest". G.K. Helleiner *The New International Order. A Canadian Perspective* 1977 (mimeographed), pp. 4–5.

11. This was made transparently clear in a recent "not to be attributed" talk by a Government official. The changes in government policy were presented entirely as a response a) to the changing circumstances in South Africa since the Soweto uprisings, b) to a concern for our good name in Black Africa and c) to the more forthright policies being developed by the U.S. since President Carter's election.

12. The sentence above is, we take it, a fair paraphrase of John Holme's:– "The range of common interests is perhaps too obvious to be apparent. It includes everything basic like the preservation of our kind of civilization, the maintenance of an international society free for commerce and ideas, and the struggle against international anarchy." John Holmes, *Canada, A Middle Aged Power* op. cit., p. 160.

V. Issues and Options

Timothy M. Shaw

Scandinavian and Canadian Policy Issues

The discussions which took place during the conference itself largely reflected the range of issues and concerns raised in the papers included in this and its companion volume.[1] Given the considerable diversity of assumptions, interests, perspectives, values and projections the conference debate was at all times lively and vigorous. It is clearly impossible to capture completely the spirit of the proceedings here. Moreover, not all of the points raised can be properly dealt with in one concluding chapter. This essay seeks merely to record one observer's view of and reflections on the conference debate; it may, therefore, be read alongside and compared with the two sets of published papers.

Although the proceedings at times went beyond the original concerns that inspired the conference, the general debate concentrated on them. These were, firstly, the distinctive relations and politics of Canada and Scandinavia vis-à-vis Southern Africa and, secondly, the prospects for change and development within the region itself. Most of the conference debate, as measured in terms of both time and intensity, focused on these two themes, although several other salient aspects of these general subjects were identified. The rest of this chapter examines these two sets of central concerns as they were raised during the conference period itself, recognising that whilst there was almost unanimous agreement that in Southern Africa fundamental "change" was both inevitable and necessary, there was considerable disagreement about its speed, scope and definition.

Scandinavian and Canadian relations, perspectives and policy options

Perhaps the fundamental question raised about Scandinavian and Canadian relations with and policies towards the states of Southern Africa was whether these countries had a distinctive role to play. One assumption underlying the conference agenda was that this group of northern rim "middle powers" tended to have interests and options different from those of any of the major powers involved in Africa, and that these would be expressed in distinctive behaviour and policies. This assumption was seriously questioned by several authors and participants who argued instead that Canada and Scandinavia are merely smaller capitalist political economies who were unable and/or unwilling to act independently of their allies and associates in the wider Western world. However, others at the conference rejected this critique, arguing instead that, not only are Scandinavian and Canadian linkages and policies different, but also they are seen by many actors in the region to be different. Still others emphasised that the role of middle powers may be important precisely because of their "in between" position. The fact that the major Western powers serve effectively as their reference group gives Scandinavia and Canada a special leverage if they choose to exercise it. These rather fundamental disagreements animated and informed much of the discussion at the conference.

A second and related point was whether Canada and the Scandinavian countries – Denmark, Finland, Norway and Sweden – were really comparable either amongst themselves or over their Southern African policies. The national attributes, political economies, foreign policies and international statuses of this group of states vary considerably (see Appendix 1). And, as several papers and points indicated, they have quite a wide range of policies towards and concerns about Southern Africa. Questions were raised, therefore, about whether all of them had an equal interest in supporting change throughout the region, and whether they had an equal level of resources or power available to effect such support. It became increasingly evident in the course of the conference, that, for instance, the domestic debate about Southern African policies and prospects was considerably more advanced, informed, intense and "progressive" in Scandinavia than in Canada.

A third set of comparisons was made, then, amongst the different combinations and balances of internal and international factors which produced the policies of Scandinavia and Canada towards the region. As the papers in this collection indicate, there is a considerable diversity amongst the linkages of, interests in and institutions concerned with Southern Africa in the five states under consideration. The importance, size and nature of trade vary as does corporate investment. Some states feel more dependent on the mineral reserves and strategic position of South Africa than do others. In some countries the internal political process – public opinion, parties, interest groups, parliaments, bureaucracies, etc. – is more involved with and animated about Southern Africa than in others. Together, then, these diverse relations, interests and activities add up to rather different degrees of concern and action about the past, present and future of the region.

A fourth issue raised, therefore, was the range of policy options available to Scandinavia and Canada. Given the diversity of linkages and concerns, are some of these states more constrained in their policy options than others? Moreover, if Southern Africa constitutes a rather marginal issue for at least some of them, is it an area in which they can afford to make either timid or determined responses? Further, in view of the essential pluralism of their policies or, alternatively, multiple and contradictory relations and goals? Will they continue, in other words, to play both sides of the street, or might we expect them, given increasing global pressure on and attention to Southern Africa, to work towards a more consistent and concerned set of objectives? And will their official policies attempt to co-ordinate or regulate nonstate, transnational linkages and relationships with the region?

A fifth, related issue is whether Canada and Scandinavia can or should develop coherent policies for the region as a whole or merely establish a set of bilaterial relationships with each of the several state and nonstate actors of Southern Africa. Given the increasing variety of social, political and economic systems in the region – majority- and minority-ruled, capitalist and socialist, industrial and agricultural, one-party and multi-party, participatory and authoritarian etc. – the formulation and execution of a single regional policy becomes rather problematic. This is especially so if any of the five countries seeks to reduce its ties with or isolate the white-ruled territories, whilst providing development and political support to the black-ruled states. However, treating each state or group of states separately may encourage contradictory positions and actions. For instance, Canada or Scandinavia might attempt to "balance" interests and pressures which seek, on the one hand, to assist the small black states of the region and, on the other hand, to maintain "business-as-usual" with the white-ruled territories. Similar difficulties could arise in attempting to reconcile aid and support for both the more "radical" regimes and movements in the area and the more conservative ones.

This leads, then, to a sixth cluster of issues about the degree of recognition of states and liberation movements and the various types of assistance that might be provided to both. Recognition is not only a symbolic act; it also opens up the possibility of other sorts of relationship, humanitarian and economic, social and strategic. Southern Africa contains a wide variety of state and quasi-state actors which may or may not be recognised – white- and black-ruled states, liberation movements and bantustans. Moreover, recognition can be withdrawn as well as offered, as in the case of Rhodesia. Clearly one option available to Canada and Scandinavia would be to reduce or even break diplomatic relations with South Africa and to go beyond informal association with the liberation movements towards some kind of formal recognition. Needless to say, in view of the universal rejection of the Homelands scheme, there was no discussion on whether to recognise Transkei and Boputhatswana.

The question of recognition is, in a sense, one aspect of a somewhat broader issue, that of whether sanctions and/or incentives are more likely to advance change in the region; this constitutes a seventh set of issues. The question of whether to recognise, not recognise or de-recognise – and the considerable range of alternatives in between, consisting of variations in the level of representation – all of which affect the nature of the international relationship, is part of a wider issue of whether contact and/or isolation, incentives and/or sanctions are more effective as threats and actions. This topic led to a debate over whether foreign investment or disinvestment is more likely to generate change. This, in turn, related to the question of whether governments such as those in Canada and Scandinavia can or should be involved in regulating or restricting non-governmental relations, whether they be social and sporting, academic or economic, technological or strategic. Clearly the continuing debates in Scandinavia and Canada over these issues of communication or disengagement have already begun to move public opinion some distance towards the latter perspective, if only on the pragmatic grounds that, since change is inevitable, it is best to maximize one's options.

Eight, a further point related to the isolation versus integration issue is that of identifying appropriate "targets" through which to support or advance change in Southern Africa. Given a critical analysis of the white-ruled territories' dependency and vulnerabilities, it may be possible to select particularly sensitive or crucial sectors on which to focus policy and action. For instance, embargoes on commercial and military trade would generally weaken South Africa's economy and preparedness over time, but ending the flow of oil and high technology inputs might work more quickly. Moreover, limits on new investment will take years to affect South Africa's political economy, whereas other tactics such as active disinvestment, making the rand non-convertible or moving away from the remaining gold-based currency dealings would have a more immediate and possibly dramatic effect. Perhaps, realistically, threats as well as their implementation, inducements as well as sanctions should all be employed in advancing change.

Related to the preceding point as well as to the first one is a ninth question of whether Western countries, especially Canada and Scandinavia, can or should attempt to co-ordinate their policies towards the region. Whilst at a very general level of analysis, they may all be part of the capitalist world system and so be assumed to act in concert, at a lower level of inquiry they do appear to have different interests, emphases and experiences. Some have taken a lead in extending support to the liberation movements or in providing assistance to the majority-ruled states; some have moved to limit investment, trade and communications more than others; and some are more prepared to consider disinvestment, oil sanctions and maybe even de-recognition. Whilst this very diffuse range of policies and activities may serve to keep the white regimes off-guard, behaviours towards the region might be coordinated with good effect, as they have already begun to be in the case of the Nordic States.

Finally, in this section, there was debate over the goals of Canadian and Scandinavian policies, given their interests and values. Could or should these states encourage gradual reform towards majority rule in Southern Africa, or stimulate more radical and fundamental regional change towards socialist societies? This issue of goal obviously relates to the first and fourth points above as, in part, it concerns the whole nature of political economy and foreign policy in pluralist industrialised states. Some participants argued that policy has recently tended to transcend internal and international capitalist interests. Others suggested that as reform was the only possible goal, tactics such as codes of conduct for corporations served merely to rationalise relations. Others insisted, however, that policy reflected broader domestic and global concerns so that more "progressive" policies such as support for the liberation movements and selected moves towards disengagement were possible despite a state's political economy. Most participants recognised that, considering the history and structure of Canada and Scandinavia, it was unrealistic to expect that these countries would support revolution in Southern Africa, although they might move towards more active promotion of social democratic solutions. In any case, given the modest international role of these actors and doubts about the efficacy of external pressures on the white regimes, it was widely acknowledged that the direct impact of any Canadian and Scandinavian policy changes is likely to be limited.

Prospects for change and development in Southern Africa

The debate about Canadian and Scandinavian policies examined in the first part of this chapter was, of course, informed by a parallel discussion about the prospects for and directions of change in Southern Africa itself. Despite the realisation that the external involvement and policies of these five states had limited impact on the region, there was considerable discussion over the nature of change in it and over the implications of this for Canadian and Scandinavian perspectives and stances. This second section concentrates, then, on alternative analyses of and prospects for development strategies and political economies in the states of Southern Africa.[2] These were made in the context of a general awareness and understanding, as indicated in this volume's introduction, that outsiders have a minimal role to play in projecting or determining the future of the region.

There was, as noted at the beginning of this chapter, general agreement, firstly, that change in Southern Africa was not only necessary but inevitable. There was also a basic consensus about the wide range of results that could eventually emerge from the present period of conflict and transition. At the same time, there was considerable disagreement over possible and preferable futures for the region. Essentially, two scenarios of desirable or probable futures for Southern Africa were debated. One consisted of a transition to majority political control and non-racialism with minimal change in the socio-economics of either the separate states or the wider region. The other consisted of a revolution to create essentially new political economies in which not only political power, but also economic, social and other goods would be redistributed and class relations transformed. These alternative visions of and preferences for formal political independence on the one hand, and socialist reconstruction on the other hand, were characterised variously as "false" as opposed to "genuine" decolonisation or "reformist" versus "revolutionary" change. In general, it was assumed that Scandinavia and Canada would tend to prefer the former variety of transition to the latter, but also that they appreciate the decision is one for the Africans in each state to make for themselves. It was also recognised that there are already considerable differences and disagreements within Southern Africa itself about which type of future political economy is both likely and desirable.

A second issue about change in the region is related to the first, namely, the speed and mode of transition. It was generally agreed that the longer delayed and more violent the process of gaining majority rule, the greater the prospects for more radical or socialist regimes, with or without further external involvement. This factor, of type of transition, already helps to explain the diversity of ideologies and structures in Southern Africa, and it will continue to affect profoundly the outcome of the present period of upheaval. Again, in general, it was assumed by participants that Canada, Scandinavia and other Western interests tend to favour non-violent reform over more violent revolution, but the elusiveness or slowness of the former tends to generate those factors that produce the latter. That poses a fundamental dilemma for policy-makers in Canada, Scandinavia and elsewhere, which may be expected to continue to inform the debates about policy options in the future. These debates will, of course, be influenced by Southern African actors, events and interests; hence the importance of recognising and analyzing these.

Thirdly, it was widely appreciated that change and development in Southern Africa as elsewhere are not unilinear and may be somewhat cyclical and unpredictable. Further, the unstable combination of a variety of internal demands in and external pressures on Southern Africa may not produce clear-cut or sustainable outcomes; as a result, the process of change may be quite protracted and indecisive. Therefore, Scandinavian and Canadian, as well as Southern African, policy responses may have to remain quite flexible and multiple.

Related to the above issue of instability and unpredictability is, fourthly, that of perceptions of Scandinavian and Canadian policies, interests and intentions held in the region. Debates over linkages, perspectives and policy options in Canada and Scandinavia may generate unpredictable images amongst different actors in Southern Africa itself. The latter may see policies to be more or less threatening than they "really" are; they may see common interests and even conspiracies where there are none. In short, perspectives and the outcomes of policies and actions by Scandinavia and Canada may have less than predictable results within the region. This possibility adds to the complexities and uncertainties of making foreign policy, particularly policy for such a diverse and volatile region.

A fifth point concerns the changeable "motif" of Scandinavian or Canadian policies towards the region. External concerns have tended to evolve from questions of decolonisation and racial discrimination to those of liberation and human rights. The fluidity of justifications or criteria for action may be unsettling for the region, although many African actors would urge that the symbolism should be developed even further, towards an expression of interest in, say, imperialism, socialism and self-reliance.

Sixthly, there remains a danger that "Cold War" imagery and interests will once again enter into policy equations over the region with implications for Canada and Scandinavia as well as for Southern Africa. The real issues of Southern Africa, it was generally agreed amongst participants, are those of freedom and nationalism, of exploitation and basic human needs. Development for most peoples is impossible under the present minority-ruled states whose influence and impact still pervade the whole region. Therefore, any intrusion of East-West politics into regional affairs tends to be unhelpful in the advancement of liberty and justice. However, it was also recognised that the exclusion of such cold war concerns was becoming more difficult, not only because of increasing external involvement, but also because of the issue of the future political economy of the region as a whole.

However, seventh, it was also recognised that the states of Southern Africa had to make their own decisions about their future political economies and ideologies for themselves, even if they are unlikely to ever be able to make such choices completely on their own. Nevertheless, it remains important that they be able to maximize their own choices about social structure and external links. And at least for some participants, part of the rationale for the continuing Canadian and Scandinavian presence might be to enhance such choice. If the new states of the region want to follow a policy of non-alignment, then the ability to enhance relations with such middle powers becomes important.

Finally, it was generally appreciated that, because of the considerable history of Western association with the region, the West's response to regional change and conflict would be quite crucial in determining its future. Once again it was recognised that, whilst Canada and Scandinavia cannot determine the West's policy response themselves, they may be able to influence it to a certain extent; moreover, they have a responsibility to exercise whatever leverage they do possess. They may be in a position to moderate or modify any of the continuing cold war components and to express and empathise with a more Afrocentric view of the conflict. To this extent, two important points follow. Firstly, the "power" of Scandinavia and Canada may be greater than at first appears; and, secondly, perceptions and expectations of their influence held in Southern Africa may be increasing. Together, these factors add to the salience of Canadian and Scandinavian policy-making towards and involvement in Southern African issues. It is these hopes and aspirations of many of the peoples of Southern Africa that need to be recognised, treated and, if possible, satisfied in the continuing evolution of Candian and Scandinavian perspectives and policies.

Conclusion: Canadian-Scandinavian-Southern African interactions

Throughout the conference debate, there was widespread recognition that, given the continuous interactions at the levels of both policy and practice amongst the regional states as well as Scandinavia and Canada, alternatives and responses were interrelated and complex. However, one concern to emerge from the discussion was that actors in Southern Africa should also be able to choose amongst their own policy options and that Candian–Scandinavian involvement and concern should recognise and appreciate this regional interest. Such an empathy for Southern Africa would also help to eliminate cold war images and rhetoric from a struggle which is essentially concerned about overcoming exploitation and repression rather than with broader questions of ideology or global politics. Moreover, it might serve to reinforce the salience of local rather than foreign decison-making and advance autonomy as well as liberation in the region.

On the other hand, it has to be recognised as well that the process of contemporary change in this region is not simply another, albeit belated, case of decolonisation. The myths of independence elsewhere in Africa have underscored the need to receive more than formal political authority but rather to achieve real control over the inherited political economy. Scandinavia and Canada are in a position not only to increase awareness of these more critical perspectives, but also, because of association with major Western countries and corporations, actively to influence their broader policy processes. Further, given African assumptions and assertions that the Western response will largely determine the future of Southern Africa – the nature of both its transition and its structures – then Canada and Scandinavia would seem to have more than sufficient motivation seriously to affect wider Western debates and involvement.

Finally, it was pointed out that, with the comprehensive nature of the contemporary world system, Canada and Scandinavia may be able both to assist in the struggle for full liberation in Southern Africa and also learn and benefit from an association with it themselves by moving from being ancilliaries to alternatives of the West. From the perspective of many participants, neither Canada, Scandinavia, nor Southern Africa, can really develop until they distance themselves from the centres of power, East as well as West. The processes of conflict and change in Southern Africa may advance this process in two ways: firstly, by giving Scandinavia and Canada an opportunity to establish policies and relations with the region different from those of other important actors in that they would be characterised by cooperation without subordination; and secondly, by demonstrating that struggle against powerful external interests is possible and that distinctive political and economic struggles can be designed and implemented to carry out a social revolution.

So, at least according to some participants, the transition to socialism in Southern Africa may serve not only to radicalise other parts of Africa, but also to afford greater prospects for significant change in Scandinavia and Canada as well. If indeed Scandinavia and Canada come to develop policies and interests separate from those of others in the world system, they will also have enhanced their own autonomy and options. In both these ways, then, the links between Canada, Scandinavia and Southern Africa may be more central, crucial and creative than they appear to be at first. Conflict and change in Southern Africa may indeed touch, involve and affect us all.

Notes

1. See Douglas G. Anglin, Timothy M. Shaw and Carl G. Widstrand (eds.) *Conflict and Change in Southern Africa: papers from a Scandinavian–Canadian Conference,* Washington: University Press of America, 1978.

2. For further details of these enquiries, see many of the papers contained in Anglin, Shaw and Widstrand (eds.) *Conflict and Change in Southern Africa.*

Appendix 1

Scandinavia and Canada:

Comparative Data (1976)
(values in US dollars)

	Scandinavia					Canada
	Denmark	Finland	Norway	Sweden	Scandinavia	
Population	5.1m	4.7m	4.0m	8.2m	22.0m	23.1m
Wealth						
GNP	$ 38.2b	$28.1b	$30.6b	$74.2b	$171.1b	$192.7b
GNP per capita	$ 7,530	$ 5,948	$ 7,601	$ 9,032	$ 7,706	$ 8.328
Trade with Canada						
Imports from Canada	$ 42.8m	$ 24.6m	$203.1m	$115.7m	$386.3m	
Exports to Canada[1]	$ 69.5m	$ 38.9m	$ 97.2m	$248.8m	$454.4m	
Trade with South Africa						
Imports from South Africa	$ 18.9m	$ 9.3m	$ 52.5m	$ 40.8m	$121.4m	$156.8m
Exports to South Africa[1]	$ 27.6m	$35.7m	$ 37.7m	$ 97.2m	$198.2m	$ 99.3m
Trade with Developing Countries[2]						
% total imports	8.8%	7.2%	7.5%	10.3%	8.8%	6.8%
% total exports	8.5%	6.4%	12.1%	12.4%	10.6%	6.6%
Foreign assistance[3]						
Net Official Development Assistance	$214m	$ 51m	$218m	%608m	$1,901m	$886m
% of GNP (rank)[4]	0.56%(5)	0.18%(15)	0.71%(3)	0.82%(1)	0,64%	0.46%(7)
Net Flows of Private Capital	239m	$ 16m	$240m	$529m	$1,024m	$1,257m
% of GNP	0.63%	0.06%	0.79%	0.71%	0.60%	0.65%
Military						
Defence expenditure	$1,080m	$426m	$1,120m	$2,830m	$5,456m	$3,610m
Armed forces	34,700	39,900	39,000	68,550	182,150	80,000
Peacekeeping forces (1978)	379	679	951	1143	3152	1629

1 FOB country of source. Costs to country of destination would be higher.
2 Excluding OPEC countries.
3 Foreign assistance to developing countries and multilaterial agencies.
4 Rank among 17 members of OECD Development Assistance Committee.

Sources: UN Yearbook of International Trade Statistics, 1976, vol. I; OECD Development Cooperation Efforts and Policies of the Members of the Development Assistance Committee: 1977 Review; International Institute for Strategic Studies, The Military Balance, 1977–1978.

Contributors to this volume

Douglas Anglin is Professor of Political Science, Carleton University, Ottawa

Georges Blouin is Assistant Under-Secretary, Department of External Affairs, Ottawa

Linda Freeman is a lecturer in Social Science, Ryerson Polytechnical Institute and York University, Toronto

Donald C. Jamieson is the Secretary of State for External Affairs, Department of External Affairs, Ottawa

Paul Ladouceur is the Chief Planning Officer of the Commonwealth Africa Division of the Canadian International Development Agency (CIDA)

Roger Leys is a lecturer in Political Science in the University of Copenhagen, Copenhagen

Robert Matthews is Associate Professor of Political Economy, University of Toronto, Toronto

Abdul S. Minty is the Director of the Anti-Apartheid Movement, London

Mai Palmberg is a doctoral student at the Department of Political Science, Uppsala

Cranford Pratt is Professor of Political Economy, University of Toronto, Toronto

John S. Saul is Associate Professor of Political Science, York University, Toronto

Timothy Shaw is Associate Professor of Political Science, Dalhousie University, Halifax

Thorvald Stoltenberg is the Under-Secretary of State, Royal Ministry of Foreign Affairs, Oslo

Anders Thunborg is the Swedish Ambassador to the United Nations

Carl Widstrand is the Director of the Scandinavian Institute of African Studies, Uppsala